Palgrave Macmillan Studies in Family and Intimate Life

Series Editors
Graham Allan
Keele University
Keele, UK

Lynn Jamieson
University of Edinburgh
Edinburgh, UK

David H.J. Morgan
University of Manchester
Manchester, UK

'The Palgrave Macmillan Studies in Family and Intimate Life series is impressive and contemporary in its themes and approaches'—Professor Deborah Chambers, Newcastle University, UK, and author of *New Social Ties*.

The remit of the Palgrave Macmillan Studies in Family and Intimate Life series is to publish major texts, monographs and edited collections focusing broadly on the sociological exploration of intimate relationships and family organization. The series covers a wide range of topics such as partnership, marriage, parenting, domestic arrangements, kinship, demographic change, intergenerational ties, life course transitions, step-families, gay and lesbian relationships, lone-parent households, and also non-familial intimate relationships such as friendships and includes works by leading figures in the field, in the UK and internationally, and aims to contribute to continue publishing influential and prize-winning research.

More information about this series at
http://www.palgrave.com/gp/series/14676

Julia Carter • Lorena Arocha
Editors

Romantic Relationships in a Time of 'Cold Intimacies'

palgrave
macmillan

Editors
Julia Carter
University of the West of England
Bristol, UK

Lorena Arocha
University of Hull
Hull, UK

Palgrave Macmillan Studies in Family and Intimate Life
ISBN 978-3-030-29258-4   ISBN 978-3-030-29256-0   (eBook)
https://doi.org/10.1007/978-3-030-29256-0

This Palgrave Macmillan imprint is published by the registered company Springer Nature Switzerland AG.
The registered company address is: Gewerbestrasse 11, 6330 Cham, Switzerland

Acknowledgements

First, we would like to thank the contributors to this volume, each of whom has worked hard, met deadlines and stayed patient with our many emails, reminders and requests. It has been a pleasure to work with you all (and to work together as editors for the first time) and we hope that we have nurtured some useful relationships within our scholarly community. It has also been good to work with Palgrave and we extend our thanks to Amelia Derkatsch for her always reliable assistance and the anonymous reviewer who provided excellent, invaluable and incredibly detailed feedback on our initial proposal: thank you. We extend our appreciation to the British Sociological Association and the Families and Relationships study group who funded the original workshop from which this project emerged back in July 2017. May their support for early career scholars fund many an edited collection. Finally, we would like to thank our families and friends for providing support when we needed it and for encouraging us in our low moments; for this, a special thank you belongs to Daniel Smith.

Contents

Notes on Contributors

Lorena Arocha is Lecturer in Contemporary Slavery at the Wilberforce Institute at the University of Hull, UK. Her research sits at the intersection of policy and practice around cross-cutting issues of modern slavery, migration, development and socio-political inequalities. She is working on a research project with colleagues based at the Advanced Centre for Women's Studies at the Tata Institute of Social Sciences in Mumbai examining the collective organising strategies of workers in exploitation in India.

Julia Carter is Senior Lecturer in Sociology at the University of the West of England. Her research interests include marriage and relationships, families and personal life, gender and sexuality and weddings. She is particularly interested in intimate relationships and the roles these play in an ever-changing social context. Her previous publications have focused on marriage and narratives of love, sexuality and commitment, and living apart together relationships, policy and social change. Her more recent publications focus on weddings, gender and race and her book *Reinventing Couples: Tradition, Agency and Bricolage* (co-authored with Simon Duncan) was published in 2018 by Palgrave Macmillan.

Charlotte Faircloth is Lecturer in Sociology of Gender in the Department of Social Science, University College London, UK. Her work has explored cultures of parenthood, with a focus on gender, intimacy and equality. She has published widely, including the books *Militant Lactivism? Attachment Parenting and Intensive Motherhood in the UK and France* and *Parenting Culture Studies*. She has also edited numerous journal special issues in addition to the volumes *Parenting in Global Perspective* and *Feeding Children Inside and Outside the Home*.

Mirna Guha is Senior Lecturer in Sociology at Anglia Ruskin University (ARU), Cambridge. Her research specialisms include sex work, gender-based violence, social relations and social justice. Mirna has a PhD in International Development from the University of East Anglia, which explored experiences and negotiations with everyday violence in the lives of women formerly and currently in sex work in eastern India. Findings from this research have been published in *Gender, Place and Culture*; *Gender and Development* and the *International Journal of Fashion Studies*. At ARU, Mirna teaches feminist theory and practice, sexuality and social control and globalisation and social policy.

Raisa Jurva is finalising her doctoral thesis in Gender Studies at the Faculty of Social Sciences, Tampere University, Finland. Her research interests include ambivalent attachments of intimacy, entanglements of power and affect in intimate relationships, feminist and queer theories and methodologies and life course perspectives on gender. She has published on discourses of heterosexuality in sex education materials, men's experiences of prostate cancer treatment and female complaint as an expression of gender inequality. Her doctoral research is part of the Academy of Finland funded research project 'Just the Two of Us? Affective Inequalities in Intimate Relationships' (287983).

Alison Lamont Having completed her PhD as part of the Universität Duisburg-Essen's "Risk and East Asia" Graduiertenkolleg 1613, Alison works on risk and modernity within the People's Republic of China, focussing on families and the role of the state in private relationships. As Lecturer in Sociology and Criminology at the University of Roehampton, she is working on a monograph exploring the rebuilding of nuclear families after the 2008 Sichuan earthquake in China.

Lara McKenzie is Honorary Research Fellow in Anthropology and Sociology at The University of Western Australia. Her research focuses on Australia, and particularly on gender, age, love and kinship. Lara's book, *Age-Dissimilar Couples and Romantic Relationships: Ageless Love?* (2015), explores age-dissimilar couples. She has previously undertaken research on inequality and cultural difference in education and is now conducting a study on precarious academics' experiences of looking for stable work in universities. Her writing here addresses the themes of gender, age, casualisation and audit practices.

Fiona McQueen is a lecturer at Edinburgh Napier University specialising in Gender and Sexuality, having finished her PhD at University of Edinburgh at CRFR (Centre for Research on Families and Relationships) in 2015. Fiona is interested in intersections between gender, power and emotion within intimate relationships. A specific interest relates to how gendered patterns of emotion serve to normalise affective inequalities within heterosexual relationships influenced by therapeutic culture, yet are resistant to changes in gender equality, making the reproduction of male power invisible.

Charlotte Morris is employed as a lecturer in education. She completed her doctoral thesis on the topic of heterosexual single mothers' narratives of intimacy in 2014 at the University of Sussex and has continued to work there in a teaching capacity. She also has research interests in gender and education, feminist pedagogies and higher education cultures.

Sharani Osborn is a graduate of the University of Edinburgh and an associate researcher with the Centre for Families and Relationships. Her research with mothers and fathers explores how parents negotiate the intersection of constructions of parenting, childhood and gender in reflections on their role, relationships and practice, with attention to the temporality of relations between generations and the interaction of contending discourses. An abiding interest is the consideration of how different conceptualisations of gender, and of masculinities in particular, theorise the de-gendering and re-gendering processes in the fine-grained practices of family life and relationships.

Lauren Palmer is a sociology graduate of Canterbury Christ Church University who has conducted research into young people's dating practices on social media, in particular the extent to which technology effects romantic relationships. She now works for the National Society for the Prevention of Cruelty to Children (NSPCC) as a Market Insights Analyst, looking at how NSPCC services ensure they meet the needs of vulnerable children and families. Her wider interests include gender inequalities, policy and public affairs and international development.

Daniel Smith is Lecturer in Sociology in the School of Social Sciences at Cardiff University (UK). His interests include the social theory and anthropology of gift exchange and its role in the sociology of class. This is explored in his ethnography of the British upper-middle classes, *Elites, Race and Nationhood: The Branded Gentry* (Palgrave, 2016). His research also extends to an interest in the sociology of comedy and humour. *Comedy & Critique: Stand-up Comedy and the Professional Ethos of Laughter* was published by the University of Bristol Press in 2018.

Rachel Thwaites is a visiting fellow at the University of Lincoln, UK, where she was previously Senior Lecturer in Sociology and Social Policy. She has research and teaching interests in gender and inequalities, identities, contemporary heterosexual relationships, early career work experiences in academia and the arts and the sociology of health and illness. She is working as a senior research officer at the Scottish Government. This role is separate from her academic interests and is unconnected to the work or views expressed in this volume.

Jenny van Hooff is Senior Lecturer in Sociology at Manchester Metropolitan University, UK. She is a sociologist of personal life and has published work on couple relationships, sexual practices, relationship breakdown, infidelity and friendship.

Kailing Xie is Teaching Fellow at the Politics and International Development at the University of Warwick, where she is the course director for gender and international development. She completed her PhD at the Centre for Women's Studies at the University of York. Her work explores the role of gender in contemporary Chinese governance. Her PhD thesis adopts a feminist approach to understanding how gender affects the lives of China's urban privileged only-daughters. Her broader research interests include feminist approaches to social justice, identity politics and race and nationalism in contemporary China.

1

Introduction

Julia Carter and Lorena Arocha

This edited collection emerged from a workshop held in July 2017 which was funded by the British Sociological Association (BSA) regional early career workshop fund. Participants at the event included some of the contributors in this volume and others joined this writing project at later stages. Authors include postgraduate and early career academics, more established scholars, not all in academia, and almost all women. The contributions to this volume get to the heart of discussions and debates central to problematisations of 'intimacy' and the sociology of family life.

This centrality of intimacy to sociological debate does not mean that 'intimacy', as a concept, is well defined and equally articulated. 'Intimacy' can often be taken for granted, a buzzword at risk of becoming meaningless

J. Carter (✉)
University of the West of England, Bristol, UK
e-mail: julia.carter@uwe.ac.uk

L. Arocha
University of Hull, Hull, UK
e-mail: Lorena.Arocha@hull.ac.uk

© The Author(s) 2020
J. Carter, L. Arocha (eds.), *Romantic Relationships in a Time of 'Cold Intimacies'*,
Palgrave Macmillan Studies in Family and Intimate Life,
https://doi.org/10.1007/978-3-030-29256-0_1

(Geschiere 2013: 24) and yet fundamental to explanations of social and personal dynamics observed across societies from the last decades of the twentieth century. It has commonly been reduced to mean sexual relations in heterosexual couples, but its etymology indicates a wider meaning, 'intimacy is to make known to a close friend what is innermost' (Kasulis 2002: 28). Hence, 'intimacy' better relates to the interaction between interpersonal relations and the public sphere and sees these as mutually constituted (Berlant 1998: 282–3). 'Intimacy' is frequently cast in positive and celebratory terms when linked to 'modern' Euro-American societies (Jamieson 2011), as in the democratisation of intimacy seen by Giddens (1992), which can serve to exaggerate and reify geopolitical differences, characterised as cultural differences along a binary logic (Khandelwal 2009). Both Khandelwal (2009) and Jamieson (1998, 2011) see, however, the potential for 'intimacy' to provide a locus from which to conduct in-depth studies, exploring differences and particularities to arrive at nuanced and intricate understandings of how we relate to others and how these everyday practices of intimacies are co-constituted and shape the state (Puri 2016).

This volume is a conversation with this body of work and with that of Eva Illouz (2007, 2012) more particularly. Illouz focuses on exploring the impact of the intensification of commercialisation and the forms and conditions of intimate relationships. She offers an explanation for how specific individuals make sense of themselves in late modernity, and how love, romance and intimacy can offer a route to salvation, even if only temporarily and ultimately leading to suffering. Hers is a theory that aims to make sense of transformations seen across societies, which have been associated with the growth and proliferation of mass and digital media, the arrival of new and improved technologies of transportation and reproduction, the expansion of consumerism and its logic and the acceleration of the individualistic 'therapeutic culture', which fosters the telling of self-narratives and self-help literature (Plummer 1996; Giddens 1992; Illouz 2007). Shifts in 'practices of intimacy' (Jamieson 1998, 2011) include the rise in non-married cohabitation, increases in childbirth outside of marriage and the use of commercial surrogacy, the legalisation of same-sex marriage, increased attention on living alone or living apart from partners and changes to 'arranged' marriage practices. Equally, these shifts lead to the creation of moral panics and subsequent moral crusades around the normalisation and expansion of commercialised sexual exchanges, trafficking for sexual exploitation, cross-border marriages and mail-order brides, forced and child marriages, sex tourism and the impact of the feminisation of migration and the emergence of transnational care systems on children left behind. Theories and explanations for these shifts tend to overstate change and underemphasise continuity along the familiar trope of geopolitical modernity (or progress narratives).

Many have contested these grand theories as they can 'provide little real aid in understanding the direct empirical world' (Plummer 1996: 37). Family sociology consequently moved towards documenting the intricacies and practices of relationships and family life (e.g. Morgan 1996; Finch 2007; Nordqvist 2010; Phoenix and Brannen 2014; van Hooff 2016; Carter 2017; Thwaites 2013; Morris 2015). Yet this narrow empirical focus, while vital in providing robust evidence for theory-testing, has also obscured the ways in which the 'family' operates in tandem with wider society. Others have, therefore, adopted a more processual concept of intimacy that allows us to explore more than one institutional framework, one idiom of representation and one orientation (Herzfeld 2016: 51) and recognise the ambivalence and tensions contained in intimacy (Berlant 1998). The notion of intimacy can therefore include attitudes, practices, desires and feelings that are safe and dangerous, that bring solace or erupt in violence, that lead to salvation or condemnation and where virtual encounters and increased internal and cross-border mobility have altered the relation between intimacy and distance. Scholars studying people on the move have contributed to a reworking of 'intimacy': 'a productive space where intimacy is shaped as much through emotion and the imagination as by structural constraints' (Bloch 2017: 118 and also Brennan 2004; Constable 2003, 2005, 2009; Cheng 2010; Faier 2009; Hirsch and Wardlow 2006; Padilla et al. 2007). Illouz, though focused primarily on Western societies and drawing on experiences of middle-class and majority groups, attempts to draw out some of these tensions and provides an explanation for the modern condition of love, focusing on why, if love hurts, many still feel it is a hurt worth suffering for.

On the face of it, her account, which incorporates the therapeutic turn and infusion of economics into romance, offers an appealing alternative lens to existing grand theory (e.g. Giddens 1992; Beck and Beck-Gernsheim 2002, 2014; Bauman 2003). Illouz draws on theories of individualisation—particularly Giddens (1992)—to coolly endorse a late modernity where the very process of choice-making has changed significantly. For Illouz, 'modern' conditions of love inevitably produce suffering due to the expansion of the logic of consumerism where 'free' and abundant choice has extended to personal relations, but the conditions of choice are imbued with uncertainty and risk. The way we make decisions about relationships speaks of an instrumental and strategic approach which is—she claims—fundamentally different to the past, where these decisions were embedded in wider moral and social communities. Now, she argues, individuals are left out in the cold to make romantic decisions based purely on their self-rational calculations. Due to these changes in the architecture (reflexivity) and ecology (social conditions) of choice, 'modern' marriage markets have irrevocably changed. And yet, the reversibility of choice in who is selected as a potential partner has increased the uncertainty and risk of every decision made. Moreover, as men and women differ in their strategies and aspirations, this ecology of choice reproduces and maintains the pervasive inequality that characterise gender relations.

Marriage markets have opened up so that class positions no longer determine suitable partners but the consequent increase in choice (enabled and encouraged by dating apps, for example) leads to greater suffering as there is less certainty and security in any choice made. This is explored by Ansari and Klinenberg (2015) in *Modern Romance*, which documents fundamental changes in our expectations about courtship because of significant changes in how people 'search' for a romantic partner (what Illouz calls the romantic ecology) and who individuals consider to be the 'right' person (what Illouz calls the romantic architecture). The seemingly endless possibilities—especially in big cities and with the use of dating technologies—mean that the stakes for making the wrong decision are necessarily incredibly high; as Beck and Beck-Gernsheim (2014: 46) say, 'the greater the choice, the stronger the temptation' to look elsewhere. Moreover—Illouz states—the considerations involved in such decision-making are different, since couple relationships ought to achieve individual fulfilment, realise individual's 'destiny' and accomplish emotional inner balance. Or as Ansari and Klinenberg suggests: coupling involves 'very deep connections between the two people that made them feel like they'd found someone unique, not just someone who was pleasant to start a family with' (2015: 20).

Illouz finds a difference in how decisions are made today about intimate coupling, decisions which are dis-embedded from groups and communities and are now located solely within an individual's cognitive calculation. This cognitive effort relies upon rational, economic balances rather than romantic visions of all-encompassing love and it is in this way that emotions have 'cooled' and intimacy became cold. It should be noted, however, that many theorists of grand social changes in intimacy, including authors mentioned above, have focused their attention on large cosmopolitan, multicultural and largely Western cities. Seebach (2016), following a long history of sociologists and anthropologists who have focused on the forms and conditions of personal relations in urban settings, notes that the dis-embedding of people from identity-providing social contexts is easily intuited in large cities.

Nevertheless, Illouz offers a nuanced account of the process of, and changes within, intimate decision-making, partly as the result of the arrival of digital dating technology, and details how this has impacted on choice, commitment and marriage markets. Illouz also does not overlook continuities in unequal gendered relations and provides a convincing explanation for the continuation of male dominance in sexual fields and marriage markets. This explanation is also unique in offering an insight into modern romantic suffering and the specific conditions which bring about this routine emotional experience. However, she does this from within particular registers, localities and anchored in majority norms.

The chapters in this volume engage with and critique Illouz's theory of the grand transformation in love and here are organised under the following sections. It is important to note that many of the chapters discuss themes that cut across these sections, and this we highlight later. The section headings below follow Illouz's (2012) in *Why Love Hurts*.

'The great transformation of love' deals with some of the underlying assumptions of Illouz's argument, in particular her conceptualisation of choice, commitment and rationality. In Chap. 2, Rachel Thwaites, focusing on heterosexual relationships in Western societies specifically, argues that Illouz's theorisation of choice does not go far enough to explain the tensions and ambiguities within this notion of choice, leaving its underlying political and gendered dynamics largely unexplored and undertheorised. Choice is also a key component in Chap. 3 by Lara McKenzie. She finds that in conversations with age-dissimilar couples undertaken in Perth, Western Australia, choice is emphasised in relation to family obligation and commitment, complicating 'free choice' decisions on whom to partner with. As a resolution, McKenzie suggests that 'free choice' on intimate relationships is co-constituted alongside commitment and obligation of family relations, and these need not necessarily be in tension. In the final chapter of this section, Julia Carter and Daniel Smith explore the limits to 'choice' by paying attention to the meanings behind the exchange of wedding gifts in conversations with couples and individuals in England. The authors take issue with Illouz's conceptualisation of choice and in particular the notion of its reversibility which—the authors argue—finds its limits within intimate consumption practices such as the exchange of wedding gifts.

'Sexual abundance and emotional inequalities' explores in some detail gender differences in dating and emotional competence. In the first chapter of this section, McQueen and Osborn engage with Illouz's conceptualisation of the therapeutic ethos which—as Illouz states—has seen a convergence in emotional competence between middle-class men and women and divergence between middle- and working-class men. To the contrary, McQueen and Osborn find no class differences in positive orientations towards emotional disclosure among men, regardless of their class position, and instead confirm differences in emotional openness between men and women among the Scottish heterosexual men and women they interviewed. Differences in the aspirations, strategies, desires and feelings between men and women are further explored by Jenny van Hooff and Lauren Palmer, who both focused on the role of Tinder, a digital application for dating. Illouz (as well as Beck and Beck-Gernsheim 2014 and Horvat 2015, among others) posits that dating technologies have enabled and promoted short-termism in relationships (or 'commitment phobia' in men) because of the appearance of abundant choice. In her chapter, van Hooff suggests a more nuanced approach among the male heterosexual participants she spoke to in England, who have not entirely rejected long-term commitment but who do tend to initiate casual relationships on dating apps in the first instance. This chapter also highlights the ongoing gender inequalities in sexual fields, a theme drawn out by Palmer in the following chapter, who notes the persistence of gender inequalities when dating through Tinder. Palmer highlights the role of traditional aspirations in dating among the young heterosexual men and women she spoke to in the South-East of England, and how these traditional registers operate alongside the rational calculation of Illouz's 'cold' subjects.

The third section of the collection 'Women's Exclusivist Strategies' expands on the theme of gender inequalities, focusing on women's orientations to love, marriage and family life. In the first chapter in this section, Alison Lamont focuses on the stigma surrounding single Chinese women in their late 20s—'leftover women' or *shengnü*. Illouz's account of decision-making in the selection of intimate partner in the context of a changed architecture and ecology of choice, where decisions are disembedded from wider frameworks and are highly individualised and reflexive, does not work beyond Illouz's researched subjects. In contemporary urban China, family, state and stigma orientate aspirations and inform decisions in intimate partner selection. Kailing Xie expands this and explains how urban university-educated middle-class Chinese men and women construct an enterprising and desiring self through state-sanctioned notions of idealised heterosexual love-marriage and employment. Like McKenzie above, Xie uncovers the tension and ambivalence that family obligations, state-regulated sexual morality and individual ambitions create in particular for women. Finally, Mirna Guha uses Illouz to analyse the conditions and forms of everyday intimacy among female sex workers in a red-light area of Eastern India. Guha identifies commonalities in the operation of the architecture of choice, but finds Illouz's framework limiting as it does not entirely account for experiences after a (failed) marriage in conditions of material and social precarity, where the mother-child relationship accrues most importance. Guha's chapter offers a discussion of the tension of ideal coupling and motherhood, something which is further explored in the final section.

The final section of this book 'From Romantic Fantasy to Disappointment' engages further with Illouz's notion of suffering in love; suffering which, according to Illouz, emerges from an abundance of choice and from men's and women's different orientations to how they choose an intimate partner. In the first chapter in this section, Charlotte Faircloth focuses on the impact of parenting among middle-class and wealthy heterosexual couples in London, couples who were committed to both gender equality and intensive parenting. She finds that the mix of institutional and emotional logics does indeed lead to suffering, particularly given the considerable gender gap inherent in parenting labour, indicating how structural constraints shape how intimacy is done, even among the financially better-off. Charlotte Morris also considers the parent-child relationship. In her narratives from heterosexual single mothers in South-East England, Morris finds that disappointment and suffering are key experiences for her single women participants, emotions which arise not from an abundance of choice or feeling of insecurity in decisions, but rather from the power of normative expectations about family life, gender equality and romantic 'happy endings'. Normative gender convention is a theme which runs into the final chapter in this collection by Raisa Jurva. Jurva, from her conversations with heterosexual middle-aged women with experiences of age-dissimilar relationships in towns and cities of Finland, argues that gendered inequalities and disappointment are an inevitable part of a heterosexual life course. However, as women she spoke to present these stories in a progress narrative, gendered inequalities are not politicised. Once again, disappointment in relationships emerges not from the abundance of choice, but from material as well as affective inequalities. This chapter brings the volume full circle as it resonates with Thwaites's warning on the depoliticisation effect of over-emphasising choice.

The task of organising these chapters into sections was not easy and an argument could be made for eliminating these divisive sections altogether. However, for ease of the reader, this breakdown offers some structure and organisation. It should be noted here, though, the dangers in producing artificial boundaries between papers which have multiple overlaps and intersections. These sections do not represent just one perspective, one cluster or one approach, they are intended merely to point to some commonalities or shared ideas. To highlight the abundant intersections that transcend section-boundaries, we outline below some of the key themes to have emerged from this volume. The first is that of *temporalities and the life course of relationships*. While in *Why Love Hurts*, Illouz is largely concerned with the very beginnings of relationships, throughout this volume we consider relationships at all stages of progression—from their beginnings and their failure to launch (McKenzie, van Hooff, Palmer, Lamont, Xie) through to marriage (Carter and Smith), first-time parenting (Faircloth) and to their endings and beyond (McKenzie, Guha, Morris and Jurva). Using this longer view on relationships and how they span across lives, we can provide a more nuanced account of the intricacies of the forms and conditions of intimacy across different contexts.

Second, contributions to this volume focus on *relationship transitions*: from single to coupled, coupled to married, married to parenthood and from married to divorced or separated and re-coupled. Again, these transitions in status, roles and ideals are not considered in *Why Love Hurts* which focuses solely on the transition from single to dating and back to single. The significance of motherhood (or parenthood) emerges particularly strongly in Guha, Faircloth and Morris, all of whom point to the restrictions that parenthood entails. These constraints or limitations find little resonance in Illouz's considerations of the architecture and ecology of choice which has decision-making as dis-embedded from moral communities and made through an individual's cognitive reflection. On the contrary, these accounts suggest both that moral communities of families continue to provide frameworks for decision-making and that decisions are often made in relational rather than individualised ways (Mason 2004).

Third, our contributors highlight the importance of the *material realities* to discussions of relationships, whether this is regarding class or family expectations (McKenzie, Xie and Lamont), gender inequalities in relating (Thwaites, van Hooff, Palmer, McQueen and Osborn, Jurva), the importance of children (Guha, Faircloth, Morris) or financial hardship (Guha and Morris). In particular, while Illouz does account for gendered differences in romantic suffering, this emerges from the riskiness and loneliness of excessive choice; as many authors in this volume stress however, gendered inequalities materialise in many ways beyond the exercise of individual's choice: through unequal access to parental leave, for example, or differential consequences of male violence against women.

A number of chapters, therefore, speak to *gendered and symbolic violence* which continues to be an aspect of intimate relating, particularly affecting women and producing disproportionately negative consequences (Guha, Faircloth, Morris and Jurva). While these material realities may be accounted for in individualised decision-making, the realities of the impact of class position, wealth inequalities and violence against women on relationship decision-making cannot, and must not, be discounted in contemporary theorising of love and intimacy. We suggest that Illouz's focus on *suffering, wretchedness and disappointment* ought to be re-centred in discussions of contemporary coupledom. However, we disagree that such suffering emerges from the move towards individualism, reflexive decision-making and dis-embedding from moral communities, but are however the result of persistent gendered violence, gendered societal norms and the material and social constraints imposed particularly on women after having children through the lack of state support and financial hardship.

One of the aims of this volume is to try to engage in existing discussion and debate on 'intimacies' and family-making in the current globalised era. Rather than confirming a clear binary between 'true love' or 'pure relationships' on the one hand, and instrumental or 'cold intimacies' on the other, the contributions in this volume provide evidence that complicate such simplistic accounts. 'Intimacy' is in transition but the emotional, material and practical considerations and negotiations of differently positioned men and women here included show that the 'when' and 'with whom' to forge relations and what form these relations should take certainly reflect the confines of people's social worlds, but also intuit a sense of possibility (Hirsch 2003, cited in Bloch 2017: 118). As Carter and Duncan (2018) suggest, 'bricolage' and 'reinvention' are crucial to understanding the role of tradition and the importance of continuity of family life, in the face of global changes in practices and formation.

Finally, Seebach (2016) proposes another reading for, and of, Illouz. Seebach points out that in *Why Love Hurts* (2012), Illouz is focused on the search for a partner, when bonds of love have not yet been created, which gives the impression that love is either 'becoming or vanishing, and exists within an individual rather than between two partners' (Seebach 2016: 51). From this perspective, love is an act of choice and imagination, and the social and moral qualities of love are obscured. Taking a different view, Seebach suggests that enduring love can create stable and durable bonds that provide a new collective form of reasoning, that is not embedded in wider communities, but that is embedded within individuals. In a geopolitical context where the global forces and new technologies of communication that once allowed for a democratisation of love and public recognition of (some) earlier marginalised forms of intimacy are now being undermined, we feel that more widely recording the strategies in negotiating and achieving love that differently positioned people take is needed. This needs to focus on the persistence in forging intimate connections that break with existing moulds despite ever-more constraining structural conditions, in turn allowing us to focus on a politics of hope (and love) that can sit alongside the suffering and misery found in contemporary modern life (Appadurai 2007).

References

Ansari, A. and Klinenberg, E. (2015) *Modern romance*. Penguin Press.

Appadurai, A. (2007) Hope and Democracy. *Public Culture*, 19 (1): 29–34.

Bauman, Z. (2003) Liquid love: on the frailty of human bonds. Polity Press.

Beck, U. and Beck-Gernsheim, E. (2002) Individualization: institutionalized individualism and its social and political consequences. Sage Publications Ltd.

Beck, U. and Beck-Gernsheim, E. (2014) Distant love: personal life in the global age. Polity Press.

Berlant, L. (1998) 'Intimacy: A Special Issue', *Critical Inquiry*, 24(2), pp. 281–288.

Bloch, A. (2017) *Sex, Love, and Migration: Postsocialism, Modernity, and Intimacy from Istanbul to the Arctic*. Cornell University Press.

Brennan, D. (2004) *What's Love Got To Do with It? Transnational Desires and Sex Tourism in the Dominican Republic*. Duke University Press

Carter, J. (2017) 'Why marry? The role of tradition in women's marital aspirations', Sociological Research Online, 22(1), pp. 1–14.

Carter, J. and Duncan, S. (2018) Reinventing couples: Tradition, agency and bricolage. Palgrave Macmillan.

Cheng, S. (2010) *On the Move for Love: Migrant Entertainers and the U.S. Military in South Korea*. University of Pennsylvania Press.

Constable, N. (2003) *Romance on a Global Stage: Pen Pals, Virtual Ethnography, and "Mail Order" Marriages*. University of California Press.

Constable, N. (2005) 'Introduction' in Constable, N. (ed.) *Cross-border Marriages: Gender and Mobility in Transnational Asia*. University of Pennsylvania Press.

Constable, N. (2009) 'The Commodification of Intimacy: Marriage, Sex, and Reproductive Labor', *Annual Review of Anthropology*, 38, pp. 49–64.

Faier, L. (2009) *Intimate Encounters: Filipina Women and the Remaking of Rural Japan*. University of California Press.

Finch, J. (2007) 'Displaying families', Sociology, 41(1), pp. 65–81.

Geschiere, P. (2013) *Witchcraft, Intimacy, and Trust. Africa in Comparison*. University of Chicago Press.

Giddens, A. (1992) The transformation of intimacy: Sexuality, love, and eroticism in modern societies. Stanford University Press.

Herzfeld, M. (2016) *Cultural Intimacy: Social Poetics and the Real Life of States, Societies and Institutions*. Routledge.

Hirsch, J. and Wardlow, H. (2006) *Modern Loves: The Anthropology of Romantic Courtship and Companionate Marriage*. University of Michigan Press.

Horvat, S. (2015) The Radicality of Love. Cambridge: Polity Press.

Illouz, E. (2007) Cold intimacies: The making of emotional capitalism. Polity Press.

Illouz, E. (2012) Why love hurts: A sociological explanation. Wiley/Blackwell.

Jamieson, L. (1998) Intimacy: Personal relationships in modern societies. Polity Press.

Jamieson, L. (2011) 'Intimacy as a Concept: Explaining Social Change in the Context of Globalisation or Another Form of Ethnocentrism' *Sociological Research Online*, 16(4).

Kasulis, T. P. (2002) *Intimacy or Integrity: Philosophy and Cultural Difference*. University of Hawaii Press.

Khandelwal, M. (2009) 'Arranging Love: Interrogating the Vantage Point in Cross-Border Feminism', *Signs: Journal of Women in Culture and Society*, 34(3), pp. 583–609.

Mason, J. (2004) 'Personal Narratives, Relational Selves: Residential Histories in the Living and Telling', The Sociological Review, 52(2), pp. 162–179.

Morgan, D. H. J. (1996) Family connections: An introduction to family studies. Polity Press.

Morris, C. (2015) 'Considerations of Equality in Heterosexual Single Mothers' Intimacy Narratives', Sociological Research Online, 20(4), pp. 1–11.

Nordqvist, P. (2010) 'Out of Sight, Out of Mind: Family Resemblances in Lesbian Donor Conception', Sociology, 44(6), pp. 1128–1144.

Padilla, M. B., Hirsch, J. S., Muñoz-Laboy, M., Sember, R.E. and Parker, R.G. (eds.) (2007) Love and Globalization: Transformations of Intimacy in the Contemporary World. Vanderbilt University Press.

Phoenix, A. and Brannen, J. (2014) 'Researching family practices in everyday life: methodological reflections from two studies', International Journal of Social Research Methodology, 17(1), pp. 11–26.

Plummer, K. (1996) Intimate Citizenship and the Culture of Sexual Story Telling. In: Weeks J., Holland J. (eds) Sexual Cultures. Explorations in Sociology. Palgrave Macmillan, London

Puri, J. (2016) Sexual States: Governance and the Struggle over the Antisodomy Law in India. Duke University Press.

Seebach, S. (2016) Love and society: special social forms and the master emotion. Routledge.

Thwaites, R. (2013) 'The making of selfhood: naming decisions on marriage', Families, Relationships and Societies, 2(3), pp. 425–439.

van Hooff, J. (2016) Modern couples? : continuity and change in heterosexual relationships. Routledge.

Section I

The Great Transformation of Love

2

Intimate Relationships and Choice in a Time of 'Cold Intimacies': Examining Illouz

Rachel Thwaites

Introduction

In a time apparently characterised by 'cold intimacies' (Illouz 2017a [2007]), the concept of choice and choice as a narrative to explain and justify individual actions has become increasingly significant (Giddens 1996; Beck and Beck-Gernsheim 2004, 2010). Sociological debate has both employed and critiqued this concept (Giddens 1996; Illouz 2017a, b [2012]; Thwaites 2017a, b). Relationships and identities are two of the major debates with which sociologists have been preoccupied, and there is empirical evidence that 'liquid' bonds and lack of interest in long-standing commitments is a false conception of the contemporary world (Gross 2005; Carter 2012; Thwaites 2017b). Nevertheless, choice remains a significant concept in everyday identity-building, relationships, politics, and economic decision-making. Therefore, in what ways and for

R. Thwaites (✉)
University of Lincoln, Lincoln, UK
e-mail: rthwaites@lincoln.ac.uk

© The Author(s) 2020   **17**
J. Carter, L. Arocha (eds.), *Romantic Relationships in a Time of 'Cold Intimacies'*,
Palgrave Macmillan Studies in Family and Intimate Life,
https://doi.org/10.1007/978-3-030-29256-0_2

what reasons it is being used and utilised remains significant to understanding interaction and identities.

Illouz's work on 'cold intimacies', which frames the interests of this volume, will be used here as the major starting point for discussion of this concept; her books *Cold Intimacies* (2017a) and *Why Love Hurts* (2017b) will form the basis of this discussion. This chapter will argue that choice is a concept used to close off a great deal of critical discussion and to mask the maintenance of the status quo within heterosexual relationships specifically. Choice does this in part by being used as a means of suggesting openness, tolerance, and acceptance of others, while ignoring the context in which decisions are made, which is patriarchal, racist, classist, and so on (Thwaites 2017a, b). By referring to 'the status quo' throughout this chapter, I do not mean to suggest that relationships, gender, and heterosexuality have not changed at all, but that change has been overemphasised at the expense of an understanding of where continuity remains. The idea of choice is implicated in the suggestion that the world is always ready for change, possibility, and renewal, when, I argue, choice is actually a more conservative concept and less emancipatory than would be hoped. It is important to continue to be critical whenever this concept is used in conversation and in discourse. This chapter will do this in dialogue with Illouz's arguments. Though I argue Illouz's ideas overplay change in late modernity, they do help us towards a renewed understanding of the continued dominance of men in heterosexual relationship decision-making.

Sociological Debate on Choice

The concept of choice[1] is slippery and has opened up a great deal of debate within Sociology. These discussions are now well worn and I will provide just a brief outline here for context as to how choice has been conceptualised by some of the major theorists of individualisation. We might hope, along with Giddens (1996, 2008), that choice is something highly positive, opening up new possibilities and life chances, and therefore to be encouraged. As Giddens argues (1996, 2008), choice can mean the ability to throw off the bonds of tradition and inequality and to think of oneself in new ways. It can actually create a new set of ontologies that people can access, opening up imagination and making new life paths seem viable. This is one way of looking at what choice 'is' and something that most people would aspire towards, particularly in social justice research and activism. This kind of choice is captivating and inspiring and, if genuine, not something to be curtailed.

However, the very extent of the positive outline of choice in Giddens' work has provoked backlash. Theorists such as Beck and Beck-Gernsheim (2010), and also Bauman (2003), are well known for their perspectives on choice and take rather different stances. Bauman (2003, 2012) takes a negative view of contemporary society, the proliferation of choice, and the impact this has had on personal relationships, as well as the intensification of commodification. His sense is that late modernity is a time of less commitment, more focus on 'lifestyles', and that the choices that come from this are focused on consumption and on individual goals. His work is full of a kind of lament for a previous, more integrated, and kinder past (though he accepts that this past may, in part, be pure nostalgia, rather than something real) (Bauman 2001). Beck and Beck-Gernsheim (2004, 2010) take more of a middle path than either of the previous theorists, suggesting that choice and change in relationships and wider society have opened up some positives and produced some negatives too. As with Giddens (2008) they see women's changing position as at the heart of this change, but also see women as differently placed within it to men: women continue to lead more relational lives and have more restricted choices to make (Beck and Beck-Gernsheim 2004, 2010).

These theorists have inspired a great deal of further theoretical and also empirical sociological work exploring these ideas (see, e.g. Gross 2005; Thwaites 2017b). Such discussion shows that scholarly debate has not been able to pin down the precise nature of choice and whether its modern iteration should be considered a positive or a negative. It is a slippery concept, able to be used for a variety of means. What is clear is that how we think of this concept can change how we consider the contemporary world, intimate relationships, social justice, and decision-making in significant ways. Rather more recently than Giddens, Beck, Beck-Gernsheim, and Bauman, the term 'cold intimacies' has emerged from Eva Illouz (2017a), who explores contemporary relationships and their saturation with the language of the market. Within this discussion the concept of choice is crucial, and it is Illouz's discussion that I will grapple with in this chapter, to examine how her thoughts and arguments may inform sociological debate on this concept.

'Cold Intimacies': Illouz's Concept of Choice

Illouz's *Cold Intimacies*, first published in 2007, and since reprinted several times, outlines her thesis that emotions and capitalism have become closely bound in late modernity. She relates this binding to the rise of a strong and pervasive therapeutic discourse, arising from psychology, which has come to shape most aspects of our lives; she also notes the impact of feminism on everyday discourse too (2017a). These discourses and the growth of internet technologies have reshaped how we love and make choices in love; in her words in *Why Love Hurts*, these have changed the 'ecology' and 'architecture' of choice (see Illouz 2017b).

To outline this thesis for the sake of the discussion in this chapter: Illouz argues (2017a) that Psychology developed as a discipline—with Freud at the heart of it—at the point in history at which professionalisation and sharpening of disciplinary boundaries was occurring. Freud marked Psychology out as a discipline dealing with sexuality, the inner self, and self-realisation. This appealed to individuals looking for new ways of understanding themselves and making sense of their emotional lives; the very focus on the individual, who has an important and 'authentic' self to 'discover' was exciting and new. However, this psychological way of thinking about and explaining the self also sets up every person within society as 'sick' in the sense that their 'true' self has been stultified behind neurosis, inhibition, trauma, family problems, and so on. Every person, then, needs the efforts of the psychologist to help them move beyond this to meet their 'authentic' self. This, Illouz argues (2017a: 28), is a real change from previous ideas of the self, which were more holistic and did not suggest layers to be discovered, but instead the need to find significant relationships through which one could communicate that self; the self was always 'true', 'authentic', and present. Essentially, Illouz argues that the mind-self was medicalised through psychology and that there are both positive and negative aspects to this; it became significant to work through one's emotions, understand one's suffering, and come to a better understanding of the self. This would mean a more fulfilling life. The ease with which modern readers can understand this discourse and see it as common sense shows the impact of this. Illouz is focusing on American society throughout this book, but the influence of twentieth-century America and the wider appeal of psychological explanations have moved beyond the USA.

Illouz continues this discussion, describing how psychologists expanded their domain of expertise (2017a: 10–11). Instead of claiming only one space of professional knowledge, they argued that therapeutic and psychological explanations and ways of tackling problems could be useful in many areas. Including, and most significantly, the world of work. This science of the mind and of emotion was taken up as a way to move beyond the sterile, system-driven organisation of Taylorism and Fordism. Psychologists turned the working world inwards, encouraging workers and managers alike to think about individuals, emotions, and relationships. Illouz argues that this is a feminisation of the workplace, but one that actually works to blur gender binaries (2017a: 16, 23) and that it was an important step in equalising relationships at work—she sees this as a part of the feminist movement's claims as to the importance of equality and rights for all (2017a: 26). Instead of complete manager control, the focus was now on good 'communication' and working out the troubles of workers to create better efficiency (2017a: 18–20). Emotion became a central part of working life and those with good 'emotional competence' could 'trade' this as a commodity leading to better assessment of performance at work, promotion, and pay rises.[2]

Following Bourdieu, Illouz argues (2017a: 63) that 'emotional capital' can be transformed into social and economic capital and this is a key change in late modernity. This sense of being able to 'trade' skills, competencies, and capitals crossed from the working life into the personal, where one now sees oneself as part of a 'market' where 'emotional competence' and 'sexual/erotic capital' are all part of this trading (Illouz 2017b: 56). One will be looking to do the best deal within this market—and be thinking about how one can trade up, or what one might lose by doing the wrong deal. This is strongly influenced by internet dating, in Illouz's discussion, to which I return below. Emotions—narrating, making objective, and 'communicating'—have become central to understanding ourselves, our relationships, and our working lives, but have also become a commodity to trade through this process, in both personal and professional spheres; capitalist, market language has saturated every part of our lives. As Illouz makes explicit in *Why Love Hurts* (2017b: 58) 'the laws of supply and demand, scarcity, and oversupply' have come to dominate our intimate and sexual lives and this has changed how we go about choosing a partner (or partners). In this sense we have 'cold intimacies', where capitalism, marketisation, trade, and commodification have become an everyday and accepted way of thinking about, and actualising, our personal and intimate lives: rationality rather than passion dominates.

Within this discourse choice becomes a highly significant idea. It is key to doing the right deal, to 'trading up' when appropriate, and to steering the course of one's relationship. We are aware that choices are about our status and the status of others and we look to trade as well as possible on the contemporary 'marriage market' (Illouz 2017b: 55). Illouz argues that contemporary life means that choices of relationship are made in a context of 'abundance', in part because of internet dating where we can see the full extent of the market before actually meeting anyone (2017a: 85, b: 78), and hence we are overwhelmed by possibility. The level of choice actually ends in a devaluing of all the possible objects of love and makes it harder to settle on one person: more people end up lonely and alone, or actually unable or unwilling to commit to another (see 2017b: 78–90 for Illouz's discussion of different types of 'commitment phobia'). Abundance of choice can actually lead the contemporary person to a place of paralysis of action or to a place where all people are made lesser because of the awareness of the relative sameness of everyone: and there is always the possibility someone more exciting and unusual will come along (Illouz 2017a: 87). From this perspective, increased choice has not made things better for contemporary individuals trying to make decisions about love.

Choice is also significant more widely, as a social and cultural ideal that is linked to agency, competence, and indeed, mastery—of oneself and one's life course. It speaks to the cultural dominance of rationality that Illouz discusses. 'Making a choice' suggests a clearly thought out and rational decision, made after weighing up the various options and choosing the correct course. It does not suggest following norms and traditions, unthinkingness (Shils 1971; see also Thwaites 2017b), the impact of others, or the impact of intangible, difficult to understand, or conflicting emotions. This agentic decision-maker is a key figure in modern Western cultures, the rational figure of economic modelling and of individualisation theory (Meyers 1997: 2; see also Thwaites 2017b: 9–10). The imaginative pull of this figure is very strong: would we not all like to think we are actively in charge of our own life?

The tension within the concept is clear, and Illouz points it out repeatedly (2017b): choice opens up possibilities but at the same time paralyses action and overwhelms, devaluing the many choices available through sheer abundance. It has connotations of activeness, thinking, and agency, but in fact can confuse and prevent action, creating a sense of anxiety and ontological insecurity. She also makes it clear that this has a gendered dimension within intimate heterosexual relationships and decisions about love: with men having no social or economic reason to marry and have children in contemporary Western societies and therefore less desire than women to do so, but women remaining desirous of marriage and children because it will improve their status in a variety of ways (Illouz 2017b: 55, 102). Freedom of choice in this situation is therefore not equal. Women's desire to commit has been documented in recent research, along with a continued sense that domesticity provides a status to women that men do not necessarily gain or aspire to (Thwaites 2017b; Carter 2012; Langford 1999). Illouz argues (2017b: 102, 106) that this desire to commit does more to create and sustain relationships, and therefore, in being more invested in the relationship, women are at a disadvantage at both the choosing stage and within relationships (see Faircloth and Morris, this volume), as men can emotionally dominate in dating and in the longer term because they have less to lose.

Throughout this discussion, Illouz attempts to explain and clarify *every stage* in the process of relationship formation in terms of institutional change. She starts to show us what choice *does* to each of us and suggests why these changes might have come about. Her argument provides a complex and insightful perspective on the concept of choice and its impact on intimate, heterosexual relationships.

Debating Illouz: Choice in Late Modernity

However, there are some aspects of her argument that give a moment's pause. For example, though evidence shows that men and boys are *more likely* to see cohabitation as an end in itself than women and girls, overall, the majority of men and women, boys and girls, continue to see marriage as something they want for their future (see Manning et al. 2017) and Illouz's claim that 'commitment phobia' is widespread is not evidenced strongly (see Illouz 2017b: 65–68). Much of what Illouz argues can be seen in earlier discussions as well, for example, Jónasdóttir (1991) exploring love power in the 1990s, arguing that men use this power in love to maintain their dominant position within relationships; while Duncombe and Marsden (1993) have looked at emotional labour within relationships and the work that women do to sustain them that ultimately leaves women depleted. Illouz's work also links strongly to previous discussions of anxiety and ontological insecurity (see, e.g. Bauman 2001; Giddens 1996). Furthermore, she overplays some of the change she describes and does not give enough space to the pull of the past or indeed to the potential for continuity in terms of choice and intimate relationships.

Illouz accepts that gender continues to play a part in unequally structuring relationships, but she also suggests that social positionings may be revolutionised through cold intimacies, with class, gender, and race all becoming less significant or new possibilities being opened for power from those who would traditionally not have it, including suggesting women dominate men through sexual/erotic capital (Illouz 2017b: 51–52, 54–55). She also argues that sexuality has become uncoupled from morality, and so opened up a sense of genderlessness in heterosexual relationships (Illouz 2017b: 49). These suggestions are simply not upheld by empirical research into contemporary heterosexual relationships; her more general point of continued, if differently structured, domination by men of women is a much more strongly evidenced point in the wider literature (Carter 2012; van Hooff 2013; Thwaites 2017b). The lack of an empirical basis for some of Illouz's points is striking, especially when the 'immanent critique' is meant, in part, to be based on empirically exploring the world so as not to privilege one perspective over another. I will return to the immanent critique below.

In one sense cold intimacies have always existed. We cannot look to discussions of marriages in the past—certainly those of the upper classes—and deny that choices were bound up with 'market' decision-making: money, status, alliances. Illouz (2017b: 58, 109) argues that it is more visible and explicit now—and in the sense of emotions being there to be inspected, discussed, and traded, with a focus on supply and demand, I can agree—but there has always been an instrumental and economic set of concerns involved with marriage, in which love and other emotions have been used as part of the bartering process (see, e.g. Erickson 2005). Marriage has always been based on an unequal distribution of (gendered) resources and choice has been curtailed for women due to this unequal distribution. Some of what we are seeing in late modernity around choice of partner and of living and making choices within longer term relationships is therefore an *exacerbation* or *extension* of ongoing concerns, rather than the contemporary organisation of relationships making the effects of choice something new. 'Cold intimacies' have always existed, but our attempts to mask this may have shifted and changed with the language and concepts around love and relationships that we use.

The love narrative—marriage for the sake of love alone—is only one way of thinking and speaking about marriage and relationships. In many ways it is an anomaly in historical time and we are *returning* to a more instrumental discussion of love and relationships. As Cancian and Gordon (1988) have argued, the more therapeutic idea of love as what will allow the self to grow and develop is a fairly recent idea, when prior to this a more rational idea of marriage—bound up with status, money, making alliances, social respectability, and having children prevailed. Therefore, we could see a growth in more economic language as an erosion of a narrative that has had its day and a *return* to a long-standing means of thinking about marriage, love, and heterosexual relationships. Choice is implicated in this returning narrative of economic and rational thought in love and marriage, but in gendered ways.

Previously there was an acceptance of relational needs and duties in an explicit way, but now, as the individualisation theorists argue (Beck and Beck-Gernsheim 2010; Bauman 2003; Giddens 1996), to a greater or lesser extent we have a discourse of individual, choice-based decision-making, where one does what is best for oneself alone when making relationship decisions. However, this works out in gendered ways within heterosexual relationships (Thwaites 2017a, b), actually helping to mask the continued existence of inequality and 'cold intimacies'. It is perhaps less the cold intimacies that are the new in all of this, and more the pulling between ideas of individual agency, relational love, and life chances that goes on: the tension between what is explicit and what is implicit in contemporary narratives of self and relationships.

Illouz's work is deliberately and carefully argued from within the confines of the psycho-social perspective—she is using the immanent critique to explore the contradictions and multiplicity of contemporary intimacies and the psychological and therapeutic narratives that create, recreate, and frame these intimacies. Her arguments are therefore intended to be contradictory, in an attempt to explore complexity and not pre-judge what might be emancipatory or oppressive in contemporary intimacies. This style brings the complexity to the fore and explores a number of perspectives, opening up the possibility of alternative viewpoints. However, its limitations are also made clear. Remaining within the confines of the framework one wishes to explore—and even, in fact, critique—prevents one from taking a fully critical look at that framework. When this is done deliberately, as Illouz does, not because she agrees with the boundaries of thinking that framework creates but as a means of critique, it acts to curtail and depoliticise her argument: she could go further. Yes, contradictions and complexities are exposed and explored, but there is a lack of political scope.

The immanent critique also aims to explore empirically, rather than dogmatically, any idea put forward—this is intended to stop the privileging of ideas that may have been accepted over time without any basis in real lives or because they have power behind them. First, considering my own critique of Illouz falls on an ultimately evaluatory framework, which cannot be described as 'immanent', it is perhaps important to state that my comments on choice come from empirical work exploring lived lives and choices within heterosexual relationships (Thwaites 2017a, b) and not purely from dogmatic posturing. However, in reading Illouz's work, though empirical research is mentioned, there is little explanation of how this work was done or how it has been interpreted. The reader is not given information to guide their judgement of this work, nor of how Illouz has used it. How this empirical work fits with or informs the theoretical discussion is not clear; it is therefore also not clear how fully the empirical side of the immanent critique has been fulfilled. Every author has a set of beliefs that will have an impact on their reading of contemporary society, including its complexities and contradictions. Ultimately Illouz *does* have a position on contemporary relationships: they are unequal and men continue to dominate women in a variety of ways. How her beliefs and the aims of immanent critique sit together remains unexplored.

In reading Illouz it is striking how much of what she examines, explores, and exposes makes sense and speaks to the contemporary reader as an explanation for modern intimate lives. Yet the points I raise above also show the limitations of the discussion. By remaining within the confines of the psycho-social perspective there is an acceptance of choice in terms of how it has been defined by this perspective: as a means of creating *change*. Change for the better or change for worse, but *change*. This perspective does not allow Illouz to take the immanent critique further and explore the tensions and contradictions within choice itself, merely the positive or negative outcomes of what has been pre-judged and defined.

Choice is therefore not changing the underlying dynamics of heterosexual intimate relationships, instead it is helping to mask inequality and the status quo, and it is this tension that is the most significant aspect of choice and the use of choice in everyday discourse for late modernity. A tension Illouz alludes to, but does not explore in enough depth to give its full political due.

Exploring Choice

In this section I wish to take these tensions and contradictions within choice and explore them and their meaning for late modern individuals in more detail, before going on to look at the gendered aspects of this within heterosexual relationships. The aim is to build on Illouz's discussion and add a more political dimension. This is done out with the framework of the immanent critique however, and this means a more evaluatory perspective is brought to bear. I accept this itself is a tension between my own critique and Illouz's, but argue that the need to go beyond the framework of the psycho-social perspective is pressing when thinking about choice.

Choice is bound up with our sense of ourselves as *individuals*, leading lives that we govern and steer; it suggests an active, purposeful life and an agent who makes decisions that are rational and reasoned. This agentic person would be an ideal interviewee, able to fully justify their life course and decision-making. They are similar to the rational decision-maker that is the centre of economic models and fit the idea of the modern individualised agent. In short, this person knows what they are doing and why they are doing it. However, this person is also not real, but an ideal. Without emotion, intangibles, and indeed, sheer luck and hope, the reality of human decision-making is not fully understood or holistically explained. Humans are not fully rational beings who always know what they are doing. And yet, 'choice' is an incredibly important idea and a word that can be used to explain and justify decisions as if they were rational and clearly made: 'it was my choice'. Within this phrase many things are hidden.

As a speech act, invoking 'choice' tends to mean the end of discussion. If someone has made 'a choice'—active, considered, agentic, personal— then to argue with them is to argue against their personal circumstances and to suggest they are incorrect on an individual level. To suggest you know better than another person about their own life can be considered a rather strange argument. Choice is therefore difficult to argue with, certainly without making it sound like a personal attack, and therefore debate can be silenced. Also, as Illouz argues (2017a: 65–66), the saturation of our lives with the idea of emotional capitalism makes the idea of choice even more significant and understandable as a speech act: making sensible choices is the central discourse of contemporary Western societies. When linked to therapeutic narratives, it suggests healthy selves, who have come to understand themselves clearly and are therefore 'successful': they have achieved better self-realisation and are working to maintain and improve their lives and relationships through this.

Craib (1994) argues that this framing of what it means to be 'successful' tends to mean that late modern selves see negative emotions and experiences as 'failure'. He, like Illouz, comes from a psycho-social perspective but stresses that, though there are many positives to psychological therapies—which need to be taken into account when thinking through their effects (Illouz 2017a: 71)—there can also be a significant downside to focusing on the individual in so much depth. It takes away from the interconnected nature of every person and from the structural. As the individualisation theorists have argued (Beck and Beck-Gernsheim 2010; Bauman 2003), we come to think in the main of our own goals and aims, while having increasingly limited thought about others and relational goals. Craib manages to avoid the deep gloom that Bauman (2001, 2003, 2012) casts over modern society, while making it clear that he feels this is not a positive path. This idea of 'success' needs to be interrogated and ways found to bring in disappointment, negativity, and failure as normal parts of human experience, without blame or pathologising the self. Choices are not always clearly made, and they are not always made to help ourselves or further our life chances.

A means to do this is to explore the concepts of happiness and success in more critical detail, giving us a sociological perspective on why we make the choices that we do. As Illouz makes clear (2017a, b), emotions are a significant part of all that we do, whether at work or in our personal lives. 'Cold intimacies' may mean an attempt to trade emotion rationally and carefully to get the best deal, but it does not mean we can be sure of a successful outcome. This is why failure is so difficult to accept: there is no one, in this set up, to blame, except the self. Therefore, *hope* remains a strong part of making the right deal, of making the right choice. Emotion is not usually something the concept of choice is associated with—emotion and rationality are separated as a binary in Western cultures, despite the historical complexity of this cultural construction (see Reddy 2009). Binaries are constructed as mutually exclusive and therefore emotion and rationality are not seen to mix. There is a further aspect to this, which is that emotion is gendered. Throughout history emotion has been feminised (with gender also constructed as a binary) and emotion and femininity closely aligned, while rationality and masculinity have been set against them (Reddy 2009: 309). Nevertheless, as shown by exploring Illouz, Craib, and Ahmed, emotion is interwoven into the choices that we make and how we can come to understand ourselves as successful actors within late modern capitalism.

Such desire for positive emotional lives, to achieve happiness, and to be seen as a success are powerful means of social control. Acting outside the boundaries of norms is not only difficult but actively unpalatable. As Ahmed argues (2010: 64), this turns us from certain objects and life paths, towards the normative (though not necessarily consciously). We are not making choices free from the influence of others and/or of society in choosing a partner or within a relationship. To use Sara Ahmed's phrasing, 'the promise of happiness' (2010) has already been given to us: if we associate ourselves with certain objects we will be happy and therefore, we will be successful (and intelligible to others or 'normal'). This means the 'choices' we have open to us are immediately narrowed and founded on normative ideals. The idea of 'abundance' in choice of partner, or free choice in the decisions we make once in a relationship, is an overstatement—there are limits to this choice and these limits are socially governed by traditions and norms.

Hence, choice manages to *suggest* possibilities, careful consideration, and success in late modern capitalism, and yet what it *does* is shut down discussion, stifle debate, and even exacerbate gendered and other inequality. Along with the emotional dominance of men that Illouz discusses, which leads to their having more say in decision-making and therefore more say on material and everyday aspects of the heterosexual relationship, Illouz points out (2017a: 69) that therapeutic narratives are middle class (see also McQueen and Osborn, this volume): having access to the language and the therapy itself to create these narratives requires a particular set of capitals. By maintaining that emotional competence is a sign of a successful and healthy self, inequalities are engrained. Without wider recourse to social structure—bringing decisions down to the individual—and without the chance to debate decisions as 'choice', discussion shuts down: we lose the ability to consider why choices are made, why social patterns and trends remain, and why social justice can be slow to materialise. This is why it is important to continuously be critical of choice and to explore how it is being used and for what means. This allows for more discussion of why we make the choices that we do and why sometimes these result in negative or difficult experiences. In the next section I will focus in more detail on the gendered aspect of choice and the need for a more political perspective in Illouz's discussion.

Choice, Gender, and Heterosexual Relationships

Specifically, choice can be used to maintain the gendered status quo in relationships, masking the power involved in decision-making and the patriarchal history of heterosexual relationships. Illouz accepts that change in the contemporary world holds within it tension and contradiction, and she accepts, in *Why Love Hurts* (2017b), that love and heterosexual relationships are unequal. She posits that choice devalues individuals to such an extent that everyone feels less sure about commitment to one other person, and that people are always thinking about the possibilities that someone better—a better deal—will come along. As discussed above, she sees this as highly gendered, with men at an advantage in any deal-making and decision-making. This advantage continues within the relationship and this power allows men to emotionally dominate their partners (Illouz 2017b: 82). Although Illouz posits (2017a: 92) that there is no direct continuity between social spheres, she accepts emotional dominance and inequality in heterosexual relationships and, when it comes to decision-making about any aspect of life in a long-term relationship, the ability to dominate emotionally allows greater decision-making power. This in turn has an impact on dominating material and social life more widely, though the extent of this will inevitably vary. The suggestion that emotional dominance cannot have a direct impact on other social spheres makes little sense in intimate relationships. This chimes with previous research, where emotional domination exists and does have material impacts (Thwaites 2017b; Langford 1999). Illouz's explanation for continued gendered inequality within relationships, despite much wider change, is useful to work with, but with a stronger political edge relating to the potential for impacts on wider material lives.

Part of this dominance of emotional lives appears to come from the very tension between the romantic/spiritual and the sober/modern. Illouz argues (2017b: 8) that late modernity, complete with 'cold intimacies', turns us away from romance and spiritual ideas that gave life a sense of meaning, fun, and ritual, lifting one out of the boredom of the everyday. In late modernity we must look soberly at ourselves and calmly justify our choices and decisions by weighing them up and talking them out, clearly and coherently, from among the range of possibilities open to us. Illouz's female respondents seem caught between these two worlds, wishing for romance and transcendence, while knowing they should be able to think soberly about their relationships, taking into account equality and tolerance of others; in Illouz's own (rather psychological) terms:

> Women's emotions and desire for commitment are often *a priori* inscribed in their strategy of pairing and, as a result, women are more likely to experience conflicting desires, employ confused emotional strategies, and be dominated by men's greater capacity to withhold commitment through serial sexuality. (Illouz 2017b: 106)

As Langford (1999) shows in her research, women want love to act as a transcendental moment in their lives, lifting them from boredom and drudgery, and giving them a new status. The strongest tension lies in making sense of oneself when caught between the pull of contradictory social norms in love and relationships: being female means looking after everyone's emotional needs, yet feeling that you are entitled to as much care and attention from your male partner as equality in relationships commands—wanting to be swept off your feet and cared for, but being aware this would suggest you may be old-fashioned, lacking in agency, or actively unable to look after yourself. These tensions pull at the heart of many romantic relationships, particularly for women (Illouz 2017b: 106).

As equality and liberation narratives become subsumed by a wider neoliberal choice rhetoric (Heron 2008), linked to a therapeutic agenda that channels energy into normative success, and increased focus on the individual, this has its impact on intimate heterosexual relationships. Individuals strive to find love and happiness and realise their authentic selves through making good choices and working through their options in life to get the best deal for themselves. However, this ignores—or masks—the ongoing structural inequality. If we accept this market in intimate relationships exists, we should perceive that it is not one of *free* trade in commodities or capitals, but one that rests on inequality (as does the wider economic market!) as well as on normative action for perceived happiness and success as a neoliberal subject. This is why we have seen so little change between genders in terms of their power within intimate relationships, despite legal and social changes in a more equal direction, and it links to emotional dominance of decision-making. Bringing the emotional, material, and structural together is key for making political claims for continued gender inequality in heterosexual relationships.

Conclusion

Illouz's arguments offer challenging insights into contemporary intimate relationships. She works deliberately within a framing that explores the complexity and contradiction of contemporary love, dating, and relationships. She explores the impact of choice on everyday lives in love and how technology is wrapped up in these choices. However, she leaves the tensions within choice itself opaque, not stepping outside the psychological and therapeutic framing of choice to explore how it can in fact work to maintain continuity and the status quo nor examining the discourses on choice within her own data. Choice is not all about change and in fact, in intimate heterosexual relationships it tends towards keeping traditions and norms in place, because our decisions are so deeply embedded in our emotional and relational—as opposed to rational and individual—lives. Though this is a deliberate choice of framing by Illouz it leaves the argument stranded without a political-critical edge. The gendered aspect of these tensions makes this a significant social justice issue for late modernity. The limits of people's lives are being defined by choice and its use in everyday discourse. When the stakes are this high, such a political-critical edge is essential.

Notes

1. Choice could be put in inverted commas throughout this chapter—it is an idea as socially constructed as any other. For ease of reading the chapter I have only put the word in inverted commas when I want to strongly highlight my argument that choice is not something free and open, but something that is frequently curtailed in some way, or when choice is almost invoked as a kind of talisman against more detailed discussion.

2. This leads to jobs that focus on 'emotional labour', as discussed by Arlie Hochschild (1983). Though Illouz is largely positive about emotional competence in her discussion, Hochschild's analysis of the interlinking of emotions and labour is worth remembering and should give some pause for thought.

References

Ahmed, S. (2010) *The Promise of Happiness*. Durham, N.C.: Duke University Press.

Bauman, Z. (2012) *44 Letters from the Liquid Modern World*. Cambridge: Polity Press.

Bauman, Z. (2003) *Liquid Love*. Cambridge: Polity Press.

Bauman, Z. (2001) *Community: Seeking Safety in an Insecure World*. Cambridge: Polity Press.

Beck, U. and Beck-Gernsheim, E. (2010) *Individualization*. London: Sage.

Beck, U. and Beck-Gernsheim, E. (2004) *The Normal Chaos of Love*. Cambridge: Polity Press.

Cancian, F.M. and Gordon, S.L. (1988) Changing Emotion Norms in Marriage: Love and Anger in U.S. Women's Magazines Since 1900. *Gender and Society*. 2 (3): 308–342.

Carter, J. (2012) What is commitment? Women's accounts of intimate attachment. *Families, Relationships and Societies*. 1 (2): 137–153

Craib, I. (1994) *The Importance of Disappointment*. London: Routledge.

Duncombe, J. and Marsden, D. (1993) Love and Intimacy: The Gender Division of Emotion and 'Emotion Work'. *Sociology*. 27 (2): 221–241.

Erickson, A. (2005) The Marital Economy in Comparative Perspective. In M. Agren and A. Erickson (eds). *The Marital Economy in Scandinavia and Britain 1400–1900*. Aldershot: Ashgate: 3–20.

Giddens, A. (2008) *The Transformation of Intimacy*. Cambridge: Polity Press.

Giddens, A. (1996) *Modernity and Self-Identity*. Cambridge: Polity Press.

Gross, N. (2005) Detraditionalization Reconsidered. *Sociological Theory*. 23 (3): 286–311.

Heron, T. (2008) Globalization, Neoliberalism and the Exercise of Human Agency. *International Journal of Politics, Culture, and Society*. 20 (1/4): 85–101.

Hochschild, A. (1983) *The Managed Heart: Commercialization of Human Feeling*. Berkeley: University of California Press.

Illouz, E. (2017b [2012]) *Why Love Hurts: A Sociological Explanation.* Cambridge: Polity Press.

Illouz, E. (2017a [2007]) *Cold Intimacies: The Making of Emotional Capitalism.* Cambridge: Polity Press.

Jónasdóttir, A. (1991) *Love Power and Political Interests: Towards a Theory of Patriarchy in Contemporary Western Societies.* Örebro: University of Örebro.

Langford, W. (1999) *Revolutions of the Heart: Gender, Power, and the Delusions of Love.* London: Routledge.

Manning, W.D., Longmore, M.A., Giodano, P.C. (2017) The Changing Institution of Marriage: Adolescents' Expectations to Cohabit and to Marry. *Journal of Marriage and Family.* 69 (3): 559–575.

Meyers, D.T. (1997) Introduction. In D.T. Meyers (ed.) *Feminists Rethink the Self.* Boulder, CO: Westview Press: 1–11.

Reddy, W.M. (2009) Historical Research on the Self and Emotions. *Emotion Review.* 1 (4): 302–315.

Shils, E. (1971) Tradition. *Comparative Studies in Society and History.* 13 (2): 122–159.

Thwaites, R. (2017a) Making a Choice or Taking a Stand? Choice Feminism, Political Engagement, and the Contemporary Feminist Movement. *Feminist Theory.* 18 (1): 55–68

Thwaites, R. (2017b) *Changing Names and Gendering Identity: Social Organisation in Contemporary Britain.* London: Routledge.

van Hooff, J. (2013) *Modern Couples? Continuity and Change in Heterosexual Relationships.* Farnham, Surrey: Ashgate.

3

Making Up and Breaking Up: The Changing Commitments of Age-Dissimilar Couples

Lara McKenzie

Introduction

In recent decades, there has been much theorisation of love and couple relationships among social scientists, emphasising the growing idealisation of romantic love, greater personal autonomy and choice in relationships, and the rising significance of distance and divorce (Bauman 2003; Beck and Beck-Gernsheim 2013; Giddens 1992; Hochschild 2003; Illouz 2007). Modern relationships, it is argued, are intertwined with democracy, individualism, commercialism, and capitalism and are

I wish to thank my interviewees and participants for opening up their lives to me. Many thanks also to the editors of this volume, for their patience, dedication, and feedback. I am grateful to my former PhD supervisors, Katie Glaskin and Michael Pinches, who played a key role in the development of this project. Some financial support was provided by The University of Western Australia, through the Social and Cultural Studies Postgraduate Research Fund and the Graduate Research School Completion Scholarship Program.

L. McKenzie (✉)
The University of Western Australia, Perth, WA, Australia
e-mail: lara.mckenzie@uwa.edu.au

© The Author(s) 2020   **37**
J. Carter, L. Arocha (eds.), *Romantic Relationships in a Time of 'Cold Intimacies'*,
Palgrave Macmillan Studies in Family and Intimate Life,
https://doi.org/10.1007/978-3-030-29256-0_3

becoming increasingly fragile. A key theorist here is Eva Illouz (2007), who introduces the notion of 'cold intimacies', arguing that capitalism and intimate life are now converging. Capitalism, she says, is deeply invested with emotion, while intimate life draws increasingly from economics and politics. She asserts that relationships' increasing rationalisation—and the growing significance of 'choice, rationality, interest, [and] competition' (Illouz 2012: 10) within them—has led to the destabilisation and 'cooling' of intimacies.[1] Similarly, Zygmunt Bauman (2003) posits that modern love relationships are 'liquid'. He suggests that people are more and more 'desperate to 'relate', yet 'wary of the state of "being related"' (Bauman 2003: viii). As a result they form loose ties rather than fixed, durable bonds. Both Illouz (2007, 2012) and Bauman (2003) are thus especially concerned with how capitalism and its logic disrupt enduring intimacies.

Indeed, it is frequently claimed that companionship, obligation, and commitment to both kin and non-kin are increasingly losing out to individualised relationships and short-term pleasure, with couplings being less and less subject to 'traditional' social constraints (see also Beck and Beck-Gernsheim 2013; Giddens 1992). The growing prevalence and apparent acceptance of age-dissimilar couples is often taken to reflect this shift. Likewise, rising divorce rates and the burgeoning of short-term and casual sex relationships is seen as evidencing cultural change (Amato et al. 2009). In my qualitative interviews with different-sex (heterosexual) age-dissimilar couples in Australia, however, I find that, alongside fulfilment and free choice, commitment and obligation remain enduring themes in people's accounts of their love and family lives. In this chapter, I explore how age-dissimilar couples talk about the beginnings and ends of their relationships. Such talk reflects a dual logic: that love and its attachments should be lasting *and* fulfilling. In doing so, I draw particularly on the anthropological work of Naomi Quinn (1996) and Claudia Strauss (Strauss and Quinn 1997), who rather point to the historical continuity and complementarity of the supposedly competing expectations of lastingness and fulfilment. As such, I challenge the claims of Illouz (2007, 2012), Bauman (2003), and others that modern relationships are increasingly 'cold' or 'liquid'.

I begin by exploring two key concepts that I utilise throughout this chapter: age dissimilarity and love. Following this, I provide a brief outline of my research methods, participants, and analysis. Next, I investigate cases where interviewees encountered family disapproval, and use these to illustrate the continued relevance and importance of commitment and obligation in people's personal lives. I then draw on interviewees' accounts of forming and ending relationships to show how lastingness and fulfilment were sometimes compatible, but were thought undesirable if a relationship was not based on love. Ending a relationship was thus justified on the basis that love had never been present, and therefore an 'unsuccessful' relationship could not have been lasting or fulfilling. In my final discussion, I question whether interviewees' understandings actually contradicted one another. I ask if relationships can be characterised by enduring commitments, or by choices to remain together based on ongoing enjoyment. I suggest that these understandings of love are complementary rather than contradictory. As such, I argue for an approach that accounts for complexity and contradiction in how age dissimilarity and love are understood.

Conceptualising Age-Dissimilar Couples and Love

Little qualitative research has been undertaken on age-dissimilar couples. While the definition of an age difference has been debated at length, most detailed studies have been quantitative, drawing largely on marriage statistics in so-called global North contexts (Berardo et al. 1993). The few qualitative studies to date tend to focus specifically on same-sex relationships, as well as on couplings where the man is older (Leahy 1994, 2002; Pyke and Adams 2010; Yuill 2004). Examples of age-dissimilar relationships also appear in classic anthropological works, with the topic most often being discussed in relation to marriage and kinship (e.g. see Lee [1984] 2013). More recently, anthropologists have explored couple relationships characterised by difference, yet this work focuses largely on inter-cultural, inter-racial, and bi-national intimacies (Bulloch and Fabinyi 2009; Cole 2014; Constable 2003).

Moreover, conceptions of what constitutes an 'age difference' can vary wildly (Berardo et al. 1993). Most scholars define age-dissimilar relationships as involving a ten-year or greater age difference, while others suggest that much smaller age differences might be deemed 'significant'. In general, older man relationships tend to have larger age differences, and many argue that it is therefore necessary to apply different measures to older man and older woman couplings (Amato et al. 2009; Berardo et al. 1993). Others note that understandings of age differences are culturally and historically contingent. Based on these arguments, I define age dissimilarities fairly loosely, as 'dependent on factors such as gender and partners' social roles' (McKenzie 2016).

My conversations with couples revealed that they saw their relationships as based, ideally or to begin with, on love. The feeling of love is commonly presented as unique, distinct from other emotions (Illouz 1997).[2] As such, the topic was poorly researched until relatively recently, and its meaning tended to be assumed rather than explicated (Evans 2003). William Jankowiak and Thomas Paladino (2008) outline two types of couple relationships that they posit are universal, aside from solely sexual ones. These are romantic or passionate love relationships as well as comfort love relationships, which are based on companionship, friendship, affection, and understanding. Jankowiak and Paladino (2008: 3) define romantic love relationships as involving 'the idealization of another, within an erotic setting, with the presumption that the feeling will last some time into the future' (see also Lindholm 1998, 2006). While I take issue with their claims regarding the universality of romantic love (at least in any meaningful sense), Jankowiak and Paladino's (2008) definitions of love adequately explain couple relationships in the global North.

While many were in what Jankowiak and Paladino (2008) would call *comfort love* relationships, all of my interviewees expressed the view that the absence of romantic love *early on* in a relationship meant that a union would not endure. Likewise, they informed me that the existence of such love between themselves and their partners—either in the past or in the present—would mean that they should continue their relationships. They also spoke about how feelings of passion occasionally re-emerged, unexpectedly, although this happened less frequently over time. Thus, romantic love was understood as the basis for a lasting relationship.

A number of anthropologists and sociologists have elaborated on this theme of 'lastingness' and its decline, focusing largely on contexts like North America, Western Europe, and their former colonies. In her book, *Why Love Hurts*, Illouz (2012: 89) acknowledges a 'cultural ideal of a long-lasting committed relationship' yet adds that presently there are 'sparse resources for achieving these ideals', leading to couples' rising fear and anxiety. It is crucial, she continues, to comprehend the many ways in which the 'cultural resources required for commitment' are being depleted (Illouz 2012: 89). For her, the intrusion of capitalism into people's intimate lives, and the commodification of relations that accompany this, play a key role in this depletion. Social scientists like Illouz (2007, 2012) as well as Bauman (2003) tend to envision this purported shift away from long-lasting relations as detrimental to people's social lives, yet others have more positive assessments. For instance, sociologist Anthony Giddens (1992) suggests that people are now moving beyond romantic love relationships towards 'pure relationships': family relations, friendships, and partnerships that can be freely entered into and exited. He sees fulfilment and ongoing choice—or contingency—as increasingly central to modern social relations. Yet, as with Bauman's (2003) 'liquid love' and Illouz's (2007) 'cold intimacies', he posits the decline of commitment and lasting, love-based relations, and ultimately assumes that the ideals of lastingness and fulfilment are necessarily opposed and contradictory.

Meanwhile, anthropologists Quinn (1996) and Strauss (Strauss and Quinn 1997) point to an ongoing, historically based tension between expectations of lastingness and fulfilment in people's shared understandings of marriage. Despite this tension, they argue, we should not assume we are moving from one ideal of love ('lastingness' fostered by commitment and obligation) to another ('fulfilment' fostered by choice). Rather, they introduce the notion of 'socially approved synthesis'—a concept theorising that *apparent* contradictions in people's cultural understandings are not necessarily experienced as such—in order to explain the co-existence of these ideals (Strauss and Quinn 1997: 22). They posit that there are culturally patterned means of resolving tensions between ideals, including those between lastingness and fulfilment (Strauss and Quinn

1997: 213). I thus draw on Quinn (1996) and Strauss' (1997) anthropological work in order to challenge Illouz (2007, 2012) and others' polarisation of lastingness and fulfilment, an argument strongly supported by my own findings regarding age-dissimilar couples.

Methodology: Researching Age-Dissimilar Couples

In my analysis below, I draw on twenty-four semi-structured interviews conducted in 2008 and 2009, undertaken in Perth, Western Australia. As part of a broader project on age-dissimilar couples, I also undertook group interviews, surveys, and some historical and media analysis, which I do not include in my analysis here. In my interviews, I spoke with people who were or had previously been involved in different-sex (heterosexual), age-dissimilar couplings. This included eleven men and thirteen women, nine of whom were in older woman couplings and fifteen of whom were in older man relationships. I did not include same-sex relationships because of the issues associated with finding a suitable, and representative, sample, and because there are a number of studies that already focus on age-dissimilar, same-sex couples (Leahy 1994, 2002; Yuill 2004).

Interviewees' ages ranged from twenty-two to seventy-six years old, and, at the time I spoke with them, their relationships had lasted from two and a-half months to twenty-nine years. Their age differences were between seven and thirty years. However, relationships between older men and younger women tended to have much larger age dissimilarities than those between older women and younger men, with the largest gap being thirty years in an older man relationship and eighteen years in an older woman relationship. I interviewed people from various socio-economic, racial, and cultural backgrounds (see McKenzie 2016), yet the majority of those I spoke with were white, middle-class, and had grown up in cities.

I recruited interviewees in a number of ways, including through my acquaintances, snowball sampling, magazines and radio, online, and using flyers. Partners were interviewed separately or together, depending on their preferences. Where possible, I interviewed both partners in a relationship, but this was sometimes not feasible; for instance, when couples were in distance relationships, had since ended their relationships, or if one partner was unwilling to be interviewed. I interviewed each partner or couple once, and our discussions lasted for approximately one hour, but were sometimes two or three hours long. I then transcribed the interviews and undertook a thematic analysis. Throughout this paper, I use pseudonyms when referring to my interviewees.

Challenging Commitments Among Couples, Families, and Friends

Those I spoke with often made comments to the effect that their relationships were freely chosen. When they reflected on the element of choice, they tended to focus on choice unencumbered by family members, friends, and wider society. In our discussions, it quickly became evident that, in many cases, partners' family members or friends had reacted negatively to their relationships. Much of the time, this had been due to couples' age differences, although this was not always the case. Disapproval was also common when one or both partners had recently broken off a marriage, had engaged in an affair, or had left their previous partners for one another. Here, I examine how understandings of commitment and obligation informed interviewees' talk about their families and partners.

Shaun and Linda's relationship illustrates this well. Shaun, who was twenty-four years old when we spoke, was married to Linda, aged thirty-three. Linda had grown up in Australia while Shaun had attended an international school in England, then later moved to Australia. They had been together for three years and married for seven months when we spoke one afternoon at a local pub. During my interview with Shaun, he spoke about his family's disapproval of their relationship. I had asked him a question about his relationship with Linda's family—and her relationship with his family—and he responded:

Shaun: My family… it's a bit of a disaster area… my mum, the second I mentioned to my mum that I was, that I hooked up with my housemate, my mum was like, 'oh right, oh that's not very smart of you, rah, rah, rah'. My mum's a bit, you know, traditional, orthodox Latin, pain in the arse. And the second I told her how old Linda was, that there was a nine-year age difference, there was a problem. And we're married now, almost three years down the track and my mum still has not met my wife.

Lara: Really?

S: But like I said, it's a very exceptional case, like it's… I don't think anybody would have had this much family drama like… Linda's mum gave me a chance, her old man gave me a chance and his current wife gave me a chance. Their whole family, Linda's step-brothers, step-sisters, we all get along fine… But my family's just, like I said, it's a bloody disaster zone. They haven't been accepting at all and I said to them quite bluntly, 'well take it or leave it. You can't determine who I want to be with, and you're gonna have to deal with it'. And I haven't spoken to my mum since before, about two months before me and Linda got married. I never even told her we were getting married.

I asked Shaun if his mother had since learned of their marriage.

Ah, I dunno. It doesn't bother me. I don't care. If you can't accept your child's partner, that they have chosen for *themselves* at a mature age [his emphasis] … It's not like I'm fourteen years old and it's some 'oh my first girlfriend', whatever… I'm a grown man, for god's sake, you can't make my choices for me. And if you want to try then it's not going to happen.

Here, Shaun emphasises his freedom of choice when it comes to selecting his partner, Linda (for further details see McKenzie 2015). He argues that family members and friends should give one's partner a chance, as Linda's family had done for him. If they fail to do this, they are not living up to their familial obligation: to be supportive. Shaun's attitude was mirrored by many other interviewees, especially those who faced, or had anticipated facing, criticisms of their relationships from family or close friends. Indeed, around half of my interviewees received negative reactions from family and friends when they had first informed them of their relationships. Most of these issues were resolved once relations and friends realised their error and recognised the chosen partners' suitability for their loved ones, and Shaun's was the only case where an interviewee had been estranged from their family over the long-term.

Another interviewee, Mark, spoke in similar terms to Shaun about his children's obligation to support his relationship with his new wife, Khiem. Mark was aged fifty, and Khiem was aged twenty-three, and the three of us spoke at their house. Mark had lived in the United Kingdom and Australia throughout his life, and had met Khiem on a trip to Vietnam. They had been together for two years when we spoke, and the couple had successfully applied for a visa so that Khiem could move to Australia and marry Mark. Mark's children by his previous marriage were twenty-one and twenty-three years old, around the same age as Khiem. Of his daughter, the youngest, he said:

> When Khiem and I told her we were going to get married... she's not very supportive, or she hasn't been in the past, and... I would suggest by her behaviour she still is not that supportive of the marriage. She tolerates it.

Mark continued, discussing his son's reaction to their relationship:

> I think [my son] is socially a very astute person and he certainly doesn't show any signs of any displeasure or any irritation or any embarrassment or anything like that really ... I'm not quite sure he's accepting of it, but certainly his outward display to me and to Khiem would lead me to believe ... [that] if he's not accepting of it he's far more accepting of it than his sister.

In relation to both his children, he added that 'I think [my son and daughter] both support me as their dad', once again highlighting the notion of support. Like Shaun, Mark frames family as ideally supportive. However, he interprets support from his children broadly, to include supporting him 'as their dad', tolerating his marriage, and not outwardly expressing any disapproval they might feel. It is noteworthy that Mark labelled his son as a 'socially a very astute person' for his ability to mask his (possible) disapproval. This highlights the link Mark draws between support and social acceptability: it is a social obligation to ostensibly support one's family.

In contrast to Mark, Shaun repeatedly stated that he 'did not care' what his mother—who had failed to live up to her social obligation as a family member—thought of his relationship. His claims, however, were at odds with something he later told me. For two years, he had attempted to get his mother to accept Linda as his partner. While Shaun's words might lead us to think that he did not value family commitment, his ongoing struggle with his mother, and eventual justification that she was not behaving as a relative should, points to the significance of commitments to kin. Social disapproval might lead some people to cut off contact with their kin, yet it was clear that such relations were maintained wherever possible.

The experiences and understandings of Shaun and Mark in many ways run counter to Illouz's (2007, 2012) arguments regarding 'cold intimacies'. In her discussion of freedom and 'rational' choice, Illouz (2012: 59) begins by claiming that 'sexual and emotional freedom generate their own forms of suffering', such as the rise of competitiveness in people's sexual lives, men's 'commitment phobia', and the gendered inequalities they foster (2012: 107). Her broad argument that freedom causes suffering initially appears to be supported by my participants' accounts, as their ability of choose an age-dissimilar partner does indeed bring about difficulties in many cases (although, historically and cross-culturally, their capacity to make such choices is by no means unusual (Fielder and Huber 2007; Hancock et al. 2003; Qu 1998; Van de Putte et al. 2009)). Moreover, if necessary, they appeared more than willing to sacrifice their relations with family and friends in order to be with their chosen partners.

Yet this kind of suffering and sacrifice does not fit comfortably with Illouz's (2007, 2012) arguments regarding the rise of 'cold intimacies'. She insists that it is the elevation of choice and rationality, rather than the unacceptability of particular 'irrational' choices over others, that brings about suffering. For her, difficulties come about due to the lack of commitment, monogamy, and sexual honour in contemporary relationships. Commitment, she argues, is 'a cognitive, moral, and affective structure that enables people to bind themselves to a future, and to forgo the possibility of maximizing their choices' (Illouz 2012: 89). Here, choice is seen as rational and instrumental, while commitment defies such logics.

Fragile Bonds or a Lack of Love? Beginning and Ending Relationships

When discussing their previous relationships, interviewees frequently informed me that, without love, lastingness and fulfilment were both impossible and undesirable. The account of one participant, Anna, illustrated this point. Anna was aged thirty-seven and was recently single when we spoke. Her ex-boyfriend, Karl, was aged twenty-seven. Anna had migrated from the United States to Australia, while Karl had grown up in Australia. They had been together for two-and-a-half months but, when I spoke with Anna, had recently ended their relationship. Anna initially supplied a practical reason for their break-up: Karl was not ready to have children, and Anna felt she had 'better get moving at having kids'. When I asked her if there was anything a couple should consider at the beginning of an age-dissimilar relationship, she replied:

> I think they'd both have to acknowledge the fact that it's there [the age difference]. Maybe talk long-term about what that age gap might mean. We talked about it probably several weeks in, I brought it up. I said 'I know you want to have kids some day and you realise if you want to have them with me you're gonna have to get a move on. Is this something that you've thought about?' He said, 'yes, I've thought about that'. So, I think that that needs to be discussed fairly early on, especially if it's the girl that's older. And if one of them wants to have kids soon and one of them wants to have kids in five years' time it's obviously an issue that I think you should deal with fairly early on.

Elaborating on the end of their relationship, Anna noted that it could have continued for longer. Yet, she emphasised, when Karl broke up with her it was not explicitly due to their different views on children. Rather:

> We split up because he figured out that he didn't like me enough... I'm the older one and he wants to get married some day and have kids some day, but he's not ready to yet. And with my ancient eggs, if I want to have kids, I better get moving at having kids.

According to Anna, their partnership had ultimately ended not because of their different ages or desires, but because their relationship lacked the love that would enable them to set aside such differences. Such issues could have been overcome if Karl had liked her 'enough', she said. Thus, contrary to Illouz's (2007, 2012) suggestion that relationships are increasingly rational and instrumental—or 'cold'—here Anna frames rational choice as relevant only where there is a lack of romantic feeling between partners. In short, purely rational decision-making equals a lack of love.

My interview with another couple, Suzie and Peter, revealed a similar logic. Suzie was thirty-five years old, while Peter was fifty-one. Both had grown up in Australia, and they had met at work. When I spoke with them together in a café, they had been together for seven months. However, their relationship had begun while they were both married to other people. I spoke with them together and, during our conversation, Suzie told me about her previous husband. She had been pregnant when they had married, she told me, and her family had pressured her into the union. She and her previous husband had been twenty years old at the time, and she spoke of their marriage as the result of social pressure and familial obligation. In contrast, her relationship with Peter was described as resisting such pressures. Like many others I spoke with, Suzie and Peter spoke about their family and friends' initial disapproval of their affair. Suzie's family had been especially disapproving.

Suzie said she had never been happy with her ex-husband, although they had been married for over fourteen years. Indeed, she failed to mention ever having loved him, although this may have been due to Peter's presence when she spoke. Suzie's comments about her previous relationship mirrored a fairly widespread cultural understanding that partners should be freely chosen and rejected (Illouz 2007; Giddens 1992). Likewise, it is considered unacceptable and undesirable to enter into (or remain in) a couple relationship out of social obligation, as Suzie had. This could be seen as confirming Illouz (2007), Bauman (2003), and others' assessments of love and emotions as increasingly 'cold', 'liquid', and contingent, in that the desirability of obligation and commitment were questioned and relationships conceived as ideally based on free choice. Yet Suzie's point was that her marriage 'failed' not due to a lack of commitment, but because the relationship should never have begun in the first place.

Thus, romantic love and obligation—to family or wider society—were seen as incompatible. As outlined above, this imagined disjuncture has likewise been theorised by Illouz (2007, 2012) and others. For Illouz (2012: 9), romantic love has been irrevocably altered by a series of cultural revolutions: 'the individualization of lifestyles and the intensification of emotional life projects', as well as 'the economization of social relationships', including within the realm of intimate life. She argues that people lead increasingly individualised lives, and that there has been a corresponding diminishment in the 'moral resources' and 'social constraints' that construct people's movements, ideas, and activities within social contexts (Illouz 2012: 14). This loss, and the 'freedom' resulting from it, creates and obscures gendered inequalities much like neoliberal 'freedom in the economic realm creates inequalities and [then] makes them invisible' (Illouz 2012: 240). Yet Illouz (2012: 242) argues that individualised intimacies lead people to make particular choices: encouraging open-ended relationships; lengthier, more complex courtships; a focus on individual 'tastes'; the evaluation of others; and raising opportunities for constantly 'improving' upon one's choices. These free choices, it is implied, discourage commitment, obligation, and lasting relationships.

Likewise, Robert Bellah et al. (1985) suggest that the 'expressive individualism' characteristic of today's romantic relationships has led to the downfall of commitment. They describe expressive individualism as emphasising sharing feelings, individual satisfaction, psychological growth, and mutually fulfilled desire. Ulrich Beck and Elisabeth Beck-Gernsheim (1995) similarly argue that there has been a breakdown in modern relationships as binding social obligations, and a shift towards the 'individualisation' of relationships. This individualisation, they argue, means that people's behaviours are less and less bound by traditional norms, values, and sources of collective identity.

As alluded to earlier in this chapter, the changes posited here have been interpreted more positively by Giddens (1992). In Giddens' (1992) work, lovers are seen as free and active agents, and modern love is contingent and contractual. Giddens (1992) suggests that this signals a 'democratisation' of people's personal lives, which are increasingly characterised by autonomy and choice regarding whether they form or continue a relationship. In my own research, however, Shaun's efforts to overcome his mother's disapproval, as well as Suzie's lengthy relationship with her ex-husband, suggest that claims of a shift away from obligation, commitment, and enduring familial relations may be exaggerated. Rather, it appears that interviewees shared deeply held understandings about the importance and obligations of familial and couple relationships, and that these were unlikely to be violated.

While people spoke of their relationships in terms of choice—that is, as choosing to be with a particular person—love was also seen as an uncontrollable, overwhelming force. Suzie and Peter provide a good example of how love is comprehended in this way. As mentioned previously, their relationship had begun as an affair. In the following exchange, they recounted how they had first met and gotten together. Peter began:

Peter: Basically we did meet at school [where they both worked]. I took on a deputy role and we.

Suzie: Within that school.

P: Within that school, and basically we had to get somebody to come in take my position at the school as a teacher, the person happened to be Suzie. Um, now that was last year and basically from the day I met Suzie there was an attraction there. But for the whole of the year we just simply.

S: We gelled.

P: We gelled, we clicked. We clicked very, very much so. And then at the end of the year.

S: Staff party, it's always those damn staff parties [laughs].

P: Basically it was just too much.

S: Mmm.

Lara: What about you [Suzie]?

S: Ever since I've been married not a year's gone by where I haven't gone to somebody to say 'I'm not happy'… when I met Peter it was just an instant, just a kindred spirit. So it was very hard to avoid and deny and it sounds very cheesy when you're trying to explain, but it happened and that's that, so yeah. So without mixing our words we kind of had an affair. I left home when I realised I just couldn't be in the marriage any longer, and then he finally left his wife and that was that. Nothing to really be proud of, but you know, it's happened, so yep.

Here, Suzie and Peter discussed love as something they had no control over. Other interviewees spoke in similar terms, using commonplace phrases like 'falling in love', talking about their couplings as 'just happening', or speaking of love as 'sneaking up on them'. One might argue that these claims were a matter of convenience: a way of denying responsibility for their earlier actions.[3] By questioning obligation and commitment to a spouse, for instance, they were able to ultimately suggest that some relationships were not chosen for the right reasons, and were therefore problematic. Thus, they should not last. Regardless of their motivations in making such claims, however, this is far more in keeping with Quinn (1996) and Strauss' (Strauss and Quinn 1997) concept of socially approved synthesis, whereby notions like lastingness and fulfilment are able to co-exist relatively unproblematically. In the case of interviewees, synthesis was achieved through the logic that commitment was (and should be) optional without freely chosen love. In the discussion below, I close the chapter by emphasising how ideas about commitment and free choice complemented rather than contradicted one another.

Conclusion: Changing Commitments? Relationships as Lasting and Fulfilling

Throughout this chapter I have argued that participants' uses of ideas such as *obligation* and *commitment*, as well as *free choice* and *love*, were in many ways highly consistent. These understandings initially appeared to contradict one another: how can relationships be both lasting and fulfilling, or characterised by enduring commitment and ongoing choices to remain together? Yet these tensions did not necessarily create problems for those who simultaneously held such understandings. Rather, it was acknowledged that people should act autonomously from family members and friends when 'choosing' a partner, effectively ignoring such ties in their 'decision-making'. Restrictions regarding partner selection were seen highly negatively, and people frequently asserted their own freedom of partner choice. Here, choice was envisioned as enabling people to enter into romantic unions. Their comments suggested that a truly free choice was one based upon uncontrollable romantic feeling.

The theses of the best-known love theorists—Illouz (2007, 2012), Bauman (2003), Giddens (1992), Beck and Beck-Gernsheim (1995, 2013), and Bellah et al. (1985)—do not fit comfortably with these findings. Their assumption is that companionship, obligation, and commitment are declining, while individualised, instrumental relationships and an emphasis on short-term pleasure are ascending. I argue that these theorists tend to oversimplify the relationship between historical continuity and change, drawing attention away from cultural complexities. Accordingly, relationships characterised by difference are advanced as evidence of a push towards individualisation—or what Illouz (2012) calls individualised intimacies—epitomising free choice and pleasure, and defying permanency. Disagreements among the proponents of these arguments tend to centre on whether these shifts are positive, negative, or represent two equally un/desirable alternatives.

Moreover, for Illouz (2007, 2012), who deems modern intimacies 'cold' or 'liquid', the pressures of 'rational' decision-making causes widespread suffering, as it disrupts previously stable relationships. These disruptions are imagined to relate to couple relations, but the endurance of these relations, as well as of familial ties, is less well considered. This is at odds with many of my observations: for instance, that supporting and being supported by family remains an important obligation. In contrast, while she acknowledges that the ideal of the long-lasting relationship endures, Illouz (2012: 89) concludes that there are now limited means of achieving such ideals, in large part due to commodification and capitalism.

My findings instead reflect Quinn (1996) and Strauss' (Strauss and Quinn 1997) suggestion that commitment and familial obligation—and the corresponding idea that relationships should last—are enduring themes in people's accounts of their love and family lives. Discussions of love and relationships that focus primarily on autonomy, free choice, and individualisation—and imply that relationships are now largely about pleasure and fulfilment—tell only half of the story (see also Hirsch 2003; Holmes 2004; Jamieson 1999; Roseneil 2007). Obligation, commitment, and responsibility to others should continue to be emphasised in theorisations of relationships. As such, I argue for an approach that foregrounds cultural continuity, and accounts for complexity and contradiction in people's understandings of their relationships.

Such an approach allows ideas of lastingness and fulfilment to co-exist. Strauss and Quinn's (1997) notion of 'socially approved synthesis' is an appropriate means of understanding this co-existence. To reiterate, Strauss and Quinn (1997: 22) posit that what appear to be obvious contradictions in people's understandings are not necessarily felt as such, nor recognised as likely sources of tension. Seemingly contradictory ideas can be ignored, marginalised, or 'selectively synthesised' (Strauss and Quinn 1997: 213). 'Socially approved synthesis', they argue, ensures that there are widely shared and readily available means of resolving potential conflicts in people's cultural understandings (Strauss and Quinn 1997: 213). When faced with apparent tensions between ideas of lastingness and fulfilment—in their relationships or beyond—interviewees are therefore able to resolve these conflicts in culturally patterned (and socially acceptable) ways. This explains why, according to my participants, a relationship that does not last is not considered to be evidence that relationships are increasingly temporary; rather, it shows that only (inherently fulfilling) loved-based relationships can be expected to last.

Notes

1. Illouz (2008, 2012) further argues this rationalisation and cooling is tied to the rise of popular psychology and the purported focus of feminism on autonomy rather than relatedness. I do not explore these elements of her argument in this chapter. However, see Twamley (2018), Thwaites (this volume) and Jurva (this volume) for further discussion.

2. Gaining scholarly attention in the 1980s, some academics argued that growing interest in emotions (such as love) reflected the individualised, depoliticised interests of capitalist societies (Rose 1999), a claim somewhat related to Illouz's (2007) notion of 'cold intimacies'. Others, however, have argued that this growing field was the result of 'the increasing impact of (and continuing backlashes against) scholars previously underrepresented in the academy, as well as broader social and political struggles' (McElhinny 2010: 311). Here, examining the emotional dimensions of social life is understood to be highly political and potentially transformative, due to longstanding connections drawn between rationality and masculinity, emotionality and femininity (Jackson 1993; Lutz and White 1986; Svašek 2005).

3. In a previous study, Illouz (1997) draws attention to how free choice, and the absence of choice, is applied unevenly when people talk about love. Her interviewees, she says, instead deployed the concepts that worked best for their arguments, thus using ideas pragmatically.

References

Amato, P.R., Booth, A., Johnson, D.R. and Rogers, S.J. (2009) *Alone together: How marriage in America is changing.* Cambridge: Harvard University Press.

Bauman, Z. (2003) *Liquid love: On the frailty of human bonds.* Cambridge: Polity Press.

Beck, U. and Beck-Gernsheim, E. (1995) *The normal chaos of love.* Cambridge: Polity Press.

Beck, U. and Beck-Gernsheim, E. (2013) *Distant love: Personal life in the global age.* Cambridge: Polity Press.

Bellah, R.N., Madsen, R., Sullivan, W.M., Swidler, A. and Tiptop, S.M. (1985) *Habits of the heart: Individualism and commitment in American life.* Berkeley: University of California Press.

Berardo, F.M., Appel, J. and Berardo, D.H. (1993) Age dissimilar marriages: Review and assessment. *Journal of Aging Studies.* 7 (1): 93–106.

Bulloch, H. and Fabinyi, M. (2009) Transnational relationships, transforming selves: Filipinas seeking husbands abroad. *The Asia Pacific Journal of Anthropology.* 10 (2): 129–142.

Cole, J. (2014) Working mis/understandings: The tangled relationship between kinship, Franco-Malagasy binational marriages, and the French state. *Cultural Anthropology.* 29 (3): 527–551.

Constable, N. (2003) *Romance on a global stage: Pen pals, virtual ethnography, and 'mail-order' marriages.* Berkeley: University of California Press.

Evans, M. (2003) *Love, an unromantic discussion.* Cambridge: Polity Press.

Fielder, M. and Huber, S. (2007) Parental age difference and offspring count in humans. *Biology Letters.* 3 (6): 689–691.

Giddens, A. (1992) *The transformation of intimacy: Sexuality, love and eroticism in modern societies.* Cambridge: Polity Press.

Hancock, R., Stuchbury, R. and Tomassini, C. (2003) Changes in the distribution of marital age differences in England and Wales, 1963 to 1998. *Population Trends.* 114: 19–25.

Hirsch, J.S. (2003) *A courtship after marriage: Sexuality and love in Mexican transnational Families.* Berkeley: University of California Press.

Hochschild, A. (2003) *The managed heart: The commercialization of human feeling*. Berkley: University of California Press.

Holmes, M. (2004) An equal distance? Individualisation, gender and intimacy in distance relationships. *The Sociological Review*. 52 (2): 180–200.

Illouz, E. (1997) *Consuming the romantic utopia: Love and the cultural contradictions of capitalism*. Berkeley: University of California Press.

Illouz, E. (2007) *Cold intimacies: The making of emotional capitalism*. Cambridge: Polity Press.

Illouz, E. (2008) *Saving the modern soul: Therapy, emotions, and the culture of self-help*. Berkley: University of California Press.

Illouz, E. (2012) *Why love hurts: A sociological explanation*. Cambridge: Polity Press.

Jackson, S. (1993) Even sociologists fall in love: An exploration in the sociology of emotions. *Sociology*. 27 (2): 201–220.

Jamieson, L. (1999) Intimacy transformed? A critical look at the 'pure relationship'. *Sociology*. 33 (3): 477–494.

Jankowiak, W.R. and Paladino, T. (2008) Desiring sex, longing for love: A tripartite conundrum. In W. R. Jankowiak (ed.) *Intimacies: Love and sex across cultures*. New York: Columbia University Press: 1–36.

Leahy, T. (1994) Taking up a position: Discourses of femininity and adolescence in the context of man/girl relationships. *Gender and Society*. 8 (1): 48–72.

Leahy, T. (2002) *Negotiating stigma: Approaches to intergenerational sex*. Victoria Park: Books Reborn.

Lee, R.B. [1984] (2013) *The Dobe Ju/'Hoansi*, third edition. Wadsworth: Cengage Learning.

Lindholm, C. (1998) Love and structure. *Theory, Culture and Society*. 15 (3): 243–263.

Lindholm, C. (2006) Romantic love and anthropology. *Etnofoor*. 19 (1): 5–21.

Lutz, C. and White, G.M. (1986) The anthropology of emotions. *Annual Review of Anthropology*. 15: 405–436.

McElhinny, B. (2010) The audacity of affect: Gender, race, and history in linguistic accounts of legitimacy and belonging. *Annual Review of Anthropology*. 39: 309–328.

McKenzie, L. (2015) *Age-dissimilar couples and romantic relationships: Ageless love?* Basingstoke: Palgrave Macmillan.

McKenzie, L. (2016) Love from afar: Transcending distance and difference in age-dissimilar couplings?. *Sites: A journal of social anthropology and cultural studies*. 13 (1): 198–221.

Pyke, K. and Adams, M. (2010) What's age got to do with it? A case study analysis of power and gender in husband-older marriages. *Journal of Family Issues.* 31 (6): 748–777.

Qu, L. (1998) Latest trends: Age differences between brides and grooms in Australia. *Family Matters.* 49: 27.

Quinn, N. (1996) Culture and contradiction: The case of American reasoning about marriage. *Ethos.* 24 (3): 391–425.

Rose, N.S. (1999) *Governing the soul: The shaping of the private self,* second edition. London: Free Association Books.

Roseneil, S. (2007) Queer individualization: The transformation of personal life in the early 21st century. *NORA: Nordic Journal of Feminist and Gender Research.* 15 (2–3): 84–99.

Strauss, C. and Quinn, N. (1997) *A cognitive theory of cultural meaning.* Cambridge: Cambridge University Press.

Svašek, M. (2005) Introduction: Emotions in anthropology. In K. Milton and M. Svašek (eds.) *Mixed emotions: Anthropological studies of feeling.* Oxford: Berg Publishers: 1–23.

Twamley, K. (2018) 'Cold intimacies' in parents' negotiations of work–family practices and parental leave?. *The Sociological Review.* Online First. https://doi.org/10.1177/0038026118815427.

Van de Putte, B., Van Poppel, F., Vanassche, S., Sanchez, M., Jidkova, S., Eeckhaut, M., Oris, M. and Matthijs, K. (2009) The rise of age homogamy in 19th century Western Europe. *Journal of Marriage and Family.* 71 (5): 1234–1253.

Yuill, R.A. (2004) *Male age-discrepant intergenerational sexualities and relationships.* Ph.D thesis, University of Glasgow

4

The Transformation of Love? Choice, Emotional Rationality and Wedding Gifts

Julia Carter and Daniel Smith

Introduction

The wedding is an important symbolic ritual in contemporary British society. Despite changes in form, content and format, evidence shows that the wedding retains meaning for British couples that extends beyond its associations with consumerism and commercialisation (Carter and Duncan 2017, 2018). Yet the wedding is often overlooked in current discussions of coupling in sociology, as much of the wedding research takes place within media and cultural studies or marketing and consumption. This is a significant oversight since the wedding is an ever-evolving social ritual which in every different and unique guise speaks volumes about couples, family relationships, emotions, rituals and relationality.

J. Carter
University of the West of England, Bristol, UK
e-mail: julia.carter@uwe.ac.uk

D. Smith (✉)
Cardiff University, Cardiff, UK
e-mail: SmithD34@cardiff.ac.uk

© The Author(s) 2020   **57**
J. Carter, L. Arocha (eds.), *Romantic Relationships in a Time of 'Cold Intimacies'*,
Palgrave Macmillan Studies in Family and Intimate Life,
https://doi.org/10.1007/978-3-030-29256-0_4

While the number of marriages taking place each year in England and Wales continues to decline, the significance placed on the wedding appears to grow. For example, while the marriage rate dropped to its lowest on record in 2015 for England and Wales (ONS 2018), almost 18 million British households tuned in to watch the wedding between Prince Harry and Meghan Markle in 2018 (Waterson 2018). As the need for marriage as a rite of passage or social necessity disappears, the wedding reconstitutes and reinvents its meaning in a society with an increasingly playful approach to its traditions (Gross 2005; Carter and Duncan 2018). What Carter and Duncan argue is that rather than declines in marriage rates reflecting a decline in adherence to traditional values, traditions are played with and reinvented so that individuals can recreate 'traditional' looking relationships in novel ways. Thus living apart together (LAT) relationships are very far from traditional co-residential marriage in form but in practice, traditional married-like couples replicate practices of marriage while living apart (Carter et al. 2015). What this means for weddings is that while some may interpret the increasing commercialisation of weddings as an emptying out of meaning and traditional values, the evidence shows that for couples, weddings retain their traditional meaning, which is combined and enmeshed with new meanings, including aspects of consumerism and consumption (Carter and Duncan 2017, 2018).

What has been overlooked by this research is, however, the meaning and process of gift-giving in weddings. Whilst as a component of weddings we could interpret contemporary gift-giving as another element in the wedding bricolage process, on the other hand, gift-giving has its own ritualised history and meaning-making tradition. Thus, the intersection of weddings, bricolage, gift-giving and ritual tradition offers a unique and under-explored avenue for further investigation. Along with many other traditions associated with weddings, the growing importance of buying gifts for wedding couples really took hold during the nineteenth century when 'the celebration of nuptials was seen by commentators as being irreversibly transformed into a vehicle for business interests, class aspiration and fashion' (Penner 2004). Again, this does not mean, however, that gifts are without special meaning and value to both the giver and receiver. Indeed, Rebecca Purbrick (2003, 2015) has studied wedding gifts extensively and writes that wedding gifts can convey social approval, and that in the act of giving and within a particular context—a wedding—otherwise mundane (often household related) objects become imbued with special, sacred meaning. For example, Purbrick provides an account of a housewife aged in her 30s from Durham whose wedding gifts are intricately linked to her family history (2003: 217). Thus wedding gifts, as with other aspects of weddings, convey particular and special meanings, about family relationships, social bonds, status and approval.

What is interesting about the wedding gift is how it has changed over time and adapted with the change in meaning around weddings and relationships more generally. As Penner (2004) notes, in the nineteenth century it was appropriate to gift decorative non-essential household items (at least among the middle and upper classes) as the assumption was that land, property and household items were provided by close family (usually parents). Moving into the twentieth century, household items became the staple of wedding gift lists amongst the 'ordinary writers' in Purbrick's study of Mass Observation respondents.[1] This was at a time when the wedding represented the start of cohabitation for many couples who required or desired help in setting up an entirely new household. Now, attitudes have changed and the vast majority of wedding couples in England and Wales have cohabited prior to marriage (Barlow et al. 2005) and therefore do not require the same provision of household items. We may, therefore, see a reversal to the nineteenth-century standard where wedding gifts are largely luxury items, designed to go beyond the everyday.

This rise in cohabitation and shift in the purpose and meaning of weddings (and by extension weddings gifts) is the result of a number of changes in contemporary intimate life. For Illouz (2012) these changes emerge because of shifts in the 'ecology' and 'architecture' of choice: the context in which choices are made and the individual process of decision-making. Illouz explains that modern subjects are defined by their ability to choose, especially in relation to consumption, politics and also in love. While marriage decisions were once made within wider moral communities, these have since broken down so that individuals are free and disconnected, at a loss for a legitimating ideology into which they can embed their conjugal and romantic decisions. Thus individualism has come to replace wider community moral frameworks as decisions are made by self-reflexive individuals. According to Illouz, therefore, 'it is the fine-tuned compatibility of two constituted selves that makes up a successful marriage, not the display of roles. The fine-tuning of the emotional makeup of two persons becomes the basis for intimacy' (2012: 39). This reliance on individual preference means that while we have more choice now, this has led to greater ontological suffering as these decisions are dis-embedded from a community and are therefore less certain or secure. As a consequence, decisions come to be based upon rational, economic, balances and psychological reasoning rather than romantic visions of all-encompassing love. In this way, emotions have cooled, and intimacy has an economic rationale and basis in reason, not emotion.

This theoretical approach is appealing, not least because it captures the ephemeral changes in our decision-making processes as well as the per-ceived 'cult of the individual' (Durkheim 1997) modernity induces. There is substantial evidence for a change in the way decision-making happens within the therapeutic turn (Illouz 2008; Giddens 1992). What is less evident is the dis-embedding of individuals from wider moral com-munity frameworks (Dawson 2012). While the decline in marriage rates, high divorce rates and growth in family types outside the traditional nuclear family are often used as prima facie evidence for this dis-embedded thesis, change in form does not always equate to change in practice. Likewise, as Gross has suggested in the US context, a decline in regulative traditions (such as traditional heterosexual marriage) does not necessarily lead to a decline in meaning-constitutive traditions (such as practices of relating; Gross 2005). Thus, there remains evidence that individuals con-tinue to be embedded in communities defined by traditions and crucially rely upon these in making decisions about their lives and future life course (see, e.g. Mason 2004).

That said, our argument has many points of convergence with Illouz; for example, we agree that modern intimacy appears to prioritise 'choice' and its reversibility, and we agree that individuals act as if their romantic partners exist on a marriage market rather than being embedded in local or social communities (see also Ansari and Klinenberg 2015). Within this chapter, however, we seek to highlight some of the limitations to Illouz's overarching claims. We do so through a focus on weddings gifts and their meanings, highlighting: first the capacity for wedding gifts to provide a route to transcend the market logic of romance; second, the importance of wider moral community frameworks in making sense of weddings and gifts; and finally, the possibility that self-gifting reveals an ethical life appropriate to the new romantic architecture of choice that is not the individualised self-determined project hypothesised by Illouz. This chapter addresses these issues using data from research projects outlined below.

Researching Weddings

The data for this chapter was collected in two projects, the first an interview study conducted in 2008 as part of a wider project on marriage and relationships. This project aimed to interview young women between the ages of 18 and 30 to find out about their relationship aspirations and experiences and in particular their attitudes towards marriage. The second project from which data was gathered took place in the summer of 2014 and was specifically concerned with wedding practices, therefore only those planning for or recently having had a wedding were recruited. This project involved interviews with 15 individuals (5 couples and 5 individuals) ranging in age from 22 to 58. Six were men and nine were women, all couples were living together except Cathy who was living apart from her partner at the time. This combined sample covers a range of class and socio-economic groups although almost all participants were White (except Mandy), heterosexual (except Shirley) and all were British. Interviews took place in provincial towns in the South of England and across two larger cities in the North of England. Both studies utilised convenience and snowball sampling which have limitations but are useful in providing an easy to access group. To this end, data discussed here is not intended to indicate national or cohort trends but instead may point to nuances within theory-making.

Both studies utilised semi-structured interviews which were recorded and transcribed. Analysis of interview data was grounded in the material and organised thematically. An important point to note is that at no point were wedding gifts specifically asked about by any of the researchers in the interviews. Therefore the data presented here offers spontaneous mentions of wedding gifts—times when gifts occurred naturally in the wider interview setting and in the context of what was otherwise being discussed. While a number of women spontaneously discussed gifts, none of these spontaneous mentions was by a male interviewee. Nevertheless, as Purbrick has also noted, more detail was often provided by her female Mass Observation writers than male writers who tended to 'discuss fewer objects, focusing on those they liked and had something to do with or were expected to like and forced to know about' (2003: 217). On the other hand, women were much more likely to know about, have used and cared for their wedding gifts. It is therefore reasonable to conclude that by not asking directly about wedding gifts, we have effectively excluded men from this discussion. The result being that this conversation continues to reflect a division of labour 'where women are much more likely to have a daily and durable relationship with domestic objects' (2003: 217) including wedding gifts. Participants' relationships with weddings gifts are discussed in more detail in the following sections.

The Wedding Gift and Rationality

Illouz's account of modern romance relies upon the claim that the 'cultural organisation of choice' in marriage partners has undergone transformation. In some respects marriage has always been about individual choice, but the meaning and conditions of choice has not always been the same. It is the *ecology* and *architecture* of choice which Illouz claims have transformed dramatically (Illouz 2012: 40). Reframing Polanyi's *Great Transformation*, Illouz speaks of the 'great transformation of romantic ecology' with the emergence of the marriage market. In this new romantic ecology, the choice of one's partner is deregulated from one's immediate social group and dis-embedded from a shared moral/normative framework. For her, the 'triumph' of romantic love is to be seen in the cultural belief that our romantic decisions are the result of individual, introspective consideration in the face of an 'open market' of potential partners, a decision separated out from wider normative frameworks of appropriateness.

Within this ecology of choice, the architecture of decision-making for individuals carries the existential problem that decision-making is never final or absolute. The reflexive monitoring of one's own emotions combines with the general spread of rationality which Weber diagnosed for modernity: people need to respond to their own individual desires and emotional needs; likewise they need to engage with another's equally individual will and emotionality; and they must be constantly alert to renewing decision-making. In romance this means that relationship decisions are never final, can always be revised or revoked, when judged rationally by individuals through their emotional reflexivity. For Illouz (2012: 91f) this architecture of romantic choice mirrors the centrality of choice to consumer markets. Those who have explored choice in consumerism have noted that the 'romantic ethic' which underlines consumer purchases is not a longing for *the commodity*, more the *idea* of the commodity (Campbell 1987; Slater 1997; Varul 2015). Modern romance may well be inherently dissatisfying, according to Illouz (2012), as it suffers from the same problem of the 'romantic consumer': part of the pleasure of romance is the dream itself, not the reality experienced. In this regard, an emotional hedonism results where desiring is, in part, autonomous from the desired object and, what's more, desiring itself becomes pleasurable (over and above its satisfaction in experience) (Campbell 1987: 85–86). In such circumstances, Illouz (2012) sees commitment as inherently difficult for late-modern couples when their romantic choices are subject to ideals over actualities: the idea of the perfect relationship takes precedence over lived experiences.

For us, however, we detect within the new romantic ecology of choice a subtle and implicit salvation story which resists the ontological suffering in love and commitment. While Illouz (2007, 2012: 159) is right to see rationality infused in emotional fields, the point we wish to make is that individuals can find the limits to this market logic of choice (and reversibility) in romance through gifting. For instance, take Penny's (27, engaged cohabiting) statement on what her wedding means: 'my feelings won't change, I don't think …you know my views of him wouldn't change it would just literally be those things [what she already has], and hopefully a lot of presents'. It is in the promise of presents that we detect less the profusion myth of a consumer society infecting romantic couplings, more gifts announcing the *end* to choice and market logic.

This view of gifts sees a process of re-traditionalisation within the great transformation of romantic ecology. Our participants, as noted, organically brought up a discussion of gifts in the context of discussing their wedding choices and decisions. It was in their spontaneous reasoning on the nature of wedding gifts that we felt the presence of both the great transformation of romantic ecology and, equally, gifting scripts taking on special significance to limit such rational, calculative decision-making on the 'marriage market'. These came in the form of two different narrations on gift-giving: one by the currently unmarried (or not-yet-married) who (anxiously) viewed the wedding through the lens of commercialisation and one narrated by the soon-to-wed who viewed the wedding gift as moving beyond the commercial features of weddings. Below Eleanor reflects the first narrative while Susan exemplifies the second.

Eleanor (26, cohabiting) remarks:

> I don't see the point in having lots of peripheral friends and things there because, well, because it's an intimate thing, and while it's a public declaration, it's kind of, I don't know, it's a thing for families um... So I think there's a lot of fuss and it's very expensive, and I think money can be put to better use, and the whole tradition of wedding gifts... is a bit strange now as well, I think. 'Cause it used to make sense in that you get married and then move in together, so you wouldn't have anything so you'd need crockery and everything to start up with. But now you have two sets of crockery before you've even got married 'cause you've both lived by yourselves, and then you've both moved in together... So, in a way, wedding lists seem a bit greedy because there isn't the need there now [for] what it was supporting before

Eleanor's talk relates 'fuss' with 'expense' and conflates gifts of expense with the corrupting presence of 'peripheral friends'. She talks with a market coolness: 'money for better use'. Yet this is not cool intimacy and neither is it wholly reducible to rationality infecting romance. Such an interpretation would be a misplaced slippage from the commercialisation of 'the wedding' to the commercial cooling of intimacy. Eleanor's talk in 'cool, market' logic is there for boundary work to avoid a commercialisation of romance and an extending of such commercialisation to *her* (potential future) wedding. Commercialisation not only corrupts intimacy with 'greed', it also encourages reading a 'big do' as itself an expression of such greed. 'Peripheral friends' only become 'peripheral' when they could potentially be seen as being invited more for their presents than their presence, as such.

We detect in Eleanor's talk an anxiety that a cooling of intimacy could be found in the cooling of gifting practices. In so doing, Eleanor conflates two distinct traditions of gifting in her talk. Purbrick's (2015) study of c.1945–2003 UK wedding gifting practices distils these two traditions. The first, arising out of post-war (1945) necessity, are domestic gifts to establish a couple in their new domestic setting. These gifts are given by close and extended kin (Purbrick 2015: 86). The second, dated c.1980, is the 'commercial gift list' tradition where couples write a list of desired consumer goods from department stores for guests to purchase. Eleanor's talk conflates these two, and her conflation signals their normative 'out of place' corruption of the wedding as a marker of intimate coupling. Eleanor's 'opposition to the list is an embodied and intellectual response to ritual undermined...' (Purbrick 2015: 91). A gift is defined by the act of giving and receiving, therefore, a list of 'gifts' (as in a wedding gift list) defines objects as gifts prior to the action that would socially mark them out as gifts. In this way, wedding 'gift' lists are a corruption of the moral script of disinterestedness inherent in Western gifting imaginaries. And, the provision of domestic necessities as 'gifts' once utilised scripts of (disinterested) 'giving' to conceal their source in interested calculation. For Eleanor, weddings gifts are out of place as they are neither one thing nor the other. They now have to create their own justification for existence which may, within the market logic, be said to be 'greed'. Eleanor's talk is not, therefore, a mere rejection of the market logic of romance but registers instead an anxiety on the part of modern couples that the boundaries between markets and romance are, normatively speaking, perceived to be porous.

Susan (20, engaged cohabiting) offers instead a resolution to the anxiety of the market logic of gifting:

I mean even just the basic cost of an actual ceremony is now like hundreds of pounds and that's like, only when we're young, and on like a fairly reasonable wage, it's quite a lot of money. And it's a lot of money for everything else as well. And there's the expectation of a honeymoon and like, the gift list, has changed probably quite a lot as well people didn't used to register for gift lists and sort of say I want this, this and this. They used to sort of accept anything that anyone gave them whether it matched or not. That's kind of changed as well. But I think it has escalated in what is expected to happen in a wedding. So I'm looking forward to the week afterwards 'cause, we like, get to play with our new stuff like [laughs], our new presents and things, and then we've got a week off work which will be nice to just unwind.

Here, we find the language of calculation is situated within the language of equally normative expectation. For with the emergence of the marriage market and the *perceived* dis-embedding of romance from moral-normative frameworks, the new ecology of choice has obliged the couple to pursue a repertoire of ritual aspects—the registering for wedding gifts and the honeymoon—which legitimate the couple. In this account, rather than gifting being left out in the cold world of market logic (greed), it is firmly embedded within kinship practices and social norms. The perception of being dis-embedded from moral communities leads individuals to find new ways of re-embedding connectivity with others. Moreover, the gift of the 'new things' and honeymoon to 'unwind' is understood to be precisely for the *couple* and, because of this, announces a denial of the commercial, acquisitive logic by which the wedding is defined.

In a dis-embedded 'marriage market' it is telling that the most common gift that was brought up by our participants was the honeymoon. Fiona (23, married cohabiting) says:

We were quite lucky, 'cause we'd been living together, we didn't need anything so for wedding gifts we set up honeymoon accounts. I think the honeymoon cost £2,500, and rather than people buying us gifts they were paying into that account. So we ended up only paying about £1,000 for the honeymoon in the end.

While Claire (24, engaged cohabiting) said of her fiancé:

> My boyfriend got it into his head that he wanted to go to Iceland for honeymoon. So that was his big incentive to get married [laughs]. …He keeps joking now about the reason we're getting married is 'cause we're going on a honeymoon … we want it to be part of our wedding present.

While gifting of money contributions towards a honeymoon might be perceived as the height of wedding market logic, we instead argue that the honeymoon as gift is the exemplar for *transcending* such a market logic.

Notably both Fiona and Claire speak of the honeymoon as a gift, and as an incentive for the wedding. In Fiona's case the honeymoon gift appears alongside quantitative reckoning (£2500 becomes £1000), and in Claire's case the incentive ends with a present. While the ideal 'gift' in Western imaginaries, its fictive generosity and symbolic efficacy, is in the spontaneity of its being given (Mauss 1990), the honeymoon's fiction seems to be that the recipients tell themselves that what is subjected to quantitative reckoning is in fact beyond the logic of the market. One of the foundational assumptions of gift analysis is the question, why would gifts be given if the people receiving them do not need them? The answer being that giving creates obligations—that people need social relations more than they do things. Yet the fiction of treating honeymoons as a promissory gift, an expectation or investment, with all the assumptions this has of 'yield', 'interest' and notions of capital accumulation, insists upon a similar question: why treat as a gift that which is subjected to commodity logic? The answer, we argue, is that the honeymoon's symbolic fiction is that it announces the end of being 'on the market'. The honeymoon as *the* wedding gift is a gift whose elaborate and excessive quality, is money spent without return, wasted and squandered, money spent on a memory, is entirely *for the couple*.

The honeymoon is given such high value precisely because it evidences less the coolness of romantic relationships nor their contamination by consumerism's logic of reversible choice. Rather the honeymoon, a unique holiday chosen by the couple, gains its exceptional quality because it epitomises the *limits* to rational accounting and calculation in marriage markets and sexual fields. The honeymoon is the conversion of acquisition and getting, into the realm of getting without payment or giving. In the romantic ecology of choice, the honeymoon is both the highest expression of the economic competition and consummation of couples as well as its negation by way of transcending the logic of acquisition.

Re-embedding in Moral Communities

For Illouz, one unintended consequence of the emergence of the marriage market within the new ecology of choice is that it leaves individuals vulnerable and open to the re-evaluation of their choices. While, of course, the existential question 'Did I make the right choice?', much like the individualistic nature of Western societies, is not confined to the present, what does result from 'the great transformation of romantic ecology' is the over-riding sense that one's *own* actions and decisions are ultimately responsible for success or failure. Furthermore, the moral and normative frameworks that underline weddings, and marriage's ritual facets, become devoid of meaning and significance. The dis-embedding of the individual from an embedded marriage economy, in part, strips away the substantive rationality of marriage decisions and choices. Given this existential consequence for individuals in the new romantic ecology, the tendency to draw upon and redeploy facets of 'tradition' (invented or otherwise) has become evident in marriage and wedding practices. The appeal to tradition in 'individualised' conditions of romance gives rise to a process of 're-traditionalisation': a perceived decline in tradition results in the reselection of aspects of tradition at a time when choices are felt to have their origin in individual desire (Carter and Duncan 2018; Carter 2017).

In the past, Illouz argues, love was ritualised and followed a proper sequence: 'emotion confirms commitment as much as commitment confirms emotion' (2012: 30). She argues that this regime is in contrast to what we have now—a regime of emotional authenticity where: '[a]uthenticity demands that actors know their feelings; that they act on such feelings, which must then be the actual building blocks of a relationship; that people reveal their feelings to themselves (and preferably to others as well); and that they make decisions about relationships and commit themselves based on these feelings' (2012: 31). This inevitably leads to the contingent commitment and confluent love of Giddens' (1992) 'pure relationship' which need last only as long as the couple are satisfied with the relationship. Thus while relationships are supposed to be built on emotion, this emphasis on emotional authenticity is actually obscuring the role of rationality in relationship decision-making where degrees of happiness and satisfaction are weighed against the possibility of finding a better partner in the extensive and easily accessible new marriage market. The emphasis on emotions therefore, in fact obscures the cooling of emotion that has taken place and the replacement of emotion with rational calculations.

A problem with the logic of this argument occurs when you consider the conclusion drawn by, among others, Dawson (2012) who notes that it is a mistake to see the claims to individuality and individual justification for action as a 'faithful depiction of how people act' (2012: 314). Rather, the increase in claims to individualism reflects a 'shift in the common vocabulary' in an era where individuals are increasingly called upon to account for their behaviour (Dawson 2012: 314). This argument is leant further weight when we consider the breadth and depth of additional research pointing both to the ongoing class, gender and wealth inequalities which continue to enable or disable access to free choice (e.g. Carter and Duncan 2018; Thwaites 2016, this volume; Smith 2016; Jamieson 1999; Skeggs 2005), and to the continuation of social categories in defining and guiding behaviour. On this last point, for example, Carter (2010, 2017, 2018) has demonstrated how the social role of 'wife' is used by young women to guide their attitudes towards marriage. This use of 'wife' is social and relational: it depends upon an agreed collective understanding of the role, as defined and recognised by others but especially important others such as close friends and family.

Illouz concludes thus: 'what has been lost in the modern experience of romantic suffering is the ontological security which derives from the organization of courtship in a moral ecology of choice, commitment, and ritual and from the embeddedness of self-value in the social fabric of one's community' (2012: 155). From the above discussion we would take issue with the assumption that an apparent change in the moral ecology of choice and dis-embeddedness from a wider community has led to a change in actual behaviours. This issue is twofold: first that changes in the vocabulary of choice equate to changes in the operation of choice, second that changes in the vocabulary of choice, where it appears to be the sole responsibility of individuals, result in a disconnection from wider moral frameworks in which choices are made. For it is our contention that while the vocabulary of choice promotes individualism, the operation of choice continues to happen in reference to wider social moral frameworks: they are not just individual cognitive efforts. The changes in the ecology and architecture of choice are, therefore, more about perception than operation (see Dawson 2012).

There are a number of examples of this embeddedness in wider moral frameworks in our data regarding wedding gifts. The first comes in the form of the wedding itself being a gift for those attending. Emily (32, engaged cohabiting), for example, explained:

> the food is nothing spectacular, but the idea that you will pay any amount because you're getting married. We wanted to have a much more relaxed approach so most of our money is being spent on providing our friends and family with a wonderful weekend rather than spending it on chair covers and ribbons to tie around chairs

Helen (21, LAT) echoed this sentiment:

> I think I probably would spend quite a bit of money on it, still not anything stupid and OTT [over the top] but spend quite a bit of money on it so it was like the perfect day for everybody but that's the thing about weddings, you're not sup—not please everybody but I wouldn't see it as *my* day or anything like that I'd want everybody to have a good day and have a good time so I think most of the money would probably go on the bar: Champaign for everybody!

These examples illustrate that while perhaps not operating under the same moral frameworks as in the past, there is clearly a wider normative guide for behaviour which frames the wedding as an essentially social event and one that is 'for' the guests: family and friends. While couples continue to be embedded within communities, weddings are events which bring together a celebration of couples, individuals and groups.

Thus a new moral order is apparently established, one which neither relies solely on individuals nor communities for validity but instead incorporates both: wedding guests become key components of the ritual.

The presence of wedding guests operates as legitimation and confirmation of a couple relationship at a wedding. But the role of guests—and their gift-giving—can extend further to provide the very moral framework for action at weddings. Gift-giving creates and cements relationships between people and so large gifts made to a wedding couple cements both the importance of the couple as the centre of the ritual and the importance of the relationships between the couple (receivers) and gift-givers. Once again, the gift becomes the means through which to transcend the infiltration of market logic into romance. For example, Mandy (30, married cohabiting) explains:

> it wasn't a traditional wedding like there was a dress and there was a cake but it was all very, we did it on like on a budget and put all the money into the reception so that we could have loads of friend there rather than into fancy stuff and like I wasn't going to have flowers and then like my auntie said 'well for your present I'll buy you flowers'

This gift of wedding flowers here emphasises the importance both of the wedding couple—who deserve a large economic gift—and the relationship between the giver and receiver (auntie/niece). In this respect both the choice to gift a particular item, and the choice to provide a wedding reception 'for' friends, are not just choices based on personal reflection, rational logic or economic reasoning—they essentially involve relationships to others and a moral framework which promotes the valuing of those same relationships.

Lucy (30, LAT), for example, explains at some length the obligations and manipulations at work within her immediate family:

> mum said to dad have you thought about putting money aside it's like traditional and my dad probably like my mum says was really like ignored my mum and was just like phew what like how old are you and then mum said well your parents did it for your sister and then he went quiet and then apparently a couple of years later mum said that dad turned round her and

said yeah I've been putting stuff aside and he's not told me this yet yeah so… it's I'm just and my mum and mum spilt the beans so don't tell him I told you act surprised but I was so surprised absolutely amazed because I wouldn't expect anything from them 'cause they're so untraditional um not not because of that just 'cause I I just wouldn't expect anything from them I would hate for them to feel obliged and he obviously does… but yeah I'm sure he knows that I would never expect that and would never ask for that… so it's just hilarious

Even though her parents are not 'traditional' they are saving up money to give her for her wedding. Such gifts connote parental (or social) obligation, responsibility, approval, love and connectedness. While the architecture of choice may have become individualised and infused with rationality, the gift of a wedding from parent to child offers salvation from such market logic. Illouz overlooks the importance of emotional connections, relationality and kinship in her theory construction. For while individuals may increasingly be required to make decisions independently, lacking the wider social scripts from the past, and living with greater uncertainty, the gift of a wedding, for example, can re-embed a couple within a moral community which uphold traditions (fathers paying for the weddings of their daughters), creating a sense of security in a world of uncertainty.

As gifts can operate to create transcendence from economic market logic infiltrating romance, we can likewise see through the lens of gift-giving the continued importance of, and our embeddedness within, moral communities. In fact, the social, normative work of 'the gift' becomes the figure and ground for such moral communities to be activated and given shape. These may not be the moral communities of the past (Illouz uses the example of the small communities depicted in Jane Austen's novel), yet they are moral communities nonetheless: passing judgement on appropriate behaviour (as Lucy's mum does for Lucy's dad), communicating traditions (for fathers to pay for daughters' weddings), forging connections (between family and friends) and promoting self-sacrifice (making weddings *for* others). The claim of complete disembeddedness from moral communities and normative frameworks is unfounded; such claims are blind to continuities in personal life. An alternative approach to understanding the ongoing significance of moral communities is outlined below.

Self-Gifts or Love's Law of the Individual

With the couple at the centre of the wedding, our final critique of Illouz's account of modern romance is the place of, and the inevitable suffering bestowed upon, the self in late-modern love life. For Illouz, the problem is that love has become a site for the affirmation of the self at the expense of other social sources of recognition. Love is capable of this supreme metaphysical task of self-affirmation precisely because contemporary individualism rests upon people being seen as singular, unique and differentiated from others (Illouz 2012: 111–121). To be loved is to be affirmed for one's uniqueness. But the dialectic that Illouz explores is that love is unable, in the end, to affirm the self. The form of recognition that love entails is dyadic. When love becomes recognition of a unique individual self it equally runs up against the problem that the lover must not sacrifice themselves completely to their beloved, and neither must the beloved be only an object of desire, affection and emotional validation for the lover. There is a tension between autonomy and recognition of self-other that modern romance suffers from. We suggest a reconciliation to this dialectic of autonomy and recognition in Simmel's inversion of Kantian ethics, 'The Law of the Individual' (e.g. Nielsen 2002: 89; Lee and Silver 2012; Barbour 2012).

Of course, Illouz is not denying that other sources of recognition exist in late-modern societies, and neither is she denying the possibility of satisfying romantic relationships. However the problem with Illouz's diagnosis of modern suffering is that it is unable to accommodate a positive vision to the existential significance placed upon love as a source of the self. Today the moral substance of love is without an anchor:

> What has been lost in the modern experience of romantic suffering is the ontological security which derives from the organisation of courtship in a moral ecology of choice, commitment, and ritual and from the embeddedness of self-value in the social fabric of one's community. (Illouz 2012: 155)

Simmel certainly would have been sympathetic with this view of modern love, however he would not have longed for the pre-modern certainty of one's social fate. Simmel's moral philosophy is opposed to the substantive morality Illouz follows[2]: Simmel knew that reason alone could not save the modern soul. With this, Simmel inverted Kant's 'categorical imperative'—moral laws universally applicable to all particular persons—because it denied an essential part of our humanity: our emotional life. As modernity affirmed reason above all other dimensions of the human subject, Simmel argued moral decisions (as Illouz notes of emotionality being incorporated with rationality) would be stifling when conducted with reason alone. For Simmel, reason *and* a deeply 'sensuous' (i.e. emotive) dimension were required for a properly *individual* moral law (Lee and Silver 2012: 132f). Our decisions to commit to certain actions are not to be predicated upon a rational, universal moral law but the obligation for 'each of us to form our deeds into a coherent narrative that defines the person we are living to be' (Lee and Silver 2012: 133).

We find such an individual law within the modern marriage market: weddings are defined by the annulment of choice; a decision to commit in the face of choice. The highest value of romantic life is the decision to cut off all other choices in an ecology where choice is defined primarily by individual, emotional and rational reflexivity. As we have argued, the vocabulary of motives which pervades romantic relationships is premised upon individual desire and emotional reasoning, but this has not meant the wholesale takeover by either a consumerist ethics of reversibility or a removal of moral obligations to others. Weddings come to be expressions of individuality ultimately because they are a decisive plot-point in our individual moral narratives. They provide us with a cultural space to express, to ourselves as much as others, what our choices mean.

Consider Jane's (22, engaged cohabiting) statement about the wedding as a 'self-gift':

> I just think it's a gift to myself. Like, I've never spent this amount of money on anything. And ... to you know... I sort of thought to myself you haven't done expensive holidays, you haven't done these things. Give yourself this, give yourself this gift of this memory and this event, you know. ... But ... no it's that just that important personal step. [...] Because you're

like … 'I want my Cinderella day' [laughs]. That's kind of what it's like. […] There are things I know I could have saved money on … like my dress for instance, I know I could have got a cheaper dress. But I thought 'no, I don't want to take a chance on a dress from … the internet, they look like they make them really well…' but you have no idea what it looks like when it comes. […] So I know I could have saved money on my dress, but then I sort of think, that's the thing I don't want to get wrong … it's my wedding dress, again it's something I would have never spent that kind of money on. But it's my wedding dress. That in particular as well is my gift to myself. I mean, I'm paying for my wedding dress. Nobody else is.

Jane's statement of the wedding—the memory of the day—and the 'wedding dress', in particular, speaks to a triumph of her emotional desire, a fantasy of Cinderella that breaks through from her inner life: the sacrifice of money is transformed from purchase to donation, from commodity (defined by selfish acquisition) to gift ('my gift to myself') situated in a romance narrative (see Mick 1996: 105). Jane's insistence that the dress is hers, in the paradoxical language of the 'self-gift', is telling. Jane's self-gift evidences the ethical maxim of the individual law: that she desires to keep this memory and dress as hers beyond all other considerations. Absent from Jane's account is, crucially, others—her partner, family or friends. This is Simmel's 'law of the individual' at work; while the moral communities of the past may be fragmented, the self does not lose anchor completely. Jane acts as her own moral community: in late modernity the self becomes differentiated not only from others but 'themselves', too. As a result, the self becomes obliged to, and capable of, finding meaning 'within' through self-dialogue (Smith 2017).

We give to ourselves to maintain a boundary between our deliberative actions involving ourselves and others and that part of ourselves we reserve for ourselves. While the self-gift is logically impossible, Simmel reconciles the impossibility by allowing the self to speak to the self. Thus while gift-giving relies on the assumption that one is giving to someone else, self-gifting requires the self to be separated from the self. Illouz positions self-value within the social fabric of one's community and therefore interprets the decline of moral communities as undermining our ability to value ourselves. However, following Simmel's 'law of the individual', we see how self-value can be sourced from within the self and with it, an individual morality encompassing both emotion and rationality.

Conclusion

We hope to have demonstrated in this chapter some of the limitations of Illouz's theory of emotional capitalism, marriage markets and changes in the ecology and architecture of choice. Crucially we have used the framework of wedding gifts to demonstrate how engaging with gifting can transcend the limits of the market logic of romance: gifts can offer an end point to the perception of endless choice and choice reversibility. While wedding gifts may be redundant and overly commercialised to the anxious not-yet-married, for the soon-to-wed they represent a resolution to the rational uncertainty within the marriage market. The honeymoon as gift, moreover, may represent the ultimate rejection of the infiltration of market logic into romance since it transcends the logic of acquisition—it is a gift simply for the couple with no tangible end product.

We can also see that through the gifting of the wedding itself—to others or to the self—that this reflects the continued salience of moral communities and normative frameworks operating to guide behaviours. On the one hand, this is seen in the gifting of weddings (or elements of the wedding) from relatives or friends which reflects collective values and beliefs held by groups. On the other hand, this is demonstrated in the self-gifting of the wedding, illustrating an individual moral law that works to guide behaviour through self-dialogue. In both cases, moral and normative frameworks continue to operate in important ways in individuals' lives and decision-making processes.

Through this discussion of wedding gifts, we hope to have demonstrated that changes in intimacy practices have not resulted in the wholesale takeover of consumerist ethics nor the entire removal of moral obligations. For while individuals consider themselves individuals first, they do so in order to better embed themselves with others (their romantic partners, intimate others, even themselves). They certainly know their choices to be open and subject to rational calculation, but they equally see others having to be accommodated in these choices and courses of action. Our choices always have limits and these limits require a sense of meaningful orientation. That is, limits are longed for as much as they are a curtailing of choice. We hope to have provided one such meaningful limit to the great transformation of the romantic ecology: we may be disentangled from a communal, substantive morality, but we have ways to re-embed ourselves. In doing so we can find a morality which does have substance despite having to carry much of the burden of our choices ourselves. By using this morality of the gift—an ideal more than a reality—love's law of the individual is able to find a way for couples to be couples, families to be families and brides to be brides in a world where we are obliged to think of ourselves as ultimately individuals.

Notes

1. The *Mass Observation survey* invites volunteer members of the British public to record their responses to particular topics or questions. Participants are given no specific instruction what to record. The archives are based at the University of Sussex and contain material from c.1937–1955 and 1981–present.

2. Illouz's reading of Simmel's theory of modern alienation in *Cold Intimacies* (2007: 111–112) refers to a loss in the experience of love, as the comprehension of the whole of the other, due to the increasingly abstract ways in which we relate to one another. Our reading of Simmel draws upon his later ethical theory, not present in Illouz's sociology, which offers a means of overcoming the alienation he initially outlined.

References

Ansari, A. and Klinenberg, E. (2015) *Modern romance*. London: Penguin Press.

Barbour, C. (2012) The Maker of Lies: Simmel, Mendacity and the Economy of Faith. *Theory, Culture & Society*, 29 (7–8): 218–236.

Barlow, A., Duncan, S., James, G. and Park, A. (2005) *Cohabitation, marriage and the law: Social change and legal reform in the 21st century*. Oxford: Hart Publishing.

Campbell, C. (1987) *The romantic ethic and the spirit of modern consumerism.* Oxford: Blackwell Publishers.

Carter, J. (2010). *Why Marry? Young women talk about relationships, marriage and love.* Ph.D Thesis, University of York.

Carter, J., Duncan, S., Stoilova, M. and Phillips, M. (2015) Sex, Love and Security: Accounts of Distance and Commitment in Living Apart Together Relationships. *Sociology,* 50 (3): 576–593.

Carter, J. (2017) Why marry? The role of tradition in women's marital aspirations. *Sociological Research Online,* 22 (1): 1–14.

Carter, J. (2018) Women (not) troubling the family: exploring women's narratives of gendered family practices. *Journal of Family Issues.* https://doi.org/10.1177/0192513X18809752

Carter, J. and Duncan, S. (2017) Wedding paradoxes: Individualized conformity and the 'perfect day'. *Sociological Review,* 65 (1): 3–20.

Carter, J. and Duncan, S. (2018) *Reinventing couples: Tradition, agency and bricolage.* Basingstoke: Palgrave Macmillan.

Dawson, M. (2012) Reviewing the critique of individualization: The disembedded and embedded theses. *Acta Sociologica,* 55 (4): 305–319.

Durkheim, E. (1997) *The division of labor in society.* New York: Free Press.

Giddens, A. (1992) *The transformation of intimacy: Sexuality, love, and eroticism in modern societies.* California: Stanford University Press.

Gross, N. (2005) The detraditionalization of intimacy reconsidered. *Sociological Theory,* 23 (3): 286–311.

Illouz, E. (2007) *Cold intimacies: The making of emotional capitalism.* Cambridge: Polity Press.

Illouz, E. (2008) *Saving the modern soul: Therapy, emotions, and the culture of self-help.* California: University of California Press.

Illouz, E. (2012) *Why love hurts: A sociological explanation.* Oxford: Wiley.

Jamieson, L. (1999) Intimacy Transformed? A Critical Look at the 'Pure Relationship'. *Sociology,* 33 (3): 477–494.

Lee, M. and Silver, D. (2012) Simmel's Law of the Individual and the Ethics of the Relational Self. *Theory, Culture & Society,* 29 (7–8): 124–145.

Mason, J. (2004) Personal Narratives, Relational Selves: Residential Histories in the Living and Telling. *The Sociological Review,* 52 (2): 162–179.

Mauss, M. (1990) *The Gift: The Form and Reason for Exchange in Archaic Societies.* New York: W W Norton & Co Inc.

Mick, D. G. (1996) Self-Gifts. In C. Otnes and R. F. Beltramini (eds.) *Gift giving: A research anthology.* Ohio: Bowling Green State University Popular Press.

Nielsen, G. M. (2002) *The norms of answerability: social theory between Bakhtin and Habermas*. New York: State University of New York Press.

ONS. (2018) *Marriages in England and Wales: 2015*. [Online]. Available at: https://www.ons.gov.uk/peoplepopulationandcommunity/birthsdeathsand-marriages/marriagecohabitationandcivilpartnerships/bulletins/marriag-esinenglandandwalesprovisional/2015 [Accessed 8 August 2018].

Penner, B. (2004) 'A Vision of Love and Luxury' The Commercialization of Nineteenth-Century American Weddings. *Winterthur Portfolio*, 39 (1): 1–20.

Purbrick, L. (2003) Wedding Presents: Marriage Gifts and the Limits of Consumption, Britain, 1945–2000. *Journal of Design History*, 16 (3): 215–227.

Purbrick, L. (2015) No frills: Wedding presents and the meaning of marriage, 1945–2003. In J. Miles, P. Mody, and R. Probert (eds.) *Marriage Rites and Rights*. Oxford: Hart Publishing.

Skeggs, B. (2005) The Making of Class and Gender through Visualizing Moral Subject Formation. *Sociology*, 39 (5): 965–982.

Slater, D. (1997) *Consumer culture and modernity*. Cambridge: Polity Press.

Smith, D. R. (2016) *Elites, race and nationhood: The branded gentry*. Basingstoke: Palgrave Macmillan.

Smith, D. R. (2017) The tragedy of self in digitised popular culture: the existential consequences of digital fame on YouTube. *Qualitative Research*, 17 (6): 699–714.

Thwaites, R. (2016) Making a choice or taking a stand? Choice feminism, political engagement and the contemporary feminist movement. *Feminist Theory*, 18 (1): 55–68.

Varul, M. Z. (2015) Consumerism as Folk Religion: Transcendence, Probation and Dissatisfaction with Capitalism. *Studies in Christian Ethics*, 28 (4): 447–460.

Waterson, J. (2018) Royal wedding confirmed as year's biggest UK TV event | UK news | The Guardian [Online] 20 May. Available at: https://www.theguardian.com/uk-news/2018/may/20/royal-wedding-confirmed-as-years-biggest-uk-tv-event [Accessed 8 August 2018].

Section II

Sexual Abundance and Emotional Inequalities

5

'I Would Like to Be Better at It': A Critical Engagement with Illouz's Account of Men and Intimacy in Romantic Relationships

Fiona McQueen and Sharani Osborn

Introduction

With a focus on established heterosexual romantic relationships, this chapter engages with a specific line of argument in Illouz's work, that the predominance of the therapeutic ethos has led to a convergence between middle-class men and women and a divergence between working- and middle-class men, in terms of their capacity to achieve and sustain intimacy. These claims are set out in *Cold Intimacies* (2007) and recur across Illouz's work (1997a, 2008). In the first of three sections, we position these claims within a brief summary of Illouz's theory of emotional capitalism but also against research which contends that these claims are too sweeping. This contention is supported in the discussion of McQueen's

F. McQueen (✉)
Edinburgh Napier University, Edinburgh, UK
e-mail: F.McQueen@napier.ac.uk

S. Osborn
University of Edinburgh, Edinburgh, UK

© The Author(s) 2020   **83**
J. Carter, L. Arocha (eds.), *Romantic Relationships in a Time of 'Cold Intimacies'*,
Palgrave Macmillan Studies in Family and Intimate Life,
https://doi.org/10.1007/978-3-030-29256-0_5

(2017) original research about intimacy in couples which follows in the second section. Class distinctions between men's positive orientation to communication in romantic relationships were not found, while differences between these men and their partners in the capacity for emotional openness persisted. On the basis that these findings call into question the scope of Illouz's claims, the third section is a critical engagement with the progression of Illouz's line of argument in relation to class and gender and with the mode of analysis which led to the categorical claims qualified by our research and to a narrow and pessimistic perspective on intimacy in working-class men's relationships.

Intimacy in Emotional Capitalism

Illouz's concept of emotional capitalism is intended to capture 'the broad, sweeping movement' of the interpenetration of economic behaviour and emotional life (2007: 5). This is seen in the incorporation of emotional intelligence as quantifiable professional competence in the corporate sector, for example, and in the value of communicative competence in romantic relationships. Illouz argues for the pervasiveness of the therapeutic ethos, and the work of distinction it does, through her use of Bourdieu's concepts of field, habitus and capitals. In the emotional field produced by psychology and associated actors, the new commodity of emotional health is produced, circulated and recycled (2007: 62–3). Habitus—and particularly the habitus socialised in the workplace (2007: 68)—regulates access to emotional competence, which becomes a capital insofar as it is convertible into economic and social benefits required to 'seize what is at stake' in the emotional field (2007: 47). Illouz argues that what is at stake is advantage not only in professional but in romantic relationships.

The emotional competence relevant to established romantic relationships is the therapeutic model of communicative rationality, explored in detail in *Consuming the Romantic Utopia* (1997a). Therapeutic discourse positioned communication as core to self-knowledge, intimacy and resolving conflict (1997a: 236) but also as codified within a model of communication governed by a procedural rationality which controlled emotions and managed interactions (2008: 134). Illouz argues that contemporary romantic intimacy combines both the possibility for authenticity and pleasure, but also the demand to bargain for and monitor rights, needs and wants. In these ways, intimacy is 'cold' (2008: 130–1). Another aspect of Illouz's analysis suggests a further meaning for the term 'cold intimacies'. The communicative rationality described above is the achievement of high levels of emotional capital, largely inaccessible to working-class men (2007: 69), who could be said to be cast out into the cold in Illouz's analysis. Working-class women feel the chill in the distance of their experience from their aspiration to middle-class forms of love and romance (1997a: 278), a distance which also reflects the divergence between the emotional competence of working- and middle-class men identified by Illouz. By contrast, Illouz argues that gender distinctions have become blurred for the middle and upper classes. Men and women have come to share common understandings of, and positions within, a therapeutic discourse valued in both the domestic and professional spheres (2008: 229).

Critical engagement with this account of gender, class and intimacy is linked to the charge that Illouz overstates the prevalence of the therapeutic ethos and the implications of changes in the working environment for interpersonal relations. Illouz conceptualises emotional capitalism as a culture producing 'a broad, sweeping movement', but the claims made for the implications of this movement for gender and class identities are, we argue, too broad and sweeping. As noted by Brownlie, such totalising claims to the pervasiveness of change in understanding and especially in practice, such as a general reliance on a therapeutically informed model of communication in romantic relationships, for example, require evidence not only of the phenomenon but of its prevalence and its practice (2014: 15). Brownlie considers quantitative data from a sample of just over 1000 respondents and qualitative data in research with 52 participants. Brownlie concludes that while the therapeutic might be symbolically pervasive, reflected in its seepage into everyday language, there are those who express unease, scepticism or criticism of the discourse as well as those who invest in some of its precepts. Widespread knowledge can prompt opposition as well as acceptance and 'even where people do accept therapeutic precepts in principle, this does not necessarily shape what they then think or do in their own lives' (2014: 104).

In her analysis of attitudes to emotions and disclosure, and of engagement with therapeutic services, Brownlie found that gender, more than class, shapes our beliefs about the value of emotions talk. Men, much more than women, conveyed the belief that talk was indeterminate and ineffective in contrast to action, the desire to evade talk about emotions, and fear of loss of control, not only of their emotions and selves but also of the story. They saw a risk of being perceived as weak but also perceptions that recourse to therapeutic services *was* weak and a failure to take responsibility for oneself (2014: 99–100). Where men did take hold of the idea that it is good to talk, they generally still struggled with the idea that they themselves should talk (2014: 104). Resistance to practising the therapeutic model of communication among men did not vary significantly by class. Brownlie is explicit that her analysis challenges Illouz's claims of gender convergence and class divergence in communication within couples (2014: 70). The question of how gender shapes the relation between principle and practice in relation to communication and intimacy is explored in further depth through discussion of McQueen's study in the next section.

Men on Emotion in Relationships: Principle and Practice

The Study

This chapter draws on research conducted by McQueen involving face to face interviews conducted with heterosexual men (n = 13) and women (n = 15) in 2012 which make up the final of three stages of data collection including an online survey (n = 1087) conducted in 2010 and telephone interviews (n = 43) conducted in 2011. The interviews focused on emotion in couple relationships, although participants were not required to be in a relationship at the time of interview. Participants were recruited initially through the online survey using a combination of snowball sampling, targeted Facebook adverts and press coverage (in the Scottish Sun). Contact with the researcher was maintained via a telephone interview and email contact until interviews took place two years later. As is often the case with qualitative research, the sample presented here is self-selected so that participants may have had a particular interest in couple relationship dynamics prior to being interviewed. The length of time over which data collection took place points towards a commitment from participants to being involved in the study which may have exacerbated this bias but which also led to a high level of rapport and ease in interviews, as commented on by several participants.

The primary focus of the analysis in this chapter is data from interviews with men. The age range of men interviewed was from mid 30s to early 70s at the time of interview. Class status was chosen by participants, although this was not always straightforward due to generational transitions as described by Danny (middle-class, early 70s).

> Interviewer: If you had to describe yourself as working-class or middle-class which would you choose?
> Danny: Well I came from working-class definitely, I have probably become middle-class, as I think lots of people in my generation with free education were able to do. I have wealth that my parents simply would not understand.

Danny highlights the ways in which class divisions can be blurred due to financial, educational, occupational and cultural factors rather than stark divisions, the class status of participants was, for some, subject to evaluation. For this reason, class in not presented in this chapter as polarising or causative. For clarity, the self-ascribed class status and occupation at time of interview will be noted alongside the self-chosen pseudonym of participants.

While the empirical research presented in this chapter was conducted by McQueen, the analysis and engagement with Illouz presented here is the result of a collaboration with Osborn for this book chapter.

Research Context

A large body of sociological research was undertaken in the 1980s and 1990s to explore couple relationships as part of a well-established feminist tradition of 'examining gender power in intimate relationships beginning in the 1960s' (Segal 1990). A consistent finding across this research was that women were unhappy in their heterosexual relationships and this was directly attributable to their male partner's lack of emotional involvement (Duncombe and Marsden 1993; Mansfield and Collard 1988; Komter 1989; Benjamin 1998). Duncombe and Marsden (1993) found most women reported their male partners lacked 'emotional participation' while the men interviewed stated that they had emotional feelings but did not necessarily want to share these with their wives.

Since this body of research was conducted a discourse around the 'therapeutic' has become influential (Brownlie 2014; Furedi 2004; Illouz 2007), that suggests emotional competence is increasingly valued, by both women and men. The accounts presented in this chapter do, in part, align with this discourse. While there was no evidence of change in women's accounts of still wanting emotional closeness and sharing with their partners, the men talked of wanting to be emotional and to be able to share feelings, in contrast to the findings of the previous research mentioned above. However, there was a gap between aspiration and practice, with implications for Illouz's claims about class and gender, which we will explore further in this chapter.

Although emotion is defined here as being *in* social relationships and communicative, 'occurring between people and not expressions of something contained inside a single person' (Burkitt 1997: 40, emphasis in original), in this chapter we recognise we are principally describing how these men refer to *talking* about emotions and the potential for difficulties around this.

Gender Is Omni-Relevant

Before presenting the main argument that men's practice of the therapeutic ethos is more complex and problematic than Illouz suggests, it is necessary to address gender as the central organising factor in the analysis. Gender differences in the interview data collected were striking, with almost all women describing a sense of themselves as being aware of their emotions, being able to discuss these easily and desiring emotional closeness with their partners. The main focus of the interviews with women was on the emotional competence of their partner(s), past and present, rather than on themselves, as exemplified by Grace (late 40s, middle-class, senior manager) when she describes her current partner's prepared-ness to discuss his emotions:

> There came a point in his life long before I met him where he felt the need to go into all of that and find out what the hell was going on and sort it out … he chose to go on to understand why he felt the way he did … what I found attractive about it was the bravery that goes with that … I think men are particularly bad about it … I don't know what it is we do to men in this country but British men find it really hard.

However, several women gave accounts of male partners who remained less emotionally skilled than themselves. While women focused on their partner in discussing emotional participation, the interviews with men focused on their own emotional lives and the implications for their rela-tionships. The gendered pattern of women who believed they were emo-tionally competent, and men who considered themselves to be less so, was clear.

Gender roles were also highly marked within the accounts of the men interviewed, for example in regard to who had responsibility for raising issues and facilitating discussions of feelings. Caracticus (working-class, mid 40s, technician) described the role his female partner had in his becoming 'better' at describing his feelings:

> Interviewer: When you're looking for a partner would you rather have somebody who doesn't push you to talk about how you're feeling, or do you actually quite like it?
> Caracticus: No I would like to be better at it, so yes I like it.
> Interviewer: Does it feel comfortable?
> Caracticus: No!

This connection between an asymmetrical gendered pattern in emo-tional competence and a gendered division of the responsibility for rais-ing issues was described by almost all participants, both men and women. The strong gender differences in these accounts call into question Illouz's suggestion that 'emotional androgynization' (2007: 37) is present within the domestic sphere. Rather, gender differences were found to be omnirelevant in the interview data, both as regards the interview focus and the interview content.

Acceptance of Therapeutic Ethos

Illouz suggests that, despite its prevalence, class is an organising aspect of acceptance of the therapeutic culture among men, and that competence in the therapeutic model of communication varies according to class for men. Among her respondents, both men and women in upper-middle-classes valued 'talking', but in working-class couples it was only women who did so (1997a: 276). However, a common theme in all interviews with men in this research, regardless of their education, was an acceptance that to be emotionally competent, or emotionally articulate was a good thing. As can be seen from this quote from Mitt (middle-class, early 60s, engineer) this included a recognition of problem solving as central to emotional communication.

> Interviewer: So would you describe yourself as somebody who is quite emotionally articulate then?
> Mitt: Yes.
> Interviewer: So you feel that's an important part?
> Mitt: I think I am, I don't know if anybody else would describe me as this but I think that I am.
> Interviewer: Does that make you happy?
> Mitt: Yes absolutely I think it must be terrible to be unable to express yourself. If you can't express yourself in words then you will express yourself some other way and it's not always going to be very good.

Implied within this description from Mitt is a sense of emotions as potentially dangerous when contained, that not expressing emotions can lead to negative consequences, a point made by Biffer when discussing his view on sharing his feelings (working-class, mid 50s, manual occupation):

No it's a good thing to do, should get your emotions out in the open, the more you hide things the more they hurt you, that's always been the case, I've seen it so many times ... So yes I do think it's important to discuss your emotions, hiding your emotions is a crazy thing to do, it's like having a bag of explosives, if you don't open it up and get rid of them they're going to blow up in your face at some stage, you have to discuss things ... Yes it's good to discuss what's on your mind and you need to, because you become insane if you don't, would drive you bananas.

Both of these accounts focus on sharing feelings and the negative consequences of containing emotion, arguably because this understanding of communication is dominant within this sample of men. Despite their class differences, both Mitt and Biffer refer to emotional control in ways that match closely with the main ideas contained in the therapeutic ethos—the benefits of talking about emotions, the need to manage emotions, the potential danger of containing emotions (Illouz 1997a; Furedi 2004). While they use different language both Biffer and Mitt utilise the discourse to convey an emotional competence, a sense of themselves as knowing what is good and what is healthy. Clint (working-class, late 30s, supply teacher) highlights the importance for his sense of self as well as for the well-being of his current partner of providing emotional support:

If you are providing emotional support for them it develops you, it makes you more aware of other people's problems and shows yourself you are capable of dealing with things. It gets you more emotionally involved with that person ... It is something you do need ... providing emotional support is one of the most important things you can do in a relationship ... it's difficult to provide emotional support if you don't want to do it ... Without it, if you can't provide emotional support to your partner I don't think you're in the right relationship, simple as.

The *status* of being emotionally competent is made explicit here for Clint in that he describes wanting to show *himself* that he is capable of dealing with things, particularly in this case providing emotional support. Clint presents himself as accepting the values of therapeutic culture in both his desire to develop himself and to connect with his partner. The self-awareness and expressiveness central to the therapeutic model of love, according to Illouz (1997a), are as present in the accounts of these working-class men as in those of middle-class men.

The 'Strange History' of Felix

In line with Illouz, Felix (middle-class, early 50s, engineer) presented an account of having wholeheartedly accepted the ethos of the therapeutic discourse, and the resultant communicative rationality. Felix's first wife encouraged him to attend counselling as she felt he was emotionally unavailable. As Felix describes below, before counselling he was not able to follow the therapeutic model of communication despite his middle-class status.

> Essentially they are two different people tied together by a strange history. So Felix 15 years ago was pleasant, well-meaning, reasonably hard working, slightly selfish or self-interested man, who was largely harmless, but quite semi-detached and divorced from the rest of the world in many ways, very much in my own little bubble … I wasn't emotionally reflective, I didn't have the vocabulary, I didn't have the tools to self-reflect, I didn't know what reflection was, I couldn't name, I couldn't feel the sensations in my body and go 'yes that thing in my tummy, that's anxiety', or 'is that excitement?'

It was a conscious decision to incorporate therapeutic values into his day-to-day life that led Felix to work hard at developing an awareness of his emotions in order to become emotionally reflexive and engaged in his relationships as well as with himself, as can be seen from this description of life after therapy:

> So [life was] a little kind of a 'John Major-y' grey kind of a life, whereas now it is moonbeams and rainbows and Fred Astaire and Ginger Rogers dancing down the staircase, it's not quite, but it's certainly a much more colourful and much more powerful … yes, than I could have imagined. It's a whole new language and I literally had no idea when I started therapy that there was this whole psychological world that you could learn about and actually learn it yourself, and it was a revelation.

It is relevant that Felix identified himself unproblematically as a middle-class man, with a university level education and professional services career, and yet he describes himself (before therapy) as lacking the vocabulary (or linguistic capital) to be reflexive about his feelings. His middle-class position, and professional job, were not sufficient to provide the required tools for Felix to have this rationality, mainly due to the resistance that was generated by his gendered habitus. In order to 'achieve' the status of being emotionally competent, to be able to *talk* fluently about emotion, it was necessary to do work on himself.

The Gap Between Acceptance and Practice: Gendered Habitus

The therapeutic model of communication proposes that 'communication prevents and resolves conflicts, brings a better knowledge of oneself and others, binds two people emotionally, and serves as the basis for true intimacy' (Illouz 1997a: 236). However disclosing emotion itself may, for many men, *cause* conflict, either relational or internal, due to a pervasive sense of vulnerability. A desire to be emotionally fluent, articulate or competent did not necessarily lead to an ability to talk about or share emotion easily. Instead there was a pervasive sense of vulnerability associated with sharing negative emotions, specifically worry, upset or fear. An extract from the interview with Davie (mid 30s, working-class, senior support worker) highlights the relationship between emotional disclosure, a sense of vulnerability and resulting conflict in this discussion about talking to his partner if he was upset:

Davie: Do you know I wouldn't say that I avoid talking about it, but it would have to be on my terms and a short conversation about it—I felt nervous, oh are you all right now? Yes.
Interviewer: That short?
Davie: Yes. A sentence … I think it is probably about not wanting to put a burden on anyone, I will deal with it myself, you don't have to worry about it, it is fine.
Interviewer: So you wouldn't talk to anybody?

> Davie: I would probably speak to Megan about it this, is all jumbled up, I would speak to Megan about it if I was really upset about something that had happened, then I would speak to her, but it does have to be on my terms, finished when I want it to finish and not go on and on and on.
> Interviewer: What is that about that not going on and on thing?
> Davie: I suppose it is a bit being in control, sort of staying in control of it.
> Interviewer: What is the fear what would be bad about it going on and on?
> Davie: I don't know, I wonder if I would end up feeling exposed or I can't even cope with this or helpless, a bit pathetic, vulnerable, that would be vulnerable if I sort of said too much or it went too deeply, that sort of thing would end up feeling quite vulnerable myself.
> Interviewer: Where is that line, how would you know you were getting to the point where right I've said enough now?
> Davie: I would probably start getting annoyed and being honest, make it difficult, make it awkward, so it would collapse.

Davie described his approach to avoiding a discussion of being upset wherein communication does not prevent or resolve conflict, nor bind two people emotionally. Rather, there is a reluctance in this account from Davie to say how he feels when he is with his partner as this leads to an uncomfortable feeling of being exposed, helpless and vulnerable. The consequences of communication are problematic in this context.

What is arguably causing this sense of vulnerability is an internalised set of values associated with manliness that represent how Davie should behave, emotionally, as a man which generates resistance to injunctions of the therapeutic discourse and its model of communication. Davie's implicit ideals of self-sufficiency and self-control, of being able to cope and deal with things himself are key elements in the, implicitly masculine, model of the autonomous subject, and in many cultural representations of idealised masculinity. Where men hold themselves accountable to norms of masculinity constituted in opposition to femininity, weakness and dependence may be felt as a failure in gender competence (Connell 2002), undermining the sense of themselves as a proper man, a proper self. Thus, the unpleasant sense of vulnerability experienced in relation to disclosing he is upset is triggered by a clash between Davie's gendered habitus and his attempt to share his feelings with his partner, behaviour that is considered desirable within the therapeutic model of communication (McQueen 2017).

Illouz refers to a 'new form of masculinity' based in the norms and values of global therapeutic habitus (2008: 217). McQueen's research indicates that while the therapeutic discourse may be widely circulating, it does not follow that a therapeutic habitus is widespread. A habitus must manifest the internalisation and socialisation of the norms and values of the surrounding culture, as habitus is 'society written into the body, into the biological individual' (Bourdieu 1990: 63). Therefore, a *therapeutic habitus* would have to be shaped by the therapeutic ethos so that its values lead to action, such as sharing all feelings, and easy navigation of new conditions of intimate relationships (Illouz 2008: 227). However, neither working- nor middle-class participants had what could be described as a 'therapeutic habitus' even if they accepted much of the therapeutic ethos. We suggest that it is too simplistic to talk of an increasingly dominant therapeutic habitus for men (Illouz 2008) when what is found in this research is more an attempt on the part of men to overcome a deeply embedded *masculine* habitus to which sharing negative emotions is a threat.

To summarise the significance of this analysis for our engagement with Illouz's account of how the therapeutic ethos orders emotional competence and practices of intimacy, the acceptance of a therapeutic ethos at a discursive level among men in our sample is clear, and this ethos is recognised as being important to how 'good' relationships *should* function. Participants in this research endorsed therapeutic understandings of the necessity of disclosure of difficult emotions to sustaining intimacy and for their own well-being. Thus, Illouz is overly pessimistic about the ability of working-class men to engage with therapeutic culture. Illouz might argue some of these men do not have the cultural competence of those in her sample, but, falling as they do between the exaggerated (class) poles of her analysis, the accounts of participants presented here suggest the limits of claims and the lack of nuance in Illouz's position.

At the same time, both middle- and working-class men described contending understandings of the need to preserve themselves from vulnerability which were in conflict with, or complicated, the adoption of practices of communication. Several men in this research wanted to overcome their traditionally masculine habitus (although they did not describe it in these terms), and all were relatively reflexive about their emotional lives, but equally almost all participants still felt a sense of vulnerability in relation to sharing negative emotions. The resistance of gendered habitus even when there is an acceptance of much of the therapeutic discourse calls into question Illouz's notion that what is at issue is a therapeutic habitus (2008). Most clearly, both the indications of men's gendered habitus and clear reference from men and women to gendered roles in respect of facilitating talk about emotions, across class identifications, argue against the notions of middle-class gender convergence and class divergence among men in intimacy in romantic relationships.

The Implications of Illouz's Mode of Analysis for Her Arguments About Gender and Class

We argue that the discussion of empirical research in the first two sections of this chapter not only challenges the validity of Illouz's generalisations about middle- and working-class men from her own research but also prompts consideration of the mode of analysis which produced them. In this third section of the chapter we examine elements of the analysis which we suggest trouble the smooth progression of Illouz's arguments that there is a convergence in the emotional competence of middle-class men and women and a divergence between middle- and working-class men. The first of these is a disregard for evidence of countervailing tendencies, which we consider in respect to claims of emotional androgyny. Second, we explore the implications of Illouz's adaptation of a Bourdieusian framework for her characterisation of working-class men as a homogeneous category and the 'other' of middle-class men. We consider two adaptations in particular: The reversal of the direction of socialisation and the theorising of emotional competence as of actual rather than arbitrary value, both of which limit the forms of intimacy recognised in Illouz's account of working-class men.

The place Illouz gives the therapeutic model of communication in middle-class workplaces is intended to explain both a convergence of middle-class men and women and the distinction between middle- and working-class men. As indicated in the first section, Illouz argues for the pervasiveness of the therapeutic ethos, and the work of distinction it does, through her use of Bourdieu's concepts of field, habitus and capitals. However, Illouz is concerned with habitus generated not in the family but in the working environment:

> That is, if we reverse the Bourdieusian model and inquire about the ways in which certain professions socialize their children to a certain emotional habitus, which in turn will help them reach particular forms of eudaimonia (happiness, well-being) in the realm of intimate relationships, then we may inquire about the ways in which intimacy or friendship are, like other forms of goods, socially distributed and allocated. (2007: 68)

Middle-Class Gender Convergence: Countervailing Tendencies

As a result of changes in the composition of the economic sector, women's increased participation in paid work and the incorporation of emotional intelligence into corporate practice, Illouz identifies a symmetry in the competencies demanded in middle-class workplaces and romantic relationships. She argues that this symmetry leads to 'the cultivation of a common reflexive and communicative selfhood that in turn tends to blur distinctions of gender roles and identities'. This common selfhood 'has articulated male and female identities in a common and convergent androgynous model of selfhood, alternatively used in the home and in the workplace' (2008: 229). Illouz doesn't claim that the convergence brings equality, but neither does she acknowledge the ways in which inequality must block a genuine gender convergence in selfhood.

Androgyny is understood by Illouz as the combination of 'feminine' and 'masculine' characteristics. Illouz considers the change this model represents to be the greatest in men and characterises emotional androgyny in New Men as, perhaps a little paradoxically, new forms of masculinity (2008: 217ff). New Men are able to 'get in touch with their feelings' and the 'feminine side of things' (2008: 221) through the development and application of communication skills in both professional and intimate settings. Thus, the concept invokes the gender binary even in claiming the masculine and feminine can be combined. For example, Illouz proposes that the emphasis on emotional intelligence and communication skills in emotional capitalism frees men from having (in the words of a social skills manual) 'to be identified always with "hard" masculine qualities and women with "soft" feminine ones' (2007: 23). The presence of or demand for a characteristic thus designated as feminine, 'perceptiveness' for example, in the professional practice of both men and women is assumed to constitute a convergence of practice, and also a convergence in how others interpret that practice. The reference by the interviewee who exemplified the New Man to getting in touch with 'the feminine side of things' (2008: 221), we suggest, points to a temporary tactical overlay of the feminine/masculine binary on the category of 'men'. His purpose is to establish the distinction between culturally and emotionally inclusive and competent New Men and those limited to, and by, traditional dispositions.

What most limits the support these examples give to Illouz's claims is that she treats the meaning of characteristics such as perceptiveness as constant, rather than taking into account the relational and discursive context in which they are enacted and interpreted. Illouz suggests that emotional capitalism expands the opportunities for women to 'play a more significant role' (2008: 236). However, Adkins (2004) questions the significance for gender identities and equality of the 'feminisation' in corporate culture and the injunction on employees to aim to embody a range of appropriate characteristics or dispositions, regardless of gender. Adkins notes that women's reflexive skills and competencies, for example, are less likely to be recognised as capital to be converted than taken for granted as natural and, therefore, not requiring recognition or reward. Thus, research in the workplace has found that characteristics may be perceived differently when displayed by women and men, interpreted as they are within the context of gender relations. Hochschild (1983) found that the public afforded men flight attendants more authority than they held and more than women flight attendants, although both were trained in the same service ethos.

As for the New Men, the invocation of the 'feminine' may be understood as superficial and convenient shorthand for a cluster of characteristics, such as empathy, which are defined in opposition to stereotypes of 'traditional masculinity'. However, in being taken up by men, they are separated from the 'femininity' through which such characteristics as empathy may be understood differently in women, as noted above. New forms of masculinity may be androgynous, in Illouz's terms, but can't be assumed to facilitate recognition of the positioning of women or to be more egalitarian in practice. Although Illouz's New Men may be held accountable to traditional norms of masculinity in some contexts, they are mobilising a 'global emotional habitus' which is a source of professional advantage and thus, we suggest, consistent with supporting men continuing to hold the majority of positions of authority and power in the workplace. Furthermore, feminist researchers have found that a blurring of gendered boundaries in one area often prompts borderwork in another. For example, caregiver fathers emphasised aspects of their parenting such as playing sport or Do-it-yourself (DIY) while downgrading the significance of 'feminine' domestic work (Doucet 2006), suggesting a re-working of gender identities rather than blurring of gender (Adkins 2004: 203).

Thus, there may be little in 'emotional androgynisation' to impact on the many persistent inequalities which might block convergence of expectations of men and women. Illouz briefly acknowledges continuing inequality between men and women (2008: 236, e.g.), but not the complex interplay of factors that sustain that inequality.[1] By contrast, Hochschild's analysis in 'The Economy of Gratitude' (2003) does show how resulting disparities between the positions of men and women in the workplace and in the home might qualify claims of convergence. Men's tolerance of their wives' greater career success or higher earning was considered by men, and some women, a gift which excused husbands from addressing the consequences of a wife's working, such as limited time for housework and cooking. Men's sense of the magnitude of their 'gift' was heavily influenced by family or peer attitudes, to the link between financial provision and masculinity, for example. Women's sense of obligation shaped power relations and undermined entitlement to and demands for a more equal division of labour (2003: 104–118). Thus, while Hochschild also writes about the commercialisation of feeling, the cooling of culture and women managing risk, she does so with a greater sense of how different dimensions of unequal gender relations sustain differences between even middle-class men and women.

Class Divergence: Homogeneous Categories and Hard Boundaries

Above we quoted Illouz's intention to 'inquire about the ways in which intimacy or friendship are, like other forms of goods, socially distributed and allocated' (2007: 68). Illouz describes intimacy as a sphere of meaning in its own right, and so 'a good of a special kind' (2008: 223) but, nevertheless, one which is 'like other forms of goods' in that it is socially distributed and allocated within the emotional field. Intimacy is defined as communication, itself defined within therapeutic discourse, and, according to the principle of convertibility of capitals, access to intimacy is made subject to the possession of other capitals which it comes to resemble. Thus, under the banner of extending the analysis of inequality to happiness, Illouz brings intimacy within the remit of a Bourdieusian analysis. In this section, we examine Illouz's analysis of class distinction and, in particular, the way two innovations in her Bourdieusian analysis shape conclusions about working-class men.

Having discussed the significance of the reversal of the direction of socialisation for Illouz's concept of emotional androgyny, we move here to its significance for claims to class divergence. If the incorporation of the therapeutic habitus in middle-class work practices is presented as bringing the selfhood of men and women into closer alignment, the same process is seen by Illouz as increasing the distance between the habitus of middle- and working-class men. Her characterisation of working-class men's affective practices is based in her equation of working-class employment with blue-collar jobs on the shop-floor where '[s]kills in human relations, the ability to attend to one's emotions and negotiate with others, have little relevance' (2008: 235). However, the recurrent tendency to generalise from one part (in this case, the seven working-class men in Illouz's sample) to a much larger whole leads Illouz to overlook changes in the types of work available to men in post-industrial economies, much of it in the service economy where aspects of the therapeutic discourse operate (2007: 65–6), and the consequently increased similarity of employment for working-class men and women. Furthermore, we suggest Illouz overstates the significance of workplace culture for communication within romantic relationships. McQueen's sample included men from a range of types of employment across class identifications who showed no significant difference in their acceptance of therapeutic discourse. Understanding the distribution of intimacy in Bourdieusian terms and emphasising the formative role of a reductive characterisation of working-class men's working environment leads Illouz to construct working-class men as a homogeneous category and position them as the 'other' to middle-class men.

Writing Within the Terms of the Field: Illouz's Mode of Analysis

A number of feminist writers have adapted the concepts of field, habitus or capital in theorising the relations between emotion, class and gender. Some have reflected on the implications of a Bourdieusian framework for researchers' conceptualisation of the relation between categories and for their engagement with working-class perspectives (Adkins and Skeggs 2004). For example, Reay (2004) acknowledges the dilemma posed by the encounter with different perspectives—which have different implications of advantage and disadvantage—for the feminist researcher. Faced with the evidence of a working-class perspective which values priorities in parenting, such as the child's present happiness, which differ from the dominant (and officially sanctioned) middle-class orientation to future success, she noted the challenge of theorising outside the normative framework according to which the 'game' (2004: 194) is played and 'won'.

[A]ll too often the flip side to this reification of middle-class practices as normative has been the relegation of working-class mothering to the realms of normative deficit and pathology. I have struggled with the problematic of how to theorize beyond middle-class norms as an academic researcher;

of how to hold on to different ways of being and acting that are equally valid and appropriate for the context in which they are being enacted.

Reay's own response was to distinguish the specificities of how emotional capital is invested and to stress context in shaping what counts as emotional capital. Although Reay suggests Illouz is careful to avoid constructing a classed binary, we would argue that Illouz does not ultimately avoid doing so. She does not 'theorize beyond middle-class norms'. Rather, despite her profession of ambivalence, she writes within the terms of the 'field' she is analysing (a problem also identified by Thwaites in this volume).

In one of the few qualifications of her thesis, Illouz writes that she 'does not intend to suggest that the new definitions of intimacy exhaust the totality of working-class practices, or that pleasure and erotic creativity are absent from working-class lives'. Another is her agreement with the evaluation that 'the therapeutic is an impoverished moral language'. Nevertheless, her position, in a second departure from Bourdieu's framework, is that the therapeutic is not arbitrarily accorded value but has been 'a successful response to the current disarray of private life and selfhood' (1997b: 60–61), that the discourse is 'efficacious' (2007: 67). An important premise of Illouz's pragmatic analysis is that 'my critique of the social uses of therapy does not contradict actors' own understandings and uses of therapy as a cultural resource to improve their lives' (2008: 223).

We would argue that Illouz is writing not only about but also, to some degree, from within the terms of therapeutic discourse. The assumption of its efficacy reifies distinctions in competence so that (although their incompetence is explained by the lack of other forms of capital required to gain emotional capital) working-class men are described and positioned as if 'actually' incompetent.

> [T]he dominant definition of intimacy demands an androgynous emotional and verbal competence that has made 'obsolete' whatever erotic, amorous or marital skills working-class men may have hitherto had at their disposal. (1997b: 59)

Illouz simplifies both the relation with middle-class models of intimacy and relations between working-class men and women to isolate working-class men.

If there is a gap in romantic competence, it is between working-class men and women, a gap that was opened by the middle- and upper-middle class models of communication and intimacy that have been disseminated through popular culture and that are consistent with women's socialization at large. (1997a: 278)

Thus, Illouz has, as she argues psychology does, brought both communication-based practices *and* any alternative practices of intimacy within the remit of a Bourdieusian analysis of class inequality, the one as plenitude (capital) and the other as lack.

Attending to Other Forms of Intimacy

Skeggs (2004) deplores the construction of the working-class 'as absolute and complete lack' within a Bourdieusian 'zero sum game'. She argues that there is a need to 'pay attention to the different value systems' and 'to understand working-class relations to the dominant symbolic' (88) if researchers are to engage with positions and perspectives outside the terms set by the hierarchies of the dominant symbolic. In the matter relevant here, of seeing intimacy outside of the norms of therapeutic discourse, Brownlie (2014) endorses analytic attention to diversity of practice and understanding and, particularly, to 'doing' rather than only 'talking'. This aligns with Jamieson's (1998) position that emotional closeness happens through, and may be constituted by, doing for and being there, through shared experience and history, through privileged knowledge and by loving, caring and sharing. Intimacy may take the form of a 'being alongside' which gives one a sense of security or permission not to talk about a problem (Brownlie 2014: 147).

Several women in McQueen's study, although they did desire greater emotional openness from men partners, also referred to moments of men's 'doing for' and caring. They expressed appreciation of these alternative forms of intimacy, forms which Illouz's mode of analysis does not seem to register, as expressions of love. One example from June (working class, mid 50s, beauty professional) highlights this:

I think it's awfully nice when you're told that 'I love you' and things like that, but I think it's also nice when things are noticed and done, because somebody has just thought about you, I think is quite nice. I've had a really sore shoulder and [...] the past two nights without me even knowing, when I've been going to get ready for bed, Ali has gone and turned the bed down and arranged my pillows and made the hot water bottle and had it lying there, so the bed was just ready for me to go in and lie on and that kind of thing means a lot, that he's thought about it.

Thus, as Brownlie observes, it is not only through talk that we communicate or are understood.

It is likely, however, not only that relationships are a mix of these different types of intimacy – disclosing and practical – but that it is through interactions, and acts of caring over time, that the knowing and understanding is constituted in the first place. In other words, the practical acts of caring are, in themselves, disclosing. (2014: 138)

Thus, attention to alternative forms of intimacy in McQueen's research suggest a more optimistic reading than Illouz's account of working-class romantic relationships. Recognising that men and women understand a wide range of actions and practices (including not talking) to bear meaning and incite interpretation allows for an analysis of both communication and intimacy in the context of couple relationships which is more inclusive of the range of and variation in working-class men's practices of intimacy.

Conclusion

This chapter engages with Illouz's writing relevant to the study of emotion and intimacy in established romantic relationships in two ways. The first is the use of empirical material to qualify claims of the pervasive adoption of the therapeutic ethos on which the further claims about changes in gender and class relations, in respect of emotion and intimacy, rely. Research in the UK shows resistance as well as acceptance of therapeutic discourse among men and women and across class categories (Brownlie 2014) and that even where there is acceptance of aspects of the discourse, the progression to practice can't be assumed. Most men in McQueen's sample testified to a belief in benefits of communication for emotional well-being and sustaining intimacy in relationships. For many men in this sample, again across class categories, gendered habitus incorporating deeply ingrained conceptions of masculinity was a source of resistance to the injunction to disclosure. Gendered roles persist as women accept responsibility to facilitate communication around emotions, emphasising the relational nature of intimacy. Our finding that gender is more significant than class in shaping practices of intimacy and the emotions around them challenges Illouz's contention that there has been significant gender convergence of middle-class men with middle-class women and class divergence among men.

This challenge to Illouz's claims prompted a closer consideration of the analysis which produced them, in particular the concept of emotional androgyny and Illouz's adaptation of a Bourdieusian framework. Illouz's account of emotional androgyny and 'new masculinity' rely on a crude demarcation between masculine and feminine and, based in her reversal of Bourdieu so that the workplace habitus socialises people for advantage at home, an over-statement of the correspondence between middle-class work and home. This narrow focus ignores the gendered relational and discursive contexts in which characteristics and actions are interpreted and the persistence in gender inequalities which continue to impede convergence on equality. Reversing the direction of socialisation also shapes her account of class divergence among men. It is combined with a too narrow characterisation of working-class men's employment and too broad a characterisation of working-class men as cut off from intimacy by their lack of therapeutically defined emotional competence. Furthermore, the oppositional logic of Bourdieu's concept of the field is combined with Illouz's acceptance of the actual efficacy (as well as symbolic dominance) of the therapeutic model of communication. We would argue that her pessimistic portrayal of intimacy in working-class men's relationships in general is a product of writing from within the terms of the therapeutic. Within those terms, she 'sees' intimacy only as communication and only in terms of the emotional competence through which the advantages of intimacy, 'a good like other goods', might be gained. Attention to other forms of intimacy might open up a different perspective from which the diversity among working-class relationships and the range of men's experience of intimacy in relationships might be seen in a clearer, perhaps brighter, light.

Note

1. Illouz subsequently addressed issues of emotional inequality between men and women in *Why Love Hurts* (2017). The book extends her work on the implications of changes in romantic and sexual partner selection. As such, her focus there is not on the established couple relationships which are the subject of McQueen's research and of Illouz's exposition of the concepts of gender convergence and androgyny in middle-class couples. Illouz does not engage with those concepts in *Why Love Hurts*. However, her attention to gender asymmetries around choice and desire which inhibit communication, in respect of both long-term commitment and having children, suggests that the differently constructed relations of men and women to 'the reproductive arena' (Connell 2002), for example, pose unrecognised problems for the concepts of gender convergence and androgynisation in her earlier work.

References

Adkins, L. (2004) Reflexivity: Freedom or habit of gender? *The Sociological Review*, 52 (2): 191–210.

Adkins, L. and Skeggs, B. (eds.) (2004) *Feminism after Bourdieu*. Oxford: Blackwell.

Benjamin, O. (1998) Therapeutic Discourse, Power and Change: Emotion and Negotiation in Marital Conversation. *Sociology* 32 (4): 771–793.

Bourdieu, P. (1990) *In other words: Essays towards a reflexive sociology*. California: Stanford University Press.

Brownlie, J. (2014) *Ordinary Relationships. A Sociological Study of Emotions, Reflexivity and Culture*. Basingstoke: Palgrave Macmillan.

Burkitt, I. (1997) Social relationships and emotions. *Sociology* 31 (1): 37–55.

Connell, R. W. (2002) *Gender.* Cambridge: Polity Press.

Doucet, A. (2006) *Do Men Mother? Fathering, Care and Parental Responsibilities.* Toronto: University of Toronto Press.

Duncombe, J. and Marsden, D. (1993) Love and Intimacy: The Gender Division of Emotion and 'Emotion Work': A Neglected Aspect of Sociological Discussion of Heterosexual Relationships. *Sociology,* 27 (2):221–41.

Furedi, F. (2004) *Therapy culture: Cultivating vulnerability in an uncertain age.* London: Routledge.

Hochschild, A. (2003) *Commercialization of Intimate Life.* Berkeley: University of California Press.

Hochschild, A. (1983) *The Managed Heart: Commercialization of Human Feeling.* Los Angeles: University of California Press.

Illouz, E. (2017) *Why Love Hurts.* Cambridge: Polity Press.

Illouz, E. (2008) *Saving the modern soul: Therapy, emotions, and the culture of self-help.* Berkeley: University of California Press.

Illouz, E. (2007) *Cold Intimacies: The Making of Emotional Capitalism.* Cambridge: Polity Press.

Illouz, E. (1997a) *Consuming the romantic utopia: Love and the cultural contradictions of capitalism.* Berkeley: University of California Press.

Illouz, E. (1997b) Who will care for the caretaker's daughter? Toward a sociology of happiness in the era of reflexive modernity. *Theory, Culture & Society,* 14 (4): 31–66.

Jamieson, L. (1998) *Intimacy: Personal Relationships in Modern Societies.* Cambridge: Polity Press.

Komter, A. (1989) Hidden Power in Marriage. *Gender and Society,* 3 (2): 187–216.

Mansfield, P. and Collard, J. (1988) *The Beginning of the Rest of Your Life: A Portrait of Newly-Wed Marriage.* London: Macmillan.

McQueen, F. (2017) Male emotionality: 'boys don't cry' versus 'it's good to talk'. *NORMA,* 12 (3–4): 205–219.

Reay, D. (2004) Gendering Bourdieu's concepts of capitals? Emotional capital, women and social class. *The Sociological Review,* 52 (2): 57–74.

Segal, L. (1990) *Slow Motion: Changing Men, Changing Masculinities,* London: Virago Press.

Skeggs, B. (2004) Exchange, value and affect: Bourdieu and 'the self'. *The Sociological Review,* 52 (2): 75–95.

6

Swipe Right? Tinder, Commitment and the Commercialisation of Intimate Life

Jenny van Hooff

Introduction

Within a few years of Tinder's inception in 2012, the popular app was held responsible for the 'dating apocalypse' in a viral article by Nancy Jo Sales for *Vanity Fair* (2015). The piece deployed a familiar trope by arguing that the easy access to sexual 'hook-ups' the app facilitates has created a generation of commitment-phobic men. Various sociologists have supported this interpretation, including most notably Eva Illouz (2007, 2012) who maintains that the choice and individual self-fulfilment that consumer society is predicated on undermines commitment and encourages the seeking out of alternative partners, usually via the internet. In this chapter, I draw on qualitative in-depth interviews with heterosexual male Tinder users to explore these claims.

J. van Hooff (✉)
Manchester Metropolitan University, Manchester, UK
e-mail: J.van-Hooff@mmu.ac.uk

J. Carter, L. Arocha (eds.), *Romantic Relationships in a Time of 'Cold Intimacies'*,
Palgrave Macmillan Studies in Family and Intimate Life,
https://doi.org/10.1007/978-3-030-29256-0_6

Commitment and Individualisation

The emergence of Tinder and subsequent apps onto the dating scene has been accompanied by a record low in marriage rates between opposite-sex couples in England and Wales (Office for National Statistics 2018), prompting a media panic over the end of commitment. While commitment has become an established public and political concern, Smart (2007) notes that it has also emerged as a key theme in the sociological debate over the impact of individualisation on intimate relationships. In the context of Giddens' (1992) notion of the 'pure relationship', commitment is negotiated and contingent and comes without the guarantees of traditional ties such as marriage. Instead, 'it is a feature of the pure relationship that it can be terminated, more or less at will, by either partner at any particular point' (Giddens 1992: 137). Similarly, Beck and Beck-Gernsheim propose that young people reject traditional notions of family and marriage, instead seeking 'emotional commitment' (1995: 16), while Weeks (1995) notes that commitments within contemporary relationships are negotiated rather than obligatory.

Other theorists lament the impact of late-modern social processes upon personal life. For Lasch, writing in the late 1970s, individualisation and excessive consumerism were leading 'personal relations [to] crumble under the emotional weight with which they are burdened' (Lasch 1979: 188). Similarly, Bauman railed against the personal consequences of the individualisation process, arguing that the uncertainty which pervades consumer society works to divide individuals and undermines the 'common interest' (Bauman 2000: 148). For Bauman, the plurality of choice on offer compounds this condition of uncertainty, as 'if you may never err, you can never be sure of being in the right either. If there are no wrong moves, there is nothing to distinguish a move from a better one' (Bauman 2000: 63). The advent of a free-floating capitalism is replicated in the trend from marriage to cohabitation, which for Bauman includes the assumption that the relationship may be broken at any minute, for any reason, once the desire or need has dried up.

From this perspective human bonds and partnerships are treated as things to be consumed rather than worked on and produced, and as such are subjected to the same criteria of evaluation as consumer goods (Bauman 2000: 163). The commercialisation of intimacy is detailed by Illouz in *Why Love Hurts* (2012). She explains that the hallmarks of consumer culture, freedom of choice and individualisation have been extended to personal life, with partner choice subject to consumer logic. Early romantic attachment is often intense within this context; however, long-term commitment is undermined by the availability of an alternative, potentially more suitable partner once the initial desire has worn off. In the past few decades, traditional patterns of commitment have been disrupted with a marked decline in marriage and remarriage and a rise in divorce, singlehood and casual relationships. Conversely, men, who benefit the most from marriage, have developed a commitment phobia driven by what Illouz terms a new 'architecture of choice' (ibid: 91), which inhibits decision-making and commitment. This comes as a result of the real and imagined increase in sexual partners, facilitated by the internet, and online dating specifically, as traditional marriage markets are replaced by contemporary 'sexual fields' (Illouz 2012: 53), where sexual attractiveness has emerged as the most important criteria in mate selection. Multiple options dampen men's ability to develop strong feelings for a specific woman, with the possibility of choice fundamentally altering their ability to commit. Illouz maintains that choice is the defining hallmark of modernity, in that it embodies freedom, rationality and autonomy (ibid: 19), and is located in the present, where commitment is necessarily oriented towards the future.

Empirical evidence has not straightforwardly supported claims of a shift from committed to casual relationships. Jamieson (1998) cautions against interpreting declining rates of marriage and the trend towards cohabitation as evidence of a rejection of traditional forms of commitment. Cohabiting relationships are not homogenous and can be understood on a continuum (Smart and Stevens 2000), with a level of permanence expected at one end of the scale, akin to marriage. Lewis (2001) also takes a nuanced view of commitment, defining it as 'behaving in ways that support the maintenance and continuation of a relationship' (2001: 124). Age and generation may influence what commitment means to couples, with research into generational differences (Sutton et al. 2003) suggesting that commitment for older couples was based on traditionally gendered roles, involving elements of care and responsibility to one's spouse, while younger couples report commitment as a personal expression exempt from societal pressures.

If we are to understand commitment as a scale or continuum then we should also examine how relationships progress along it. Much of the discussion on commitment presumes that couples are matched in their desire for commitment as relationships have come to be based on 'emotional give and take' (Giddens 1991: 62) and an end to traditionally gendered roles which are renegotiated to give each partner an equal say. From the perspective that contemporary relationships are based on the principles of democracy and personal freedom commitment would be something that is mutually agreed upon, with both partners satisfied with the progression of their relationship. However, research indicates that young women lack power in heterosexual dating relationships (Chung 2005; van Hooff 2013) which continue to be characterised by gender inequality.

Research has found that couples may move between greater and lesser ties in their relationships (Smart and Stevens 2000; Barlow et al. 2005), or may have a linear vision of how their relationships will develop, with each 'step' seen as further progression to a more secure and committed relationship (van Hooff 2013). Carter (2012) distinguishes between 'pull factors' and 'push factors' in the process of developing commitment. Pull factors draw a couple together and are characterised by love, fidelity and monogamy. These usually precede push factors, which include internal and external investments and expectations and are motivated by not wanting the relationship to end. Within this model certain stages of a relationship will be reached before it can progress. Previous research on couples (van Hooff 2013) suggests that relationships begin casually, with early sexual contact and few expectations of future commitment. However once individuals had been 'seeing' each other for a certain amount of time it was generally expected that they would move to consolidate their partnerships, characteristic of the drift into committed relationships noted in Carter's (2013) research. Thus the argument that there has been a rejection of commitment and long-term relationships has generally not been borne out in sociological research, with couple relationships standing firm at the centre of intimate life (Gabb and Fink 2015; van Hooff 2017). This is supported by US-based research (Rosenfeld 2018), which also suggests that the majority of single people are not actively dating or engaging in casual sex, further challenging the representativeness of the popular 'hook-up' culture trope.

Research into commitment has generally explored the stability and longevity of long-term relationships, hence the focus on cohabitation and marriage. Media panic around Tinder has presumed a shift to disposable and temporal relationship forms, with commitment increasingly short-term. However, the early stages of relationships and more casual encounters are underrepresented in sociological research. Most notably, recent work by Wade (2017) on the 'hook-up' culture of US college students suggests that while young people are not necessarily engaging in increasing amounts of casual sex, they are reluctant to demonstrate emotional attachment, with emotional vulnerability deemed shameful. This research seeks to contribute to sociological understanding of early relationship formation and casual encounters, particularly those mediated through the internet.

Tinder

Face-to-face interaction and co-presence are often privileged in sociological discussions of personal life, particularly from the perspectives of symbolic interactionism and phenomenology; yet the internet has facilitated the development of new ways for people to form intimate relationships (Jamieson 2013). The shift from online dating to mobile apps has further accelerated this development, with location-enabled hand-held devices allowing immediate connections based on geographical proximity. While the market has become saturated with a variety of dating apps, Tinder remains the most popular with an estimated 1.6 billion daily swipes (Tinder 2018).

Early sociological research into online dating focused on the new possibilities afforded by the internet to find a 'date', whether casual or long-term (Jagger 2001), with traditional geographical constraints no longer applying (Poster 1995; Valentine 2006). The emancipatory potential of the internet was also cautiously welcomed, with arguments that online communication offers increased safety, control and freedom (Doring

2000; Miller 2011; Boyd 2007). The autonomy fostered by the internet was understood as a challenge to traditional hierarchies, including patriarchal relationships (Castells 2007). Recent research (Hobbs et al. 2016) found little evidence to support claims that Tinder users were rejecting romantic love, monogamy and commitment. While some were using the platform to engage in casual sexual encounters, the majority used the technology to pursue meaningful partnerships and welcomed the agency that it provided. Moreover, in a study of over 2000 young adults, Timmermans and Courtois (2018) found that the majority of dating app users they surveyed did not meet other users face-to-face. For those who did, a third of these offline encounters led to casual sex, while over a quarter led to the formation of a committed relationship. A detailed analysis of US survey data considered the impact of dating apps such as Tinder on relationship stability (Rosenfeld 2018). Findings confirm that most heterosexual adults are traditionally married, and interestingly that rather than engaging in a series of 'hook-ups', single heterosexuals do very little dating, with less than 20 per cent of those surveyed having a date or sexual encounter within the previous twelve months. These results challenge the argument that the emergence of dating apps has undermined commitment and suggest instead that singlehood is becoming a more widespread and stable identity.

Consumer culture has provided individuals with important cultural resources for creating personal identities and marketing themselves online. Daters can construct an idealised image, which may bear little or no resemblance to offline reality, thereby fuelling the romantic fantasies and projections of their online lovers (Albright 2007), leading to issues of trust and deception. Online dating profiles are created to represent an ideal-self, yet in the face of imminent offline interaction 'individuals had to balance their desire for self-promotion with their need for accurate self-presentation' (Ellison et al. 2006: 430). Dating apps such as Tinder present a new technological environment for impression management (Ward 2017), with users highly motivated to control the impression they create or 'give off' (Goffman 1957). Hogan (2010) argues that Tinder users are crucially different to Goffman's subjects as the context of face-to-face interaction is always reciprocal. Instead the Tinder user is a curator who filters their self-image before it is presented.

The commodification of intimacy fostered by online dating has been a focus of sociological research, with claims that dating profiles create a reflexively organised story about the user, which reflects not only how they see themselves in the present, but their life choices and who they have the potential to become. Daters have to consider how to represent themselves when assembling online identities, marketing themselves to potential partners. Research indicates that men enjoy a plurality of masculinities to select from, based on varying combinations of occupational and economic resources, lifestyle interests and bodily attributes when assembling personal identities, while women remain limited to physical ideals (Jagger 2001). For Illouz (2012), the individualisation of the criteria of choice of a mate has accompanied an increasing value placed on physical attractiveness, for both women and men. Under consumer culture the body becomes intensely eroticised and emphasised femininity and the sexual model of masculinity are rewarded on the dating market. Adherence to conventional standards of physical attractiveness then become an important currency for male and female dating app users.

Methods

The overarching aim of this research was to explore the ways in which heterosexual men use and experience dating apps. In-depth face-to-face or telephone/skype interviews were conducted with fifteen men actively using Tinder and other dating apps, between 2015 and 2017. The focus on men was motivated by the general paucity of research on men and intimacy, as Gabb and Fink (2015) note in their work on long-term relationships, with the topic area a suitable 'gap' (Alvesson and Sandberg 2013: 5) in existing research. Discussions of online dating have also focussed on heterosexual men, and their use of dating apps to access casual sex rather than committed relationships, with little empirical evidence to support these assumptions. A flier, including a brief description of research, the required demographic characteristics of participants, and my contact details, was circulated via social media and email. However, male participants proved particularly difficult to attract for interview, and the majority of the sample was recruited via snowball sampling, which meant that some participants were not unfamiliar to me, or each other. Ethical approval was granted for the study from Manchester Metropolitan University in 2015, and in order to disguise characteristics, transcripts were modified where specific individuals, places or events were made reference to.

Each in-depth interview lasted between forty-five to ninety minutes, and was recorded, transcribed, coded and analysed using thematic analysis in order to identify common themes. Interviews took place in a location selected by the participant, which was usually either my office, a café or bar, or in one case the participant's workplace, with four of the interviews taking place over skype, and two by phone. Follow up email or phone correspondence took place in the instance of five of the interviews in order to clarify points. All participants had been using dating apps for a minimum of two months, and all were employed, with the men aged between twenty-six and forty-seven years old, and predominantly white British, with one British-Pakistani and two Black British participants.

Despite the initial issues in recruiting participants, the interviews yielded a huge amount of data. Concerns that men would temper their answers to a female interviewer appeared unfounded, as most participants spoke openly about their encounters, although some were generally more taciturn in their responses.

Consuming and Being Consumed

Much of the attention and criticism directed towards Tinder centres on the user interface of the app, which encourages daters to scan through pictures of potential matches, with minimal space given to accompanying text profiles. Online dating is the leading example of the 'technologies of choice' discussed by Illouz (2007, 2012), which have fused consumer logic onto intimate relationships, as selecting a mate becomes akin to online shopping. For the men interviewed, the matches were initially selected based on appearance, which indicated attractiveness and the 'type' of person a match might be:

> She has to be 'my type' or it's not going to work, and I can tell that within the first thirty seconds. (George, 45)

As reported in other research (Ellison et al. 2006), participants evaluated matches in terms of suitability for a relationship, or casual sex, based on small cues, or signals 'given off' (Goffman 1957) unintentionally. Participants evaluated matches based on these cues as quickly as possible, motivated by fear of 'wasting time' on an unsuitable date:

> First of all you're looking at how fit she is, whether it's on Tinder, real life, wherever. That's the most important thing. Then location. You work out compatibility from chatting online so you don't waste time meeting up. (Pete, 37)

As Pete explains, dates are quickly assessed, initially on a combination of physical attraction and geographical proximity, followed by messaging. While there is some resonance with Illouz's (2012) 'sexual fields', in which sexual attraction has become the primary criteria for mate selection, participants evaluated attractiveness alongside other factors, including personality. What participants regarded as excessive displays of female sexuality were usually rejected, as women were expected to perform a normatively gendered role (Evans 2003) or risk being dismissed. Irfan describes how he navigates this through visual cues given off by women, which enables him to swipe through a greater number of profiles:

> Potential partners are anyone that doesn't have ridiculous selfie pictures or anyone not pouting in all of their pictures. No one that has ridiculous cleavage on show either. Also no hideous girls. I don't personally read the profiles because there's just not enough time in the day. (Irfan, 28)

The 'hyperpersonal' intimacy argued by Walther (1996) as characteristic of online relationships is apparent here, as the speed and depth of ties is accelerated and encourages users to present themselves in a certain way to potential dates. Time was key to all of the participants discussions of their use of Tinder, with all anxious to be as efficient as possible in their dating. Enough time is spent messaging or texting to ensure that the physical date will not be a 'waste' of time, while participants are also keen not to let this phase drag without arranging to meet. As well as being very aware of what they were looking for in a partner, which was usually based on a combination of conventional attractiveness and personality 'type', participants also invested effort in presenting particular versions of themselves. In this sense, the early stage of online dating is performance insofar as it involves presenting a gendered version of oneself that the user assumes his or her potential partner wants to see:

> Well obviously you create a brand, and my brand is not being like other men. In my first few dates I'm totally presenting a brand, I am what they want me to be, so I present myself as an intelligent, sensitive man who offers them something better. My tagline actually says that I'm not like other men. (George, 45)

The availability of various 'types' of masculinity for men to draw on when presenting themselves online was highlighted by Jagger (2001), and it appears that this has parallels here. For George, success on the app involves presenting a particular version of masculinity at odds with that identified with Tinder, and this becomes what distinguishes him from the competition. Yet, as Illouz notes, while daters may distinguish themselves in terms of their personality, or humour, in order to ensure success they must conform to physical norms, as online dating encourages standardisation. In the process of self-presentation, physical appearance takes on a new, almost poignant importance in the process of the profile picture, as daters use the accepted conventions of the desirable person and apply them to themselves (Illouz 2007: 82). Participants generally drew on hegemonic versions of masculinity, as Chris notes, 'successful, sporty, sociable':

> 'I've worked out that you've got to present yourself in certain ways, through your photos, so that's what I've done really. I want to say that I'm successful, sporty, sociable and want someone similar.' *Shows me his profile. There are photos of him alone, with groups of friends, skiing, playing football, travelling.* (Chris, 35)

All participants were aware that they presenting a particular version of themselves, to be consumed by others, with most conscious that they had to distinguish themselves from the 'competition'. This was filtered through preconceived notions of what a dateable man might be, with profiles conforming to normative versions of masculinity, usually based on resource capacity and physical attractiveness. These findings align with early research on online dating which noted that body ideals have become important for men to be successful (Jagger 2001), as the body becomes the visible carrier of the self in consumer culture (Featherstone 1991). The men interviewed were also aware that economic success was crucial to attract women, with one participant noting that during a period of redundancy he temporarily left Tinder:

> It was actually the one time I had time to use it [Tinder], but there was no point, the first thing girls ask is what you do, it would just have been awkward. (Rob, 34)

The self-presentation of the men interviewed and the presentation of potential matches became a theme of the research findings, with participants openly discussing their personal 'brand' or online attractiveness. This was usually presented and performed in normatively gendered ways, as participants quickly learn that success on Tinder involves transformation of the self into a packaged product, to compete on the dating app market. However, claims that dating apps such as Tinder have directed a shift to commodified intimacy neglect the relationship between gender, romance and performance, as explored by Evans, who explains that, 'part of our contemporary performance of gender is the performance of the lover or the loved, in appropriately gendered ways' (Evans 2003: 13). In this research, Tinder is seen to reinforce these heteronormative performances of gender, rather than represent a radical shift in heterosexual dating practices.

Hooking Up or Looking for More?

Popular understandings of Tinder suggest that it enables casual sex and disincentivises users from committing to longer term, monogamous relationships. Yet, when asked why they used Tinder, participants all described their engagement as a means to meeting a partner, for both casual and more serious relationships. The attraction of the app was its efficiency and the large pool of potential dates it afforded access to, as Irfan explained:

> Where else would I meet someone? In a bar? I'm not going to meet anyone at work. I'm on Match as well, but it just takes forever and leads to nothing. Tinder works 'cause it's fast. (Irfan, 28)

Meeting a long-term partner is presented as an ideal, although users often engaged with the app on a superficial level:

> To be honest, I use it when I'm on the toilet [laughs], I let my mates pick matches, I rarely swipe left. But when you start chatting to someone nice, you get invested. (Daniel, 30)

Tinder's gamified user interface promotes a casual initial engagement with potential matches, with participants reserving emotional commitment until a match has progressed. Some participants were keen to reject the image of Tinder as a 'hook-up' app, as George explained:

> I think there's an urban myth about people wanting casual sex on Tinder, that hasn't been my experience at all, everyone I've met has been on it looking for a long-term relationship. (George, 45)

The efficiency and availability afforded by Tinder was also cited by users as a motivation for using the app. Most participants had experienced committed relationships with women they had matched on the app, although the majority of offline encounters either resulted in casual sex or not led to anything beyond the initial meeting. Success is usually defined as a long-term relationship, with all participants professing this as their eventual goal, although all committed relationships initiated through the app started casually and typically became sexual within one to three dates. This experience is similar to research findings on the ways that heterosexual couples began their relationships in the pre-dating app 2000s (van Hooff 2013). Relationships began as casual encounters, with few expectations of commitment, only continuing if the participants wanted to see each other again. There is very little difference in the approach to sex and commitment for the men interviewed here, with the exception that Tinder affords a greater degree of choice and efficiency.

It has been noted elsewhere that relationships that begin online rarely stay there (Valentine 2006), and this was accurate for the men here, who were keen to meet up as quickly as possible, with matches based on propinquity. Early theorising on the impact of computer-mediated communication on relationships argued that as geographical distance has no bearing on the cost it plays a less important role for relationships fostered online (Poster 1995); however, for users of dating apps, distance is a deciding factor in selecting a match, as spatial proximity enables physical engagement with other users. The shift towards a 'cooler' intimacy (Illouz 2007; Hochschild 1994) is apparent here as participants make rational decisions about potential dates based on the criteria detailed in the previous section and practical considerations, such as proximity, rather than being motivated by passion.

While most of the women the participants matched with did not meet their ideal of a long-term partner, they were happy to engage in casual sex or relationships, the 'hook-ups' Tinder has become notorious for. Participants also made a distinction between women they wanted to match with for sex or for potential relationships, based on their profile. Usually the casual relationships were carried out with the consent or knowledge of both parties; however, the men interviewed described negotiating these interactions carefully. The dominant heteronormative script remains in place in participants' interactions and expectations, although they are loosened for more casual sexual encounters. For Alex, who reported using Tinder for the past three years for at least an hour a day, encounters were generally positive, and although they had not led to long-term relationships, Tinder had broadened his social network:

> A long period on Tinder would be six plus dates, usually it doesn't go anywhere. Usually relationships are sexual. I'd always chat to multiple people at once and occasionally see multiple partners at once. Most encounters have been enjoyable and interesting, some I'm still friends with, one is now our company solicitor, but most I don't speak to. (Alex, 29)

Normative gendered discourses of commitment also emerge in participants' discussions of dating, with assumptions that the women they see are always hoping for more committed relationships than they are. Farvid and Braun (2006), in their analysis of popular women's magazines, found that women were constructed as being in constant pursuit of long-term committed relationships with men. Pete describes women who 'read more into it', assuming that sexual encounters will translate into emotional commitment:

> If a guy isn't texting or calling you all the time if he hasn't made an explicit commitment, if he's not displaying a keen interest and the girl is choosing to sleep with him and read more into it then it's up to her. But it'll be over in less than a month. (Pete, 37)

Many of the participants discussed managing the expectations of the women they match, navigating between casual and committed partnerships, as Rob explained:

> But women who are too keen are off putting, like clinginess. Most are, like they tell you they love you right away, text you twenty times a day, and you have to handle that. (Rob, 34)

This is despite some participants alluding to emotional hurt after the ending of a relationship. While he displays gendered understandings of emotionality, Rob also briefly describes the pain of being 'ghosted' (the termination of all communication without warning) by a woman he was seeing:

> I had a five month relationship with someone I met on Tinder, I really liked her but I don't know what happened, I think she didn't fancy me or met someone else, so you just get back on it. (Rob, 34)

Patriarchal scripts define women as emotional and vulnerable, often leaving them humiliated, dismissed and ignored (Illouz 2012: 70), with little space for emotional attachment in contemporary displays of masculinity. Ghosting is usually seen as an example of callous male behaviour, meaning that participants are ill equipped to cope with it when it happens to them. Discussions of Tinder have focussed on the power heterosexual men have in sexual fields, to choose and casually date women, yet in the process the agency of those women involved has been overlooked, as has the emotional attachment of men. Thus, the use of dating apps can be seen as reinforcing and recreating conventional hierarchies of masculinity and femininity, rather than providing new freedoms.

Many participants described the user experience of Tinder as 'addictive', which made it difficult to abandon in favour of a more committed, sexually exclusive relationship. Thus the reality of dating for the majority of the men interviewed was a series of medium-term relationships interspersed with more casual encounters. As Illouz (2007) notes, technology encourages an increased refinement of tastes, as users aim for a match who is 'out of their league', and the participants here displayed particularly high standards about the attributes of a potential long-term partner. While several of the men interviewed had been using the app for a number of years without meeting any women that conformed to their ideal, they refused to compromise, as the internet unleashes a fantasy yet inhibits actual romantic feelings (Illouz 2007: 104). Tinder also introduces an element of efficiency into dating, with participants unwilling to 'waste time' on the wrong match, when a sea of other potential women are apparently available, a swipe away. For this reason, most participants often dated multiple women casually, with sexual exclusivity negotiated at a later stage. However, the casual start to relationships, characterised by 'hooking-up' did not preclude them from becoming more serious at a later stage, rather it appears that commitment is not assumed and has to be more formally established in relationships formed on Tinder, unlike the 'drift' into committed offline relationships (Carter 2013). Moreover, characterising Tinder as the end of commitment fails to take into account the fragile nature of the early romantic attachment of relationships formed on the app, which are likely to have a high failure rate. Those who 'successfully' navigate the app to form long-term relationships are no longer visible.

Conclusion

Enthusiasm by sociologists and cultural commentators to announce social change does not always reflect the messier, more nuanced reality. The research presented here provides limited support for the shift to a technology-enabled commercialisation of intimate life. For the participants interviewed, Tinder and other dating apps enabled access to a larger pool of potential women, in a shorter space of time than offline dating. These initial motivations align with Hochschild's posited emotional cooling (1994) or Illouz's cold intimacy (2007), with efficiency and choice ruling over passion. The intensely competitive, technology-enabled 'sexual fields' (Illouz 2012) are partially represented by participants' experiences. Although the men interviewed were strategic in the way they presented themselves and selected potential matches according to consumer logic, beyond the initial meeting, relationships were allowed to develop or fade out. While this may lead to some acceleration in relationships which sometimes begin and end more quickly than equivalent offline encounters, underlying normative gender roles and ideals about long-term relationships remain in place. The evidence that men are emotionally detached (Illouz 2012: 243) in such encounters was also limited as participants performed normatively gendered displays of emotion, but also expressed attachment and desire for commitment.

The focus on Tinder illuminates the unpredictability and high failure rate of early romantic attachment, which may not previously have been as visible, rather than a significant shift away from committed relationships as argued by Illouz (2007, 2012). It should also be noted that men are not a clear and cohesive group (Holmes 2015), and heterosexual men's use of dating apps are complex and multidimensional, with participants often ambivalent about their own use and motivations. Participants who claimed to be looking for a long-term relationship would also engage in casual sexual encounters, frequently moving between both types of relationships. Therefore, the distinction between 'hook-ups' and long-term commitment did not reflect the everyday lived reality of the men who have not rejected committed relationships, but expect all encounters to begin casually. This is not evidence of the casualisation of relationships, and instead aligns with earlier research into offline relationship formation, where commitment followed on from casual sexual encounters for most couples (van Hooff 2013). While evidence to support the commercialisation of intimate life was limited, findings suggest that the use of dating apps may reinforce conventionally gendered hierarchies, as participants' interactions and experiences continue to be framed by heteronormative scripts.

References

Albright, J. M. (2007) How do I Love Thee and Thee and Thee: Self-presentation, Deception, and Multiple Relationships Online. In M. Whitty, A. Baker and J. Inman, (eds.) *Online Matchmaking*. London: Palgrave Macmillan: 81–93.

Alvesson, M. and Sandberg, J. (2013) *Constructing Research Questions*. London: Sage.

Barlow, A., Duncan, S., James, G. and Park, A. (2005) *Cohabitation, Marriage and the Law: Social Change and Legal Reform in the 21st Century*. Oxford: Hart Publishing.

Bauman, Z. (2000) *Liquid Modernity*. Cambridge: Polity Press.

Beck, U. and Beck-Gernsheim, E. (1995) *The Normal Chaos of Love*. Cambridge: Polity Press.

Boyd, D. (2007) Why Youth (Heart) Social Network Sites: The Role of Networked Publics in Teenage Social Life. In D. Buckingham (ed.) *Youth Identity and Digital Media*. Cambridge, MA: MIT Press: 119–142.

Carter, J. (2012) What is commitment? Women's accounts of intimate attachment. *Families, Relationships and Societies* 1 (2): 137–153.

Carter, J. (2013) The curious absence of love stories in women's talk. *Sociological Review* 61 (4): 728–744.

Castells, M. (2007) Communication, Power and Counter-Power in the Network Society. *International Journal of Communication* 1: 238–266.

Chung, D. (2005) Violence, Control, Romance and Gender Equality: Young Women and Heterosexual Relationships. *Women's Studies International Forum* 28 (6), 445–55.

Doring, N. (2000) Feminist Views of Cybersex: Victimization, Liberation, and Empowerment. *CyberPsychology and Behavior* 3: 863–884.

Ellison, N., Heino, R. and Gibbs, J. (2006) Managing Impressions Online: Self-Presentation Processes in the Online Dating Environment. *Journal of Computer-Mediated Communication* 11 (2): 415–441.

Evans, M. (2003) *Love: An Unromantic Discussion*. Cambridge: Polity Press.

Farvid, P. and Braun, V. (2006) 'Most of Us Guys Are Raring to Go Anytime, Anyplace, Anywhere': Male and Female Sexuality in Cleo and Cosmo. *Sex Roles* 55: 295–310.

Featherstone, M. (1991) *Consumer Culture and Postmodernism*. London: Sage.

Gabb, J. and Fink, J. (2015) *Couple relationships in the 21st century*. London: Palgrave Macmillan.

Giddens, A. (1991) *Modernity and Self-identity*. Cambridge: Polity Press.

Giddens, A. (1992) *The Transformation of Intimacy*. Cambridge: Polity Press.

Goffman, E. (1957) *The Presentation of Self in Everyday Life*. New York: Doubleday.

Hobbs, M., Owen, S. and Gerber, L. (2016) Liquid love? Dating apps, sex, relationships and the digital transformation of intimacy. *Journal of Sociology* 53 (2): 271–284.

Hochschild, A. (1994) The Commercial Spirit of Intimate Life and the Abduction of Feminism: Signs from Women's Advice Books. *Theory, Culture and Society* 11: 1–24.

Hogan, B. (2010) The presentation of self in the age of social media: Distinguishing performances and exhibitions online. *Bulletin of Science, Technology & Society* 30 (6): 377–386.

Holmes, M. (2015) Men's emotions: Heteromasculinity, emotional reflexivity, and intimate relationships. *Men and Masculinities*, 18 (2): 176–192.

Illouz, E. (2007) *Cold Intimacies: The Making of Emotional Capitalism*. Cambridge: Polity Press.

Illouz, E. (2012) *Why Love Hurts: A Sociological Explanation*. Cambridge: Polity Press.

Jagger, E. (2001) Marketing Molly and Melville: Dating in a Postmodern Consumer Society. *Sociology* 35: 39–57.

Jamieson, L. (2013) Personal Relationships, intimacy and the self in a mediated and global digital age. In K. Orton-Johnson, and N. Prior (eds.) *Digital Sociology: Critical Perspectives*. London: Palgrave Macmillan.

Jamieson, L. (1998) *Intimacy: Personal Relationships in Modern Societies*. Cambridge: Polity Press.

Lasch, C. (1979) *The Culture of Narcissism*. London: Abacus.

Lewis, J. (2001) *The End of Marriage? Individualism and Intimate Relations*. Cheltenham: Edward Elgar Publishing Ltd.

Miller, D. (2011) *Tales from Facebook*. Cambridge: Polity Press.

ONS (2018) *Marriages in England and Wales: 2015*, available at: https://www.ons.gov.uk/peoplepopulationandcommunity/birthsdeathsandmarriages/marriagecohabitationandcivilpartnerships/bulletins/marriagesinenglandandwalesprovisional/2015.

Poster, M. (1995) *The Second Media Age*. London: Polity.

Rosenfeld, M. J. (2018) Are Tinder and Dating Apps Changing Dating and Mating in the U.S.? In J. Van Hook, S. M. McHale and V. King (eds.) *Families and Technology*. New York: Springer: 103–117.

Sales, N. J. (2015) Tinder and the dawn of the 'Dating Apocalypse.' *Vanity Fair*, September. Available at: http://www.vanityfair.com/culture/2015/08/tinder-hook-up-culture-end-of-dating.

Smart, C. (2007) *Personal Life*. Cambridge: Polity Press.

Smart, C. and Stevens, P. (2000) *Cohabitation Breakdown*. London: Family Policy.

Sutton, L., Cebulla, A. and Middleton, S. (2003) *Marriage in the 21st Century*. Centre for Research in Social Policy CRSP. Working Paper 482.

Timmermans E. and Courtois, C. (2018) From swiping to casual sex and/or committed relationships: Exploring the experiences of Tinder users. *The Information Society* 34 (2): 59–70.

Tinder (2018) 'Tinder Presents the Year in Swipe', available at https://blog.gotinder.com/tinder-presents-the-year-in-swipe-r/ [].

Valentine, G. (2006) Globalizing Intimacy: The Role of Information and Communication Technologies. *Women's Studies Quarterly* 34 (1/2): 365–393.

van Hooff, J. (2017) An everyday affair: Deciphering the sociological significance of women's attitudes towards infidelity. *Sociological Review* 65 (4): 850–864.

van Hooff, J (2013) *Modern couples? Continuity and change in heterosexual relationships*. Basingstoke: Ashgate.

Wade, L. (2017) *American Hookup: The New Culture of Sex on Campus*. New York: WW Norton & Co.

Walther, J. B. (1996) Computer-mediated communication: Impersonal, interpersonal, and hyperpersonal interaction. *Communication Research* 23 (1): 3–44.

Ward, J. (2017) What are you doing on Tinder? Impression management on a matchmaking mobile app. *Information, Communication & Society* 20(11): 1644–1659.

Weeks, J. (1995) *Invented Moralities: Sexual Values in an Age of Uncertainty*. Cambridge: Polity Press.

7

Dating in the Age of Tinder: Swiping for Love?

Lauren Palmer

Introduction

In *Cold Intimacies*, Illouz (2007) explores how capitalism has created a society in which economic behaviour conflicts with intimate relationships. She states in a culture of 'emotional capitalism', emotions, relationships and intimate bonds have become commodified whilst economic relationships have become increasingly emotional. In an era of 'cold intimacies' (Illouz 2007) and 'liquid love' (Bauman 2003), fluidity and uncertainties have led to increased insecurity, vulnerability and anxiety around romantic relationships causing social bonds to become objects of consumption, becoming easily disposable as they lose their real meaning. In line with this argument, Bauman (2003) states that while love can suddenly strike, it becomes a rare achievement, instead individuals replace the art of loving with commodified imitation; taking the waiting out of the wanting. Intimate relationships increasingly become commodities to

L. Palmer (✉)
Canterbury Christ Church University, Canterbury, UK

© The Author(s) 2020
J. Carter, L. Arocha (eds.), *Romantic Relationships in a Time of 'Cold Intimacies'*,
Palgrave Macmillan Studies in Family and Intimate Life,
https://doi.org/10.1007/978-3-030-29256-0_7

be consumed, efficiently and in great volumes (Bauman 2003; Blum 2005; Illouz 2007; Keskin-Kozat 2004).

Illouz (2007) uses the concept 'emotional capitalism' to express a culture in which emotional and economic discourses define and shape each other, leading to intimacy and emotional life becoming shaped by economic relations. Illouz (2007) points to evidence of this process of emotional capitalism in a number of different areas including internet dating, self-help literature and talk shows. She argues internet dating makes romantic encounters into economic transactions, emptying relationships from emotion and representing a significant departure from the tradition of love (Illouz 2007). Illouz (2007) characterises traditional love through the concept of 'love at first sight' and excitement, arguing this type of love happens spontaneously and unexpectedly. However, due to the mass consumption of prospective partners internet dating creates, it demands a rationalised mode of partner selection which in turn contradicts this idea of traditional love (Illouz 2007). Therefore, internet dating is seen to fulfil a new standard of rational choice, which drives out all relationships, introducing mass consumption, endless choice, selectivity, rationality and standardisation to the realm of intimacy and romantic encounters. Due to the vast volume of interactions internet dating produces, dating becomes highly repetitive, enabling users to create standardised messages to send to all potential partners and use the same talking points both online and offline. Through this the user must maximise options and use techniques to be cost effective, taking the excitement and novelty out of the equation, which characterised traditional love (Bauman 2003; Illouz 2007).

Illouz (2007) explores how internet dating has become separated from traditional forms of love in a number of different ways. For example, internet dating creates a space in which the self can visualise the market for potential partners, unlike traditional love, in which the market remains hidden. Virtual relationships are also seen to defuse the pressure 'real relationships' create; online users can date knowing they can always return to the marketplace to find something better, there is no obligation to 'buy' (Bauman 2003; Illouz 2007). Bauman (2003) is critical of online dating as he suggests it supposedly leads individuals to favour temporary connections over life-long relationships. Dating becomes a recreational activity, in which people are seen as easily disposable, as easily as pressing delete, without any mess or regret (Bauman 2003; Hobbs et al. 2016). When insecure and anxious about relationships, individuals turn to technology to find relationships and protect themselves, thus expecting more from technology and less from each other. Therefore, the ties formed through the internet are not ties that bind, but ties that preoccupy and online relationships can be put 'on hold' if better ones come along (Turkle 2011). Heino et al. (2010) investigated the use of a 'market metaphor' in online dating, comparing internet dating to the economic market, a place where people can 'shop' for potential partners. The study found that the design of online dating sites encouraged participants to adopt the marketplace metaphor when online dating. This metaphor influenced their communication and behaviour online, for example comparing choosing partners to going through a catalogue to find what you want (Heino et al. 2010).

Horvat (2016) contributes to this discussion by questioning the universality of love in an era of cold intimacies (Illouz 2007) arguing the reinvention of love, may actually just be a reinvention of free sex. The true meaning of falling in love is taking the risk of falling whatever the consequences may be; however, this becomes problematic as we live in a society which is directed against any sort of risk. Free bodies become 'fuck bodies' where anything goes, and this liberal permissiveness is a false reinvention of love. Therefore, Horvat (2016) asks, is internet dating a real reinvention of love in this technological era? The problem with online dating apps was people were trying to create real conversations and real connections, but ended up creating conversations which were much more superficial, based on sex. Everyone becomes a potential 'fuck body' (Horvat 2016).

However, the question is to what extent are we living in an era of cold intimacies? To counter this argument, there has been research which emphasises the continued importance of tradition, monogamous relationships, intimacy, love and commitment in people's lives (Carter 2012; Carter and Duncan 2016; Jamieson 1998; Smart 2007; van Hooff 2013). Duncan (2011b) argues that theorists misinterpret the change in intimacy, seeing it as a wholly reflexive process where people can freely create their biographies, separate from tradition. However, he argues that individuals consciously or unconsciously draw on tradition to piece together responses to changing situations. Individuals make decisions about their personal lives pragmatically; tradition is idealised, however becomes reinvented and reformed as a response to changing situations (Duncan 2011a). Similarly, Carter (2017) found that whilst there was this possibility for couples to live beyond the conventional family, this was not always the case. Relationships were still bound by tradition; the traditional family was aspired to. Through a process of bricolage, traditions were reaffirmed and reinvented, and the act of marriage became strengthened through this process. Love became the narrative of marriage and relationships, as relationships were less about structuring society and more about love and romance. Marriage is desired because it is assumed, traditional and normal; to not marry was seen as socially unacceptable in a culture of free choice. Whilst the transformation of intimacy may influence the ways in which couples discursively construct their relationships, in terms of lived experiences, relationships continue to be underpinned by tradition (van Hooff 2013, 2017).

This chapter examines whether the dating app Tinder, as a new phenomenon, transforms dating within an era of liquid modernity and cold intimacies, or whether Tinder extends the way we are dating, thus implying a continuity with tradition. This chapter focuses on how young adults use technology to negotiate intimate relationships; whether there is a split with tradition in which dating apps facilitate emotional capitalism, or whether traditional narratives of romantic relationships are incorporated into new modes of dating.

Tinder has become a cultural phenomenon amongst young adults; however, it is criticised for its association with casual sex and meaningless bonds. Kao (2016) argues that Tinder caters to young adults and has transformed the ways in which they seek out relationships. Whilst Tinder represents a shift in dating culture which favours instant gratification, immediate attraction and convenience, in some ways dating culture has remained the same due to the process taken when selecting partners (Kao 2016). Much of the existing literature surrounding online dating suggests a continuity with tradition, with value being placed upon romantic relationships. Hobbs et al. (2016) explored the experiences of users of online dating apps to see if technology had influenced their views of long-term relationships. In particular, they looked at whether dating apps may be eroding traditional ideals of commitment and romantic love. Through a mixed method approach of online surveys and in-depth interviews with six of the participants from the survey, they found that the majority of individuals valued romantic love and used technology as a means to pursue meaningful relationships. The participants found technology gave them greater chances of meeting new partners (see also van Hooff, this volume). Similarly, Brym and Lenton (2001) found that among Canadian users of online dating sites, the strongest motivation for using online dating services was to find dates and establish long-term relationships. These studies show that technology can give multiple choices when it comes to online dating. Whilst there may not be a single reason why individuals use dating sites, many use technology to facilitate romantic bonds amongst other motivations. Whilst these studies reflect key findings within online dating, the majority of existing literature addresses dating websites rather than dating apps, such as Tinder. Similarly, a number of previous studies on online dating focus on self-presentation rather than experiences and reasons for using online dating or dating apps.

Methods

This study aimed to look at how people use online dating apps and their experiences of using apps such as Tinder. Through in-depth interviews I was able to gain an insight into how individuals order and interpret the social world, taking into account the different viewpoints and practices in the field (Flick 1998; Ivey 2012; Rodica and Milena 2008). Whilst there are limitations in using qualitative research, such as difficulty replicating data, as I aimed to gain a full understanding of why individuals use dating apps, qualitative approaches gave me the possibility to find subtle changes, ambiguities and complexities within personal life (Smart 2007). I used a cross-sectional design, as research was collected at a single point in time, allowing the research to be carried out quickly. Thematic analysis of the interviews helped me to understand the phenomena of Tinder in terms of the meanings people brought to them (Babbie 2010; Boyatzis 1998).

Due to the time constraints of this project (which was originally an undergraduate dissertation), purposive sampling was used, the sample only included participants who were currently on Tinder or had used Tinder previously. Within this purposive sample, convenience and snowballing sampling was used; those who were available and accessible to the researcher at the time (Mason 2002). The sample included ten participants, five male and five female, all of whom identified as heterosexual and aged between 21 and 23 years old. I focused on this age group as young adults not only have access to, but use communicative technologies at a much higher rate and a higher frequency than any other age group. As online dating apps are a relatively new phenomenon these young adults are seen to be at their peak dating age when these online dating apps were produced. To understand the uses of Tinder, therefore, this age group was a good starting point (Rappleyea et al. 2014). Participants ranged in occupation and were largely working class to lower middle class (National Statistic Socio-economic classification 2010). All participants identified as White British, and one Mixed-race British, reflecting my own social network. Institutional ethics guidelines were followed throughout this study and participants have been assigned pseudonyms to ensure anonymity.

Emotional Capitalism

Illouz (2007) views online dating sites as an example of emotional capitalism; internet dating transforms encounters into economic transactions as it restructures the search for a partner into a market. Romantic relations are 'not only organized within the market, but have themselves become commodities, produced on an assembly line, to be consumed fast, efficiently, cheaply and in great abundance' (Illouz 2007: 91). According to Illouz (2007) the sheer volume of potential partners Tinder offers its users creates a highly repetitive narrative both online and offline, forcing its users to create a standardised procedure to manage large quantities of potential partners. This is seen within the interviews; Richard (23), for example, described Tinder as 'numbing'; for him the girls he swiped right and spoke to had no identities, they were just people to reply to without having a real connection. Each conversation was the same, he sent the same message to each girl, with no meaning. Richard explained how he had entered into a constant cycle of 'meeting and sleeping' with people from Tinder, which drove out any possible meaningful relationships. As Horvat (2016) suggests, the people Richard was meeting through Tinder were 'fuck bodies', conversations became less meaningful and more superficial. In line with emotional capitalism, due to the volume and frequency, the conversations and meetings through Tinder become scripted, much like telemarketing (Illouz 2007).

The idea that Tinder created too much choice was also prevalent in the interviews. According to Illouz (2007) internet sites make the market for potential partners more visible, which leads to people looking for the best value they can get, refusing to settle when something better could come along. This abundance of choice inhibits rather than enables the capacity to commit to a single relationship (Illouz 2012). Tinder created a space to go to where this was possible, you could talk to numerous people at the same time and easily terminate the conversation or tie with the click of a button, this being one prominent aspect of virtual relationships described by Bauman (2003). There was no necessity to keep talking to somebody if someone better came along, or if you got bored:

There is always someone to swipe, someone to talk to, someone to keep you entertained for a while (Harry)

It's too easy for someone to just swipe right … if they would stop talking to you, you knew full well that they had swiped right for somebody else and are talking to somebody else (Isabelle)

If it doesn't go well you can just delete and move on (Alice)

You can just walk away from it whenever you want it's not awkward to walk away from them (George)

According to Illouz (2007) unlike internet dating, in 'the real world' of dating the market of partners remains unseen, therefore the concept of too much choice does not affect relationships. This is exemplified by

Alice who compared Tinder to a 'real relationship', where this would not be as easy to do, showing the difference between 'virtual' and 'real' relationships:

> It is so easy to just get bored of talking to someone if someone new pops up, whereas if you were in a bar … that wouldn't happen, you would just be talking to one person, whereas the vast options Tinder gives you, makes it a lot less personal, you can just stop talking to someone, un-match them and never speak to them again.

Isabelle had similar views; Isabelle, who had used Tinder for a long period of time and described how her use of Tinder was 'to find somebody to love me', stated that Tinder had changed her perception of love. For Isabelle, love was something you worked for, something that you stay in for a long time when you find the right person. However, she described how Tinder was not like this, Tinder did not promote love because it was so easy not to try when there were other possibilities out there. Due to having all potential partners visible, she knew the men she spoke to on Tinder were likely to be talking to a number of people at the same time, and stated this was the hardest thing about Tinder, and was 'the worst feeling'. In line with Bauman's (2003) views that easily disposable ties are taking over from romantic love, Isabelle stated:

> The older generations are like, if it's broken then they fix it, but our generation now because they have got Tinder and what not, if it's broken then they will just swipe right and find something better, and I think that's what's hard, I think that's what's ruined my perception of it.

Examples of emotional capitalism can be seen throughout the interviews, in particular how Tinder creates a vast market of visible potential partners which causes the search for romance to become inherently unstable. Illouz (2007) states this shows a significant departure from traditional love; however, there was still, to some extent, a connection to tradition within dating explored in the next section. Interviewees still wanted love, despite the negative views they held about Tinder.

Ambivalence

The concept of ambivalence is explored by Illouz (2012) as a condition created by choice. Illouz (2012) refers to romantic ambivalence as dampened feelings, conflicting emotions and as a property of the institutions that organise our lives. There were a number of ambiguities and conflicting emotions within the interviews which were centred on using Tinder to facilitate free sex and the vast choice it created for its users. Many interviewees stated that Tinder was used as an app on which you could get free sex and create meaningless bonds which you could easily terminate if necessary. In every interview the use of Tinder as a tool for casual sex was mentioned. When asked if Tinder was a good way to meet a partner Hannah (21) was quick to say no stating that the reason for this was because everyone was only on there for one reason: 'to get laid'. For some, like Richard (23) and George (22) who explained they used Tinder to have sex, the app made this a lot easier for them. George felt that Tinder had made sex meaningless:

> You're far more willing for it to be meaningless because you're allowing yourself to go into something meaningless, you're already setting it out to be meaningless, so it doesn't bother you that it is.

This is also seen in Richard's account, the meaninglessness of sex, the becoming of 'fuck bodies' (Horvat 2016) meant that for Richard sex was just a physical thing, which has no passion or love, it was no longer a big deal to him. Previously Richard explained how he was shy when having sex, and sex used to be a major part of a relationship, something he would often play up in his mind, making him nervous, however Tinder changed that. The sacredness of sex was being removed by Tinder. Richard's account is in line with Illouz's (2012) argument that simultaneous accumulation of sexual partners, and the exposure to a large number of potential partners Tinder creates, decreases and dampens the potential feelings and commitments that individuals have towards one relationship (Illouz 2012). This detachment 'is a form of ostentatious display of sexual capital to other men' (Illouz 2012: 103), thus serial sexuality creates an emotional detachment, leading to meaningless bonds.

Whilst for some, the experiences of Tinder made them view sex in different ways, Tom (22) highlighted that perhaps it is not Tinder but the individual who creates this negative viewpoint. Tom states that whilst Tinder does make one-night-stands a lot easier, the type of person who is having one-night-stands is likely to do this, regardless of whether it is through Tinder or not. Correspondingly, Alice (21) states how although you can never know other people's motives for using Tinder, and whether it is just for sex, the same can be said for meeting someone in a club. This casual sex is not just facilitated on Tinder but also in bars and clubs; it is not the app creating a casual sex culture, but society. This idea of casual sex is not a new phenomenon created by Tinder, sexual lifestyles within the twentieth century included the idea of 'sexual freedom', and sex not being bound by feelings of love, but by casual bonds (Haavio-Mannila et al. 2001). The behaviours of young people may not have changed, however the means by which to obtain casual sex and the technology that facilitates these bonds has.

This disentanglement of sex from emotion is seen in the male interviewees' responses more than the females' responses. Illouz (2012) uses the concept of 'emotional inequalities' to describe this change in causal bonds, stating men are more likely to engage more frequently in casual sex and are much more motivated by sex than women, who tend to value intimacy and love more significantly. Sexuality is channelled differently according to different sexual strategies for gaining status, suggesting a gender difference in responses to creating these casual bonds (Illouz 2012). Illouz (2012) states that women adopt serial sexuality as an imitation of men's power. However, for women this serial sexuality coexists with exclusivity causing a mix of sexual strategies that become full of contradictions. As seen in Isabelle's response when talking about her experiences of casual sex through Tinder:

> People do it unlovingly ... I think being naive, I just thought that sex was so lovely and perfect and I honestly remember thinking I will never ever have sex with a random guy and Tinder ruined that. (Isabelle, 22)

This gendered difference in responses takes place in what Illouz calls 'sexual fields'; social spaces in which sexual desire becomes autonomised and competition generalised. Within these social spaces men and women experience their sexual freedom in competitive fields in different ways. Intimate relationships become much more difficult to achieve, especially for women. Men are more likely to view the marriage market, as a sexual market. Whilst sexuality has become a status signal for both men and women, their sexualisation, and the way they negotiate sexual fields differs. Women are more likely to be in the sexual market for a short amount of time and value intimacy and commitment, whereas men will view the marriage market as a sexual market for a longer period of time (Illouz 2012). This is seen in female responses, in particular both Alice and Isabelle's accounts; they viewed the men they spoke to on Tinder as only wanting a casual bond, which was easily broken due to the vast choice Tinder creates, which is not what they viewed as desirable. Whereas for Richard and George, the market was viewed as a sexual market, based around meaningless ties.

> Tinder has highlighted that actually boys are fickle and boys just want sex (Isabelle).

It was clear from the interviews there was a certain ambivalence around Tinder and the uses of Tinder. Interviewees would often contradict previous statements made about the app, suggesting that how they felt about Tinder was not clear cut. On the one hand, Tinder was seen as not creating 'real' relationships (i.e. long-term relationships) and was more about quick, repetitive fixes and casual sex. However, on the other hand, for some Tinder was seen as a legitimate way to meet people, with a number of interviewees entering relationships with someone they had met on Tinder. This ambivalence is something Illouz (2007) explores through feminism and the therapeutic turn; the therapeutic discourse, much like feminism, encouraged women to put together two contradictory sets of values: Independence and nurture, which constituted emotional health. However, this intertwining of feminism and therapeutic language also produced a process of rationalisation in which relationships are transformed into cognitive objects which can be compared. This rationalisation of emotional bonds means intimate relationships can be susceptible to depersonalisation and emotions detached from the individual. Intimate relationships can become both meaningful and meaningless; something which can be measurable and categorised (Illouz 2007). Interviewee's saw their own relationships being meaningful when attached to traditional discourses; however, causal bonds created through Tinder were often seen as meaningless.

Whilst this may be perceived as a progressive move towards liquid modernity, in a number of interviews the idea of creating meaningless bonds was still viewed as undesirable within dating. For example, when Richard and George described how they used Tinder for sex, they conveyed how they did not like using it for this reason, and they did not like how this changed sex for them. This suggests that whilst it is widely assumed that late modern societies are becoming more liberal and open about casual sex, there are still a number of associated anxieties around free sex. These centred on the specialness of sex; its status as extra-ordinary (Jackson and Scott 2004). Thus, whilst sex may seem more meaningless through Tinder, there is still a view that sex should be special, and there is this aspect of shamefulness in regards to free sex. Casual sex is not viewed as romantic or traditional within a relationship, therefore it may not be seen as fully socially acceptable. Casual sex was something interviewees did not want and were ashamed of, even when they chose to use Tinder in this way. Many interviewees expressed their negative views towards casual sex on Tinder:

> The type of girl you can bang instantly without having met at least once before isn't worth it. (Harry, 21)

> Tinder makes it easy, sadly everything easy is worth very little. (Tom, 22)

When asked if Tinder had changed interviewees' views on sex many acknowledged that it had because sex was so easy to obtain through Tinder. Many then stated this was not how *they* used the app and that their use of the app did not relate to the stereotypical use of Tinder, and thus, creating an 'us' and 'them' narrative. This was exemplified by Alice (21):

> I think if you want sex and just sex and you go on Tinder, you can find it pretty easy and quickly, a lot of people use it for that, just a quick fix I guess, but I don't.

Rosie's (22) response to this question was similar:

> It becomes more accessible and there are people that use it just for sex I guess … it's just easier isn't it … but I personally wouldn't use it for that, but I know a lot of people that do.

Both Alice and Rosie had distanced themselves from the sex narrative, suggesting that sex is still valued within the society as being a special aspect of a relationship. Whilst this contrasts arguments around cold intimacies and liquid love as interviewees did not want Tinder to ruin the value placed on sex and traditional ways of dating, it reinforces the gender differences within the sexual fields; female interviewees were much more likely to view casual sex negatively, compared to the male interviewees.

Lucy and Alice expressed how the view that Tinder was just used for quick ties had affected their views on their own Tinder relationships. For Alice this did not affect her use of the app, as she openly admitted that in the past she had used Tinder for the purpose of finding a partner, however stated that this is not something that many people would admit to because Tinder was seen to be used only to find sex. Alice has been in a relationship from Tinder for six months, however she disclosed that she never told her family that was how they met:

> I never say we met on Tinder, it's bad isn't it, but just because the stigma, some people, especially older generations, don't think it's like a legitimate way to meet someone, but I don't think that.

Whilst the negative perception of Tinder did not affect Alice's reasons for using Tinder, nor her relationship, there was still the underlying thought that, in some people's eyes, it was something to be ashamed of: That Tinder was not a legitimate means to find a boyfriend, and thus she kept it a secret. This is similar to Lucy (22), who met her husband, who is now the father of her four-month-old child, on Tinder. Lucy, however, never admitted to her family members that this is how they met. She stated she wanted as few people as possible to know they met through Tinder as 'it has connotations'. Throughout the interview, Lucy had a very negative view of Tinder, describing it as 'tacky', despite the fact that she is now married to the man she matched on Tinder:

> I wouldn't say it was the best way to meet a partner, I wasn't using it to look for a partner and wouldn't have ever said I'd have met someone from there, it just kind of happened … I'm sure I'm not the only one … I would never say to someone, if you're looking for someone go on Tinder.

For Lucy there was a clear distinction between the people on Tinder, herself and her own relationship. Lucy explained her use of Tinder was never serious; it was mainly something to joke about with friends. However, for Lucy to have entered a relationship which progressed into marriage, the use of Tinder must have been serious at one point in time, suggesting her motivation for using Tinder changed over time, as her relationship grew in seriousness. This was a similar theme amongst a number of interviewees. When describing Tinder, much of the negative aspects of the app were described through how 'other people' used it. When Tinder was discussed in terms of their own dating and relationships, it was seen as more acceptable. Aside from Harry, Richard and James (21), all other interviewees had dated or been in long-term relationships, which they defined as committed relationships lasting a long period of time, with someone they met from Tinder. Whilst often views of Tinder were negative, Tinder was still, to some extent, a way for interviewees to find a long-term partner. Both Tom and George described their long-term relationships through Tinder in contrast to the competing narrative of liquid love:

> I did meet an ex-girlfriend on there, and we were together for a year and a half and that was through Tinder, and we didn't use it in the context of hooking up, I think we just randomly met each other through that. (George)

> We decided to give it a go when we were both at university, so it was not like, there were no one-night-stand type things, they were actual dates. (Tom)

To some extent interviewees accept the idea that Tinder facilitates casual sex and therefore according to Bauman (2003), Horvat (2016) and

Illouz (2007) casual love. However, through the ambivalence described above and their use of the 'us' and 'them' narrative, most interviewees distance themselves from Tinder's hooking-up reputation while simultaneously using it as a legitimate dating tool, in order to find long-term relationships. This suggests Tinder does not represent a significant departure from traditional dating practices.

Bricolage

This continuation of dating traditions and practices was evident in many interviewees' responses: James, Rosie, Isabelle, Hannah, Tom and Alice all described how the idea of meeting new people was one of their main motivations for using Tinder. The idea that Tinder was a legitimate way to meet new people and date was also prominent as Rosie pointed out:

> I don't really think it's any different to meeting someone out, and I think it's just become one of the normal ways of dating people.

Whilst for some the vast choices Tinder gave its users was overwhelming, leading to easily disposable ties, this choice was also seen as a positive, opening up new possibilities for dating; contradicting previous statements, as James explained:

> I'm only ever going to meet someone like through mutual friends or via the workplace, or whatever, if it wasn't for Tinder and I think that's always been the case, but now with Tinder, you've got like a whole entire parameter of 10, 20 kilometres around of … someone that's going to be interested in you.

This account is similar to Isabelle who described how without Tinder, and the internet, she would only meet people through friends, church, school or work. Tinder now allows her to be connected with people from 'different ways of life', speaking to people she wouldn't necessarily talk to. Internet dating allowed for a much larger volume of interactions than 'real-life' dating, thus increasing the pool of potential partners in one single snapshot (Illouz 2012). Illouz (2012) compares this possibility of choice as if 'on a buffet table' (Illouz 2012: 181); for interviewees this 'buffet' of choice leads to increased opportunities for dating. For Alice, a relationship was a relationship, whether you met on Tinder, or met somewhere else, Tinder does not devalue that relationship. If you get on enough, whether you were looking for something or not, it will just happen. Interviewees seemed open to the idea of finding love through Tinder, with Lucy and Alice explaining they had found love through the app. All interviewees, apart from Tom, felt it was possible to find love through Tinder, as Alice stated:

> I think you have to find the right person, and be lucky, but yeah, I did and I know people who have, so I think it's possible.

Similarly when asked if it was possible to find love on Tinder George stated:

> yeah, for sure, it's just rare, I wouldn't expect it, but I think you could.

Whilst love may not have been a primary motive for downloading Tinder, a number of interviewees still valued love as a rare and lucky experience, which coincides with Illouz's (2007) description of traditional love, as a unique and an 'unexpected epiphany' (Illouz 2007: 90). In this sense Tinder is seen by interviewees to create the possibility to find traditional love, countering the argument that internet dating creates a significant departure from this aspiration. Furthermore, love may not have been as prevalent in interviews due to the age range of the participants and their stage in life; statistics show that young adults are marrying at a later age than previous generations. The age men and women are getting married has continued to rise since 1970 (Office of National Statistics 2015). This may be due to young adults putting off marriage and the commitments of adulthood to invest in their careers. Therefore, whilst traditional love is still idealised, it is delayed as a response to changing situations (Armstrong et al. 2010; Bogle 2008).

The concept of bricolage (the piecing together of old and new (Carter and Duncan 2018)) can be utilised to explain the incorporation of new dating technologies into traditional dating practices and aspirations. The tradition of meeting new people and going on dates is still prevalent within interviewees' experiences; interviewees still valued romantic relationships. Whilst the values of traditional romantic relationships are present, the means by which interviewees facilitate this has changed. Instead of finding dates at dances or nightclubs, young people are finding dates through Tinder. Tinder therefore becomes patched together with traditions of romantic love to form a new and reinvented way of dating (Bogle 2008; Duncan 2011a; Carter and Duncan 2018). In this way, young daters are bricoleurs:

> It is just another way to date, technology allows us to do so much and everyone is always on their phones, so it's just a new way of dating … dates are pretty standard no matter where you meet. (Alice)

> It's like a reflection of the twenty first century. (James)

> It's the modern world of dating, instead of meeting people in bars and speed dating, you now meet people on Tinder. (Richard)

The notion of standardisation of dates is explored by Illouz (2007), who argues that internet dating creates interchangeability and has introduced mass consumption to the realm of romantic encounters, which is based upon endless choice and standardisation. These standardised techniques used to deal with the volume of interactions makes dates highly repetitive. As Illouz (2007) argues, romantic relationships now face the problem of greater volume and speed of romantic consumption. It may be that the frequency of encounters through Tinder creates this scripted dating character which as Alice puts it, makes dates 'pretty standard' (Illouz 2007). Whilst this points towards aspects of emotional capitalism, it could be argued that dating in general has become standardised, whether facilitated through Tinder or not. Alongside the narrative of standardisation is the value placed on romantic relationships, thus showing the contractions and ambivalence throughout the interviews.

However, whilst there are some aspects of emotional capitalism and liquid love within the interviews, there is still a continuity with tradition, which could suggest that whilst technology is changing the way romantic relationships are formed, tradition still plays a part in this process. It is clear there is a change within romantic relationships; however, this change may not be the behaviours of young people but the options available to facilitate romantic relationships.

Conclusion

Whilst there has been a change in technology which supports Illouz's (2007) and Bauman's (2003) ideas of transient intimacy, this has not completely changed young people's romantic relationships or their aspirations. Young people are faced with the idea that sex can be simultaneously casual yet special, bonds can be easily broken or meaningful. It may be that the conflicting and ambiguous ideas the interviewees had about Tinder reflect the conflicting views around romantic relationships for young people in society generally. In attempting to resolve these conflicting ideas, interviewees created an 'us' and 'them' narrative. On the one hand Tinder creates a space which facilitates instant and quick fixes, a visual market of potential partners and too much choice (for 'them'). On the other hand, there is still this continuity with tradition and dating within Tinder (for 'us'). In this way interviewees distanced themselves from the more 'distasteful' aspects of Tinder while upholding it as a legitimate dating tool.

There was an evident gender difference in responses, which aligned with Illouz's (2012) ideas around gendered inequalities within marriage markets and sexual fields. Female interviewees were much more likely to view Tinder as a new way of dating with ultimate expectations of long-term relationships and to view the causal bonds and free sex facilitated on the app as negative. Whereas, whilst the male interviewees also viewed Tinder as a legitimate way to meet people, they were much more likely to view Tinder as a sexual market and stay in this market for a longer period of time. This demonstrates men's continued power within the dating field (Illouz 2012). It is also important to note that for interviewees who go on to form long-term relationships, Tinder no longer operates as a site of choice—love inhibits romantic choice once commitment is established and Tinder is only discussed by these participants as a tool for dating, in the very early stages of relationship formation.

This is not to say Illouz's (2007, 2012) ideas should be dismissed when discussing romantic relationships in society. It is clear that aspects of cold intimacies and in particular emotional capitalism within internet dating are prevalent within interviewees' accounts—at the early stages of the dating process. Young people in today's society are given the opportunity, through technology, to easily create meaningless, superficial bonds over romantic relationships. The degree to which this is reproduced in participants' accounts is perhaps a reflection of their age and stage in the life course (van Hooff's chapter in this volume shows a slightly different attitude to dating on Tinder among her older cohort of men). Alongside this narrative of cold intimacies and liquid love is the narrative of tradition and romantic relationships. Whilst Tinder creates the *opportunity* for casual bonds, young people still, to some degree, hold long-term romantic relationships as an ideal, suggesting instead a continuity with traditional dating practices alongside changes in dating forms; in short a bricolage of old practices with new tools.

References

Armstrong, E.A., Hamilton, L. and England, P. (2010) Is hooking up bad for young women? *Contexts* 9 (3): 22–27.

Babbie, E.R. (2010) *The basics of social research*. 5th edn. Boston, MA: Wadsworth/Cengage Learning.

Bauman, Z. (2003) *Liquid love: On the Frailty of human bonds*. Cambridge: Polity Press.

Blum, V.L. (2005) Love studies: or, Liberating love. *American Literary History* 17 (2): 335–348.

Bogle, K.A. (2008) *Hooking up: Sex, Dating and Relationships on Campus*. New York: NYU Press.

Boyatzis, R. (1998) *Transforming qualitative information: thematic analysis and code development*. Thousand Oaks, CA: Sage Publications.

Brym, D.R. and Lenton, D.R. (2001) *Love Online: A Report on Digital Dating in Canada*. Available at: http://projects.chass.utoronto.ca/brym/loveonline.pdf [Accessed 20 November 2016].

Carter, J. (2012) What is commitment? Women's accounts of intimate attachment. *Families, Relationships and Societies* 1 (2): 137–153.

Carter, J. (2017) Why Marry? The role of Tradition in Women's Marital Aspirations. *Sociological Research Online* 22 (1): 1–14.

Carter, J. and Duncan, S. (2016) Wedding paradoxes: Individualized conformity and the 'perfect day'. *The Sociological Review* 65 (1): 3–20.

Carter, J. and Duncan, S. (2018) *Reinventing couples: Tradition, agency and bricolage*. Basingstoke: Palgrave.

Duncan, S. (2011a) Personal life, pragmatism and Bricolage. *Sociological Research Online* 16 (4).

Duncan, S. (2011b) The World We Have Made? Individualisation and Personal Life in the 1950s. *The Sociological Review*, 59 (2): 242–265.

Flick, U. (1998) *An introduction to qualitative research*. Thousand Oaks, CA: Sage Publications.

Haavio-Mannila, E., Kontula, O. and Rotkirch, A. (2001) *Sexual Lifestyle in the Twentieth Century: A Research Study*. Basingstoke: Palgrave.

Heino, R., Ellison, N. and Gibbs, J. (2010) Relationshopping: Investigating the market metaphor in online dating. *Journal of Social and Personal Relationships* 27 (4): 427–447.

Hobbs, M., Owen, S. and Gerber, L. (2016) Liquid love? Dating apps, sex, relationships and the digital transformation of intimacy. *Journal of Sociology* 53 (2): 1–14.

Horvat, S. (2016) *The Radicality of Love*. Cambridge: Polity Press.

Illouz, E. (2007) *Cold Intimacies: The Making of Emotional Capitalism*. Cambridge: Polity Press.

Illouz, E. (2012) *Why love Hurts*. Cambridge: Polity Press.

Ivey, J. (2012) The value of qualitative research methods. *Paediatric Nursing* 38 (6): 319.

Jackson, S. and Scott, S. (2004) Sexual Antinomies in Late Modernity. *Sexualities* 7 (2): 233–248.

Jamieson, L. (1998) *Intimacy: Personal Relationships in Modern Societies*. Cambridge: Polity Press.

Kao, A. (2016) Tinder: True Love or a Nightmare? *Advanced Writing: Pop Culture Intersections* 16.

Keskin-Kozat, B. (2004) Liquid love: On the Frailty of human bonds. *Contemporary Sociology: A Journal of Reviews* 33 (4): 494–495.

Mason, J. (2002). *Qualitative Researching*. London: Sage.

National Statistic Socio-economic classification (2010) *National Statistic Socio-economic classification.* Webarchive.nationalarchives.gov.uk. Available at: http://webarchive.nationalarchives.gov.uk/20160105160709/http://www.ons.gov.uk/ons/guide-method/classifications/current-standard-classifications/soc2010/soc2010-volume-3-ns-sec%2D%2Drebased-on-soc2010%2D%2Duser-manual/index.html [Accessed 30 March 2017].

Office for National Statistics (2015) *Marriages in England and Wales.* Available at: https://www.ons.gov.uk/peoplepopulationandcommunity/birthsdeathsandmarriages/marriagecohabitationandcivilpartnerships/bulletins/marriagesinenglandandwalesprovisional/2015#the-average-age-at-marriage-continued-to-rise [Accessed 01 September 2018]

Rappleyea, D. Taylor, A. and Fang, X. (2014) Gender Differences and Communication Technology Use Among Emerging Adults in the Initiation of Dating Relationships. *Marriage and Family Review* 50 (3): 269–284.

Rodica, Z. and Milena (2008) Qualitative research methods: A comparison between focus-group and in-depth interview. *Annals of the University of Oradea: Economic Science* 4 (1): 1279–1283.

Smart, C. (2007) *Personal life: New directions in sociological thinking.* Cambridge: Polity Press.

Turkle, S. (2011) *Alone together: Why we expect more from technology and less from each other.* New York: Basic Books.

van Hooff, J. (2013) *Modern Couples? Continuity and change in heterosexual relationships.* Farnham: Ashgate.

van Hooff, J. (2017) An everyday affair: deciphering the sociological significance of women's attitudes towards infidelity. *The Sociological Review* 65 (4): 850–864.

Section III

Women's Exclusivist Strategies

8

Wretched? Women's Questions of Love and Labour in the People's Republic of China

Alison Lamont

Introduction

How old is 'too old' to be single? Lahad (2017) has demonstrated how gender and time intersect to create female adult singlehood as a social problem that opens women up to ridicule and prejudice. Women in the People's Republic of China (PRC) are no exception. Single, urban women with a successful career and good education are being stigmatised for reaching their mid to late 20s without marrying. The figure of the 'left-over woman' or *shengnü* presents a uniquely modern problem of romance. In a deregulated marriage market (Illouz 2012) where the dominant problem is surplus of choice, single women are derided for being 'picky'; in an environment where love is supposed to triumph all other criteria for mate selection, they are damned for being 'materialistic'. While this stigma has been criticised and plenty of women live happily in the PRC

A. Lamont (✉)
University of Roehampton, London, UK
e-mail: alison.lamont@roehampton.ac.uk

© The Author(s) 2020   **153**
J. Carter, L. Arocha (eds.), *Romantic Relationships in a Time of 'Cold Intimacies'*,
Palgrave Macmillan Studies in Family and Intimate Life,
https://doi.org/10.1007/978-3-030-29256-0_8

without marrying by the age of 27, the fear of becoming or being labelled as 'leftover' shapes women's social experiences. This chapter explores the *shengnü* stigma through the lens of modernity, as characterised by individualisation, and the very modern pains of love within the traditional concerns of family.

As a nation, China takes pride in its familism. The insistence that 'family is the basic cell of society' reflects and enacts the idea that to get society right, you must first get the family right. This has been a persistent theme in Chinese governance historically and it is again in the ascendance, with President Xi's vocal support of family being widely reported (e.g. An 2018). The 'right' family in this instance is a nuclear, able-bodied and heterosexual unit with a minimum of one, maximum two, children born of married parents who, ideally, have undergone health checks prior to marriage. A relatively late legal age for marriage is part of the attempt to slow population growth, and strong social norms against sex outside marriage means that relatively few children are born out of wedlock (Davis and Friedman 2014: 5). For the state, family ties keep individuals happy and healthy while increasing the nation's human capital (Kuan 2015). Viewed as population, family is the bedrock of China's contemporary governance (Greenhalgh and Winckler 2005) and so structurally, individuals are compelled to marry in order to access state-backed resources, particularly in regard to fertility and old age care. This produces an environment where the need to marry is experienced as almost non-negotiable by both men and women in a way more intense than the 'compulsory coupledom' that Wilkinson (2012) has documented in the UK.

Yet despite this experience of marriage as a quasi-compulsory step in the life course, as being as practical and essential as passing the competitive *gaokao* examinations, the entry routes into marriage are not as cut and dried as college entry exams. Where arranged marriages were once common, since the 1930s young Chinese people have been wrestling with the right to pick their own partner and picking their own terms for deciding what makes a good match. True love, material prosperity, political background, equal social status, captured in the popular idiom *mendanghudui*, and the ability to 'cultivate' emotions over time have all been compelling reasons for marriage, as well as for resisting and ending marriages (Honig and Hershatter 1988; Glosser 2003). Increasingly the dominant factor in deciding on a partner is expected to be emotion over duty (Jankowiak and Li 2017). Looking for love has become big business and, as Illouz (2007, 2012) finds elsewhere, increasingly the use of metrics and technology to find a partner has marketised and commodified romance in the PRC. On the surface, the tensions between gender equality, intergenerational responsibilities and the conflicting demands of love and labour seem to be replicating in mainland China what has already become commonplace in the West. Yet, as this chapter argues, the historical and institutional underpinnings to this marriage market are structurally different to that of the Anglo-American experience, rooted in fundamentally different forms of state welfare and a state that intrudes more confidently into the family home.

Individualisation, Intimacy and Their Institutions

The intimacy paradigm that has dominated the sociology of families in Western Europe since the 1990s assumes democratic social relations and gender equality predicated on a politico-economic arrangement of institutions underpinned by a welfare state (Giddens 1991). This underpinning institutional arrangement is not mirrored in the PRC, where formal gender equality is significantly stilted by discrimination, and where the universal communist state provisioning of the 1950s was dismantled in the marketisation of the 1980s reform era, resulting in what has been described as a productivist, not welfarist, state model.[1] As part of this, the family remains central to the protection of Chinese individuals from the vicissitudes of the labour market; in contrast, Western European individuals, according to theorists like Beck (1992) and Giddens (1991), are able to substantially 'disembed' themselves from these traditional structures of the life course and instead fully engage in life planning and the 'do-it-yourself-biography'. Similarly, Illouz's definition of individualisation denotes that when it comes to partner choice:

[I]ndividuals, not families, become carriers of personal, physical, emotional and sexual attributes that are supposed to constitute and define their particularity and uniqueness and that individuals take charge of the process of evaluating and choosing. (2012: 51–52)

Yet this chapter will demonstrate that the family has not been separated wholly from individuals in romantic affairs in the Chinese case and so the architecture of choice-making for individuals is shaped and oriented towards future family formation, rather than fulfilment of the self.

The continuing structural dependence of individuals on family means that the intimacy argument has struggled to find its theoretical footings in the PRC, even before having to address the critiques offered in its original formulation (Jamieson 1999; Gillies 2003). Yunxiang Yan has led the scholarly work which flexes the individualisation hypothesis, on which the concept of intimacy relies, to adapt it to contemporary PRC families. Where Beck and Beck-Gernsheim highlight an internalised culture of democracy and a welfare state as necessary preconditions for individualisation (Yan 2008: 8), Yan disentangles these two premises from individualisation's 'four basic features' of: detraditionalisation; institutionalised disembedding and re-embedding; the pursuit of a 'life of one's own'; and the internalisation of risk. He argues that with this adjusted underpinning, the individualisation hypothesis becomes relevant beyond the political realities of Western Europe (Yan 2010: 506–507). Off the back of this, and based on his long-running ethnographic work in northern China, Yan maps the shifting landscape of family formation in the PRC and argues that adult children, rather than ageing parents, are the new centre of the Chinese family, and that choice is being exercised in a more individualised way than ever before (2003, 2010).

Yan's work has been foundational to the contemporary study of intimacy in the PRC but has been challenged by other interpretations of individualisation. For example, Barbalet (2016) has recently argued that individuals have never been successfully disembedded from the Chinese family, and even under the explicit attempt to disembed individuals from tradition in the Cultural Revolution (1966–1976), individual class status was still linked to the class status of family members (Barbalet 2016: 12; see also Andreas 2009), undermining Yan's claim that individualisation can be applied smoothly to the PRC. He argues that the family in the PRC today plays a far stronger determining factor in individual lives than the individualisation hypothesis proposes; if nothing else, choices about education are made by parents and determine, in large part, the imagined future of the child (Fong 2004; Kuan 2015). In the more contested domain of marriage and relationships, there is more scope to talk of individual choice in which the family features as one of the many institutional drivers and constraints but Barbalet claims this analysis fails to recognise the unique emotional weight of family and does not adequately take into account the institutional profile of the contemporary Chinese family.

While Barbalet (2016) rightly demonstrates the continued relevance and impact of the family on individual choice, he overlooks the significance of *obligatory choice-making* in the contemporary PRC. The key shift the individualisation argument makes is that, where individuals were once born into a web of expected conditions and relationships determined by collective social structures, they are now born into a bureaucratic maze of decision-making, determined by structural demands for competition and flexible planning (Beck and Beck-Gernsheim 2002). Choices *must* be made, even if the choices being made are to uphold the 'traditional' model of the life course identified by Barbalet. In this regard, the continuing importance of the family is less about the 'obligation of need' that made the pre-modern family the necessary and dominant social institution but now one of affection and the necessary interdependence of individualised biographies (Beck and Beck-Gernsheim 2002: 107).

Illouz joins this debate to argue that individualisation in the realm of romance constitutes the development of a reflexive, emotional self which emerges as marriage markets become deregulated. In her words, there is an

> affinity between the process of individualization of a choice of a mate, the 'deregulation' of marriage markets, and the fact that the search process is structured as if on a market, each freely exchanging attributes of his or her self, conceived as an accretion of social, psychological, and sexual traits. (Illouz 2012: 54)

So while individualisation is a core to the analysis, it is the impact of this individualisation on the development of the self that is Illouz's focus. In the PRC this individualising of private life was augured in 1950 with the new Marriage Law formally outlawing arranged marriage, concubinage and giving primacy instead to love-matches. The emergence of new architectures of mate choice in the PRC has since developed as the state's reconfiguration first as a dictatorship of the proletariat and then as a unique socialist market economy wrangled with ways in which to build a 'modern' family able to serve the people (Glosser 2003). The definition of modernity is contested and the Western origins of the often normative discussion of whether or not a post-colonial country has 'modernised' is no less heated in the Chinese context than in others (Goldstein 2006). Illouz's definition of modernity as being 'based on equality, contractualism, integration of men and women in the capitalist market, institutionalised 'human rights' as the central core of the person' (2012: 12) is complicated by the widely acknowledged persistence of gender inequality (Qi et al. 2016); the Chinese state's socialist oversight and steering of capitalist markets (Heilmann and Merton 2013); and by the PRC's perspective on human rights as being rooted in social good rather than in individual liberty (Zhao 2015). Yet there is enough flex in her definition to focus on the character of modernity as being defined by the emergence of a romantic self whose self-worth is built on desirability and the ability to navigate the new architecture of choice in love. The 'penetration of economics into the machine of desire' (Illouz 2012: 58) certainly resonates powerfully with findings from research into dating in the PRC (Zheng 2019; Zhang and Sun 2014). Nevertheless, the tension between the individual and the collective will re-emerge throughout this chapter as a central challenge that Illouz's, Giddens' and other Western social theorists' work on individualisation meets when analysing Chinese social reality.

The argument I make adopts Illouz's focus on the self and sits between Barbalet's rejection of individualisation of intimacy in the PRC and Yan's wholesale acceptance of it. I argue that the Chinese state, since making the post-1949 decision to preserve the family, has acted consistently to bind increasingly individualised individuals to the nuclear family in order to create a series of policy 'breaks' on individualisation and instead obligating micro-level collectivisation. This marks the Chinese experience of individualisation of intimacy as peculiarly statist in contrast to Anglo-American experiences. While the Chinese state has withdrawn from intimacy to a large degree since the 1980s (Honig and Hershatter 1988), it still maintains structures that it explicitly intends to compel individuals to support each other. In this, the notion of 'cold' (marketised) intimacy defined by meeting material, rather than emotional needs, is supplemented by a 'steely' (state-necessitated) intimacy which is bound by population governance in a uniquely Chinese way.

The policy evidence for this statement is wide ranging: Barbalet notes that the 1950 Marriage Law[2] and its later iterations individualise mate selection but preserve intergenerational obligations, something strengthened in the 1980s' revisions (2016: 14). We may add that the 1996 Law on Protection of the Rights and Interests of Older Persons[3] formalises adult children's obligations for the provision of care to their elderly parents and has prompted some families with strained intergenerational relationships to draw up formal contracts of care (Chou 2011). Another example: rural parents over 60 who have not contributed to a pension scheme can now benefit from the New Rural Pension Scheme *if* their adult children enrol and contribute to it, in what commenters have described as a uniquely 'family binding' policy (Williamson et al. 2017: 67). Other established policies are more direct: the household registration system means that children 'inherit' their parents' household registration status (rural or urban) which determines their access to public services and benefits.[4] Children born to unmarried mothers cannot be easily registered in this system, and nor can children born 'out of plan'—that is, born to parents who have not registered the pregnancy to the former Family Planning Committees—register for a birth certificate in the usual way (Johnson 2016). These policies and practices must be considered when exploring the scope for 'individualised' intimacy in the PRC as they inform the decision-making that Chinese adults engage in around their relationships. While Barbalet (2016) places too much emphasis, I argue, on these structural constraints, Yan can be critiqued for accounting them too little. Yan (2010) documents the research into the emergence of the Chinese 'entrepreneurial self' and the 'desiring self' but is less assiduous in documenting the hard structural barriers, such as those listed here, which act as conscious breaks on individualisation and anchor individuals into the traditional family of 'need' as opposed to a fluid structure of affection and intimacy.

My aim is to demonstrate that while the state has encouraged conditions of individualisation in the labour markets, it has sought to keep 'family matters' (i.e. reproduction; childcare and education; old age care) as strictly collective issues bolted onto the nuclear family, rather than the state, via policy and emphasis on traditional virtues of filial piety. Without recognising the intersection of pressures of the individualisation experienced in education and the globalised labour market, with state welfare policies which target families not individuals, the experience and structure of intimacy in the PRC cannot be fully perceived. I argue that the case of the stigmatisation of economically successful urban[5] women who have delayed marriage until nearly the age of 30 offer an incisive case through which to explore this matrix of individualised and 'familialised' structures and how it plays out on Chinese selfhood and life planning.

The need to make a good marriage match is acute, particularly for women. A successful 20-year-old woman marrying today may be expected to quit her job (e.g. To 2015a: 74) and become entirely dependent on her husband socially and financially; but to delay marriage in order to cultivate her financial independence acutely diminishes her options on the marriage market due to the entrenched norm of hypergamy (Davin 1999). In the case of marriage breakdown, a young woman may have lost both marketable years of employment and her 'youth', and so struggle to support herself through work or subsequent marriage. Overlying these financial risks are the emotional risks of 'wretchedness' or loneliness that are feared to stem from either not marrying or committing to a loveless match.

The conflict for individuals looking at marriage, then, is three-way: between a highly individualised labour market; the emergence of a reflexive, self-actualising self who is encouraged to engage with self-development in work and in relationships; and a family of obligations which in turn overrule the demands of the self for the demands of the collective.

'Leftover' Women

The rest of this chapter explores the stigma faced by unmarried Chinese women as they approach their late 20s and face the contradictory imperatives of family and self. The derogatory term *shengnü,* or 'leftover women' took hold in the mid-2000s as a descriptor for this group of women, particularly those who are successful urban women with high levels of education and a good career (Zhang and Sun 2014). The media discourse is aggressive, accusing these women of being either 'too picky' or of having made 'poor choices', and dismiss them as having made their own bed of singlehood (Feldshuh 2017). The problem is framed as one of population and selfishness: why, in a country with a shortage of women are women failing to marry? The answer suggested by the Chinese media is effectively that urban women have standards that are too high; critiques of male norms of hypergamy are largely ignored (Hong Fincher 2014).

To date, the research into stigmatised Chinese singlehood has focussed on explorations of the 'leftover women' phenomenon as a media discourse, critiqued through the lens of gender inequality and patriarchy. Publications reflect two dominant frames for reading this phenomenon: either educated, professional Chinese women who delay marrying are the outcome of a demographic phenomenon of population change and the state's attempts to control these changes (e.g. Wei and Zhen 2014; Gaetano 2014: 126; Zhang and Sun 2014); or they are a discursively created social problem, a form of moral panic generated by the media to achieve the state's goal of social stability (Hong Fincher 2014; Feldshuh 2017; Luo and Sun 2014). There is an overlap between the two perspectives, as population exists as a form of discourse in its own right, and the discursive creation of 'leftover' women draws on demographic findings as well as gender and social norms. This is reflected in the strongest publications, and emphasis of 'population' or 'discourse' as the explanatory power of the stigma is dependant largely on the wider argument the author(s) draw.

All areas of research on the issue, to differing degrees, emphasise the key issue underlying the dilemma of unmarried professional women, which is the inherently contradictory expectations of work and family for women in the PRC. This tends to manifest as 'tradition vs. modernity' (Ji 2015), or as Confucian values vs. market values (To 2015a; Zhang and Sun 2014). The revival of Confucian-esque norms which value women as 'good mothers and virtuous wives' conflicts with the labour market which values women who are instead 'good workers and virtuous employees', active in the spheres outside the home and obedient to the imperatives of the market and bosses, rather than husbands and sons. The pursuit of education (to the exclusion of dating, Zhang and Sun 2014) is the new filial act (Fong 2004) until educational and career success intersects with deeply entrenched trends of hypergamy which demand that men marry women in relatively less capital than themselves. While highly educated, professional women can provide some social mobility for their parents by remitting good wages or the purchase of good-quality, desirable accommodation, they are out-manoeuvred on the marriage market by women who have bypassed higher education and married early. This suggests that Illouz's (2012) optimistic reflection on social mobility through sexual capital may be played out here, though more research is needed to fully understand the dynamics at play.

Regarding the stigmatisation of single women, filial piety has been revived and repurposed (Yan 2016) to add cultural weight to the state's new demographic argument for more children in an ageing population: personal choice is again linked to national risks. Where some literature has looked at this as originating in 'tradition' or 'culture', I argue instead that tradition and culture have been harnessed to the state's goals of risk reduction and population management; and that the source of the stigma of being unmarried is rooted in the concept of social risk. As shown in the discussion below, these risks are experienced as personal rather than political (despite their political roots), and as having painful consequences if handled badly.

Building on these foundations, this study explores how single women express themselves and their worries about being 'leftover' on a lively Chinese social media platform via a community question-and-answer website. Though these ephemeral online exchanges are not necessarily naturally occurring data (Marres 2017: 79–80), there is a methodologically interesting directness in the publicly available online data generated by users. Examining these sources gives an indication of how internet users engage with and understand the stigma in their own terms, away from the formal and probing context of an interview.

I advance the argument that despite the state's persistent attempts to keep individuals firmly embedded in one of the key institutions of 'tradition' (the nuclear family) the fate of individuals is now widely interpreted as the outcome of 'modern' individual characteristics and choices, even when those choices are made by a family collective rather than an individual. This can be brought into focus by using the lens of the intimacy to analyse 'love pains' (to paraphrase Illouz) management queries of urban unmarried women. My analysis emphasises emotional risk and the role of choice within constraints, where others have emphasised the role of structure without sufficient agency.

Research Aims and Methods

The aim of this study is to gain an understanding of how the stigma of female singlehood in the PRC is popularly understood through the lens of institutionalised individualisation and institutionalised collectivisation at the family level. I analyse questions posted on the Chinese-language community question-and-answer website *Zhihu* (similar to the English-language websites *Quora*, or *Yahoo! Answers*) as examples of reactions to a widely known phenomenon and as evidence that individuals situate themselves within, around and against this discourse in the process of life planning. This attends the theoretical concern of this chapter by providing insights into dilemmas of individualisation in the PRC.

I adopt *Zhihu* as the field site for this research as it represents a space where questioning netizens can spontaneously post questions and give answers on a public platform.[6] Questions can be tagged to topic-relevant categories by any user. One of the subcategories of questions on *Zhihu* is '*shengnü*' which, as of 1 April 2017, had 1142 questions tagged and was followed by 5866 users. A translation of the *Zhihu* questions analysed here can be found in Appendix 1. I have provided the 'title' question (but not the extended 'subsidiary' text which can be much longer) and assigned each question a number. The 'title' questions are short, mostly a sentence.

For ease of reading, I mark the questions analysed as, for example, Q1 indicating 'Question 1' listed in the Appendix to this chapter, rather than give a full reference to the original post in each mention. Because it cannot be guaranteed that each question was written by a specific individual (rather than say, friends working together to write and revise the question before posting it), I refer throughout to the specific questions, rather than the individuals who have written the question; yet by necessity I assume that the authors are, as they claim, single women, and use gendered pronouns which reflect this assumption.

The questions are presented here in English but have been analysed from the original Mandarin Chinese; though the subsidiary text is not included in the appendix, it formed the core of the Chinese-language analysis. Language is partly why the sample size is small: Chinese is a heavily context-dependant language in any situation, frequently enriched by literary allusions and cultural idioms. This is intensified online where netizens deploy shorthand (e.g. the number five, *wu*, often acts as a homophone for crying, as the word 'crying' is also pronounced *wu:* a sympathetic post may simply read '55555555555'), and culturally specific memes, including memes designed to evade China's hawkish online surveillance (Meng 2011). Finally, online posts tend not to be thoroughly proofread and are prone to typographical errors. In short, to fully understand questions and the subtlety of language is an act of deep reading through multiple cultural and linguistic layers. Choosing a small sample to understand thoroughly invites a richer and more informed analysis than of a larger sample in this case.

Following Recuber's (2017) digital discourse methodology, I conducted an initial sweep of questions tagged to the *shengnü* subtopic on *Zhihu*, and purposively selected ten questions posted by different users between 2012 and 2018. I focussed on questions to explore the dilemmas that troubled women in their own words in order to understand how they framed the 'pains' of love and the architecture of choice in contemporary Chinese marriage markets. This is important as Illouz (2012) explains that the 'pain' of love is timeless, but how it manifests itself is the core of the emerging modern Self: understanding how women experience these pains then becomes a window through which to understand

Chinese modernity. I therefore selected questions based on the following criteria:

1. Questions written by users identifying as single women (*danshen*) or as leftover women (*shengnü*), to address the research interest by exploring the questions single women have about their own status and what they feel is important in this context;
2. Questions which suggest conflicted feelings in order to address the theoretical consideration of the chapter by seeking out tension between individualisation and the persistence of family as an institution in which the state seeks to keep individuals deeply embedded;
3. Questions which attracted a lot of attention, and those which attracted very little; while there is no formal attempt here to rigorously compare between widely answered questions and barely answered questions, the selection was motivated by a curiosity about whether 'popular' and 'unpopular' questions were markedly different in content or presentation. The main observation that has come from this is that questions which are shorter, less detailed and give less emotional content from the author tend to receive fewer responses from the *Zhihu* community. The sample of ten questions analysed here range from long to short questions, from popular to unpopular.

I follow Recuber in selecting a small sample of questions and arguing for the 'transferability' rather than 'generalizability' of my findings (2017: 51). Key to this approach is the transparency of the small case selection and limitations and arguing that the findings can be compared across research (web)sites (Recuber 2017: 52–55).

The ten questions selected for analysis range in the author's self-identification as 'leftover'; their stated relationship status; their age; and their employment status. Only two questions use the term *shengnü* to describe their own situation. Q2 ironically states that in the eyes of the public she a 'proper' leftover woman, though her tone suggests that she desires to contradict the 'picky' connotations of this label. By contrast, Q10 labels herself an older *shengnü*. This question is also different from the others in this sample in that the author clearly states that she is unemployed, and that what she really wants is to get married and have children.

All other nine questions in the sample specify that the author is either in employment or education, and do not mention childrearing as a goal. Of the ten questions analysed, four described past relationships or discussed relationships they were leaving at the risk of becoming 'leftover'; four self-declared never being in a relationship and two did not detail their own relationship status.

Findings

A thematic analysis brought out key emotions described in the sampled *Zhihu* questions, revealing that emotional risks (of future loneliness and wretchedness) are juxtaposed against financial risks (of future destitution), complicated by a need for familial approval. All questions in the sample present a fear for the future, even when inquiring about a present dilemma, which motivates the decision to solicit advice on a public forum. Questions frequently ask for, for example, 'an able person to put me on the right path' (Q1). Advice is sought in the face of a 'vast and perplexing' future (Q6) as individuals seek to colonise their future life with planning and expert advice (Giddens 1991).

The risk that overshadows all of the questions raised is emotional, rather than explicitly financial, and can be analysed along three axes: loneliness, wretchedness and the pursuit of love (*ai'qing*). A successful relationship premised on intimacy is framed as a strong guarantor against the risk of misery, particularly in old age. Backing this is the idea that the active pursuit of love is what a well-adjusted individual must do in order to achieve the outcome that the traditional kin network would have secured when arranged marriage was legal; indeed as Zhang and Sun (2014) document, many Chinese parents still maintain that it is their duty to assist their children in this pursuit.

Loneliness

The pursuit of a partner to forestall old age loneliness is a dominant theme, rather than the traditional fear of childlessness in old age.[7] Q1 worries about 'loneliness and isolation' (*gudan jumo*) and the 22-year-old writer of Q4 frets that her last years will be spent in a 'lonely and solitary' state (*gudu zhonglao*) but neither specify what is meant by loneliness; in a later edit she makes to her original post, Q4's author says she is still afraid 'that this state [of singlehood] will continue without end'. Neither question entertains the possibility of wider networks of friendship to alleviate loneliness in old age, framing their choice as binary: marriage or loneliness. The threat of loneliness posed here is shaped as attempts by the writers to identify strategies of self-enrichment through their decision-making at this stage in their career of intimacy. Loneliness motivates self-reflection and personal consideration of the sexual capital the writer judges their self to possess, in ways resonant with Illouz's findings. Q4 edited her question a year later from the original posting, commenting that the situation had not changed and that although 'I really am pretty commonplace (*pingyong*)', she was nevertheless 'improving' and considering buying a cat. As Lahad comments 'the unmarried woman is regularly stereotyped as lonely, miserable and with no alternative but to fill her empty life with cats' (2017: 55); it is possible that Q4's author is choosing to self-reflexively opt into this stereotype as an 'owning' of her undesired single status.

This question and the others which project a lonely future based on current singlehood embody a self-reflexive building of a life trajectory (Giddens 1991: 73–77) which links the specific past of the self to the future, where 'self-actualisation is understood in terms of a *balance between opportunity and risk*' (Giddens 1991: 76, emphasis original). The balance of risk is centred on the experience of the self as desirable (Illouz 2012: 41ff), and the strategies employed are intended to either increase the self's desirability (hence appealing for help to understand why they are single, so better to address the problem) or to seek out new anchors for self-worth through other, less unpredictable forms of affection (pet ownership).

As discussed in the next section, the possibility of negative outcomes is fully recognised and, particularly the younger authors of these *Zhihu* questions, individuals are seeking to reflexively identify their weaknesses and inform the choices they have to make to prevent loneliness and misery. This introspection and fear of future loneliness is rightly complicated by Illouz who points out the contradiction between the image of a self-actualising individual who changes over time and the static 'promise' of eternal commitment to another changing, mutable individual (2012: 98ff.). In parallel, singlehood demands continually renewed self-improvement strategies over time to cure the chief love pain of eternal loneliness.

Wretchedness

Q1 and Q5 both ask if their situation is, or could become, 'wretched' or 'miserable' (*can*). The difference is quite marked between the questions; Q1 is comparing between her older women friends' belief that 'women must have a family!' to her peers, who seem unbothered by marriage due to their economic security. She is worried that making the wrong choice now and being 'picky' about her choice of man will make her miserable in old age, as her seniors predict. In contrast Q5 asks bluntly, 'I'm 20 years old and I've never dated. Is that wretched?' She wants know if she *should* be worried, if she is already lost, even though she is a good seven years away from 'officially' qualifying as 'leftover'. The responses posted to her question seem flippant but unequivocal, with commenters stating, for example, that 'it is more wretched to have no money'. Indeed, the attitude of needing either love or money (but preferably both) to have a happy life is a running theme through the replies and is echoed in the tension between 'family' and 'career' that is present in the majority of questions (see also Guha, this volume, Chap. 10). The possibility of anchoring self-worth through economic rather than emotional success is offered up as an unequal alternative: while financial security secures basic needs, emotional security should offer both emotional *and* basic needs. Unlike poverty in singlehood, poverty in marriage (and more particularly, parenthood) offers access to forms of state welfare which are precluded by childlessness, and marriage is the gatekeeper to parenting (see discussion above). The questions and responses analysed are not so naïve as to suggest marriage as a solution to poverty, but closely connect these two experiences under the umbrella of forms of wretchedness. This experience of love pain challenges the class blindness of some of Illouz's analysis (Klesse 2014).

The highly reflexive practice of questioning future happiness emerges in a post-traditional order in which choices within constraints *must* be made in light of new flexibility and availability of information, and successful choice-making is facilitated by wealth. However, having no money does not remove the need to make choices and to plan, as shown by the distraught writer of Q10 who asks 'how can life continue?' in the face of her singlehood, age of 29 and unemployment. The active telling of her life history as a poor, and now unemployed, migrant worker demonstrate a 'reflexive shaping of self-identity' which, in the context of such suffering means that the making of choices she is faced with is 'an almost insupportable burden, a source of despair rather than self-enrichment' (Giddens 1991: 86). This question is unusual in the sample (and in wider understanding of *shengnü*) due to the author's self-declared poor, migrant status. However she faces the same issues as her richer, urban sisters and deploys the language of being 'leftover' to communicate her dilemma. In Illouz's language of the sexual field, this question reflects the author's lack of 'sexiness', and low sexual capital. Across several of the questions analysed here, the authors go out of their way to state that they are 'ordinary looking' in effect. However, while sexual appeal in modernity is 'an autonomous criterion for selection of a mate' (Illouz 2012: 54) in the Chinese context at least this sexiness is determined by life choices beyond physical appearance, and must be understood in the matrix of family as the central pillar of welfare, hence the swift financial commentary given by many commenters to these questions.

The quasi-interchangeability of a good financial footing and a secure family life is not painted so simply as to suggest that happiness can be bought, but a persistent theme is found to the effect that, so long as you have money, then at least wretchedness can be averted. Financial security on the individualised job market is earmarked as the primary goal in this dyad, perhaps because it may seem as more achievable as one can do more to prepare for a job than a marriage; it is easier to change jobs and upgrade them; the figure of 'destiny' is less central to employment than romance, and so on. The tension evident in these findings resonates strongly with Illouz's (2007) work on emotional capitalism in which she argues that the practices of finding a partner have come more and more to resemble finding a desirable job. However, while employment trajectories increasingly improve with regular changes in jobs, and changing career is increasingly possible even later in life, relationships are more hedged by the desire for stability and commitment. This is particularly the case for women and the potential for women's bodies to be 'spoiled' by 'use' (Xie 2018 and this volume, Chap. 9).

Love

Of the ten questions analysed here, four make no mention of romantic emotions, three directly refer to 'love' (*aiqing*) or 'dating' (*tan lian'ai*), and three use the more euphemistic terms such as 'like' (*xihuan*) or 'cultivate emotions' (*peiyang ganqing*). Q2 reflects a dilemma: the author is 29 and is seeing a man for whom she has no strong feelings but with whom, conscious of her age, she has persevered. Yet despite her efforts, she cannot seem to 'cultivate emotions' for this man. Her question is whether she should continue the relationship. The expression 'cultivate emotions' harkens back to the 1950s' government marriage campaigns which encouraged couples already in arranged marriages to aim for a form of friendship in marriage rather than using the new legal right to divorce to seek love (Friedman 2005: 320). The author of Q2's difficulty in reconciling her willingness to compromise on a romantic match with the lived reality of spending a lifetime with someone for whom she does not experience at least *some* romantic feelings founders her stoic attempt at compromise. This difficulty is matched in Q1, which notes that the author's peers are unwilling to marry someone who will 'drag them down'; and in Q8 who says she simply wants to meet her 'other half' in the course of living her own life, and then asks if she should change her attitude. The attitude of the friends of the author of Q8 is indicative of the modern need for romance to validate the self, and to constitute self-worth (Illouz 2012: 119) rather than the 'traditional' impetus to settle down quickly. In modern terms, the willingness to settle for an 'other half' suggests then either low self-worth or the continued option of a second, older frame for romance framed around the cultivation of emotion for the sake of wider family.

By contrast, Q3 and Q5 explicitly draw on the romantic term to '*tan lian'ai*' which translates clumsily to 'dating', the process of testing romantic waters before committing to lifelong partnership. Q6's author writes of a man who has broken up with her despite his declaration that he 'really loved' her and that he had 'pledged undying love'. These explicit framings of love read less as instrumental pursuits of a relationship as financial and emotional security (in contrast to the fear of wretchedness), and more like the construction of a pure relationship in Giddens' sense, or a pillar of self-worth in Illouz's sense. It is not the 'demand for love' that is the key issue, but the use of love as a 'codifying force organising the character' of the relationship (Giddens 1991: 91) that is striking. Unlike a purely instrumental marriage of either convenience, or of instrumental value, the drive to 'cultivate' feelings or to start a relationship because of existing feelings is the *raison d'être* of the whole endeavour.

Of the four questions which make no mention of love there is instead a construction of 'lifestyle' in the sense of having had to choose a set of practices as an expression of self-identity. For example, Q7 mentions her work and her 'improving' hobbies (learning English, working out) and Q8 feels that going on blind dates is 'not her style' and that she instead is focussed on getting a raise at work. There is a connection between love as an organising construct for a relationship and the development of lifestyles focussed around career achievements which can be explored through a reflexivity of self: these women are asking questions which reflect their struggle of shaping their identity, and of generating sources of self-worth independent of romance. Q2 and Q10 both self-report as 29-year-olds and label themselves as *shengnü* but they appeal very differently to love as a framework. Q2 is calling off a relationship which has failed to cultivate feelings, whereas Q10 is desperately wondering how to continue a life without marriage or employment. For Q2, the lack of emotion cannot outweigh the reduction of risk of being 'leftover' that comes with breaking up. Yet for Q10, emotion seems entirely secondary to a feeling of total despair discussed earlier, and the need to address one or the other, or both, of her sources of identity urgently to bring meaning to her project of self.

Discussion: *'But My Family Is Anxious'*

The role of the parents of unmarried Chinese women in their late 20s in intensifying the pressure between work and mate selection is well documented (see particularly To 2015a). Four of the sampled *Zhihu* questions directly mention their family's expectations, mostly couched in terms of anxiety. Family anxiousness is raised in conflict with a decision to end a loveless relationship (Q2) or long-term singlehood (Q10, Q8) but in this sample, it is not the engine of conflict. Instead the conflict is framed as being powered by the contradictions between the marriage market and job market; of the pursuit of intimacy (emotional security) and the prospect of a career (financial security). Both paths lead to self-realisation, whereas parental anxiousness instead speaks of non-individualised obligation. Women's compliance with their parents' interventions in their relationship issues has been taken by some authors to be signs of 'traditional' attitudes (To 2015a: 143) in a way which perhaps challenges Illouz's (2012) argument that the emotional, managerial self is constitutive of a society's modernity. Instead, I argue rather than tradition, this strategy is better captured by Yan's (2016) analysis of 'descending familism' which posits that filial piety has been re-orientated around the adult child, rather than the traditional focus on the eldest generation. This retains the PRC's modernity in Illouz's sense, as the adult self is here still emotional and self-actualising, constituting a deregulated, individualised modernity, but gives it cultural specificity by demanding recognition that the governance of self is done in conversation with governance by family.

Yan (2016) has documented how adult children have successfully labelled their own happiness as an act of filial piety towards their parents, as it reduces the amount parents have to worry about them. Contra to a 'return' to tradition, he argues that this is a sign of intensifying individualisation as the state seeks to limit the 're-embedment' of individuals in anything that might emerge as a threat to the state, leaving 'the disembedded individual stand[ing] alone, between the mighty powers of the state and the market' (Yan 2016: 252) with no one to turn to but the family. Based on the discussion presented here, while I agree with Yan's diagnosis of deepening individualisation, I would argue that the state has taken meaningful steps to ensure that the individual is still embedded in the *nuclear* family as a unit by which the state can maintain effective regulation of individual behaviour, while still avoiding funded social policy welfare measures. In evidence for this I point to the revival of strong Confucian discourses (even if the content of signifiers like 'filial piety' have had new content poured into them) and the continued use of formal laws and policies to bind an individual's life trajectory to their family fortunes, as discussed above. This manifests in the continued parental investment in their adult children's marriage prospects and stands apart from the self-realisation project of pure relationships. However, unlike Barbalet (2016) who rejects the individualisation hypothesis on the back of evidence of collective decision-making at the family level, I witness the *Zhihu* questions as anchoring the reflexive self as the final decision maker: women seek advice from experienced others on their life plans and lifestyle choices, centring on their emotional self. This behaviour emerges in response to a society that has, to a large degree, made the family (*not* the individual) the responsible institution for mitigating the risk of old age insecurity. The women interrogate their future as an autonomous agent in a maze of individualised choices, into which they must factor their parents and their future selves as parents.

The seeming autonomy of choice-making in intimacy is deceptive as it paints an independent, reflexive self, navigating choices within constraints set by markets and gender norms. Yet there is a persistent preoccupation with family in these *Zhihu* questions and an acknowledgement that the outcomes of these decisions impact beyond the trajectory of the self. This preoccupation cannot quite be captured by Beck and Beck-Gernsheim's description of an 'altruistic individualism' (2002: 162; To 2015b) which reiterates that, in the same way Durkheim identifies greater interdependence in regimes of high divisions of labour, those in individualised societies must cooperate more. Legal provision for old age care provided by adult children, for example, is not altruistic and cannot be negotiated through life planning or decision-making. The state has tied its individuals to the lifeboat of family by the continuation of the family's institutionalised role in key welfare provision roles. Likewise, filial piety, even if focussed on adult children, cannot be understood as a simple choice or a constraint but must be recognised as a system of obligation and opportunity into which individuals are born. The nuclear family anchors urban, successful women facing the individualisation of risk for their future financial security and emotional equilibrium into a structure of traditional values against the backdrop of modern aspirations.

Conclusion

This chapter contributes a new analysis of the stigma of female adult singlehood in the PRC by drawing on the hypothesis of individualisation of intimacy. Exploring single women's questions about their relationship prospects demonstrates that they are experiencing individualisation of intimacy and that they are to a large degree disembedded from old structures of kinship. However, I argue that the state has maintained embedding mechanisms to tie individuals in the institution of the nuclear family, which still functions as a significant guarantor of welfare in mainland China, particularly for care provision. Therefore Yan's (2016) analysis of descending familism holds when extended to explore the *shengnü* stigma but, I argue, should be amended to take into consideration the state's persistent policy manoeuvres that keep the family firmly in the frame for individual decision-making and life planning.

The reflexivity embodied in the questions posted to online forums reveals relationships to be increasingly valued for themselves as Giddens-esque pure relationships, rather than as instrumental to other means: to the point that relationships can be dispensed with, in the eyes of some, in favour of financial security which would enable the individual to provide for herself and her family independently. However, this financial 'get-out' clause from family points to the crucial welfare and care role that the family plays, and which can only be bought out of by the most financially successful. Within this framework we can see women's questions about their decision-making as a choices made under constraints, where women become stigmatised by their lifestyle choices, understood as the reflexivity of self, demonstrated by life planning in modernity. The central emergence of a desiring and desirable self, in line with Illouz's analysis of love pains in modernity is echoed in a fear of 'wretchedness' which ties the pains of love to the pains of poverty, pointing to a class dimension that is perhaps deeper than what Illouz's analysis of sexual capital and social mobility can account for. The market of marriage choices may make mate selection 'cold' and rational but the experience of a culture of compulsory coupledom makes the urgency of intimacy 'steely', state-mandated and compulsory. Within this architecture of choice, determined by uncertain futures within a welfare regime which changes a-democratically to adapt to market needs, romance in mainland China has become a painful source of self-worth and of modern anxieties about selfhood while retaining the traditional pain of suffering for love in the context of family obligation.

Appendix

Translations of the questions analysed
Zhihu data correct as of: 04/04/2018

Q1. Must women marry and start a family? Is it really miserable to be a single woman in old age?
https://www.zhihu.com/question/28480369/answers/created

Q2. I am a leftover woman, facing a boyfriend that I've never had any feelings for, what should I do?
https://www.zhihu.com/question/35938530/answers/created

Q3. Single for a long time, should I despair of love?
https://www.zhihu.com/question/26376529/answers/created

Q4. I'm 22 years old and I think it's not possible for me to marry, what should I do?
https://www.zhihu.com/question/23897077/answer/27514788

Q5. 20 years old and I've never fallen in love. Is that wretched?
https://www.zhihu.com/question/265662723/answer/297233777

Q6. I'm a 27-year-old female Masters student, is it really going to be hard to find a partner?
https://www.zhihu.com/question/55205246/answer/146881891

Q7. I am 27 this year, female. Due to a narrow circle of friends, and that all the people I come into contact with at work are women, I'm seeking ways I can break through my current [single] situation?
https://www.zhihu.com/question/48137877/answer/116000259

Q8. 26-year-old single woman is just focusing on getting a good career, developing naturally, but family is worrying about marriage: Why?
https://www.zhihu.com/question/20484861/answer/28252599

Q9. I'm single woman and 25 years old. Should I study overseas or work here in China? Since the dawn of time, why is the biggest problem not how to study or work, but how to find a partner?
https://www.zhihu.com/question/28597021/answer/57126042

Q10. Older leftover woman without work, how can things continue like this?
https://www.zhihu.com/question/38990753/answer/79208472

Notes

1. The 'productivist state' is one in which state welfare such as health insurance is offered where it is anticipated to promote or protect economic growth (e.g. Hwang 2011).
2. Available: http://www.china.org.cn/china/LegislationsForm2001-2010/2011-02/11/content_21897930.htm. Accessed: 04/04/2018.
3. Available: http://www.china.org.cn/government/laws/2007-04/17/content_1207404.htm. Accessed: 04/04/2018.
4. This status can be changed through marriage or meeting the (typically financial and residential) criteria of the receiving area, but this is limited by quotas (Young 2013).
5. By 'urban' I refer specifically to women who have a household registration in an urban centre, rather than any women living in the cities; 'rural' likewise refers to registration, rather than physical location. For the complexities of China's household registration, or *hukou* system, see Young (2013).
6. This methodology does fall within the purview of the British Sociological Association's ethical guidelines for digital research, available online here: https://www.britsoc.co.uk/media/24309/bsa_statement_of_ethical_practice_annexe.pdf
7. The elderly childless are generally pitied in China, and were one of the core demographics identified as deserving of welfare in the 'Five Guarantee households' in the earliest building of state safety net in the People's Republic of China (Davis-Friedman 1991: 87–101).

References

An, B. (2018) Family binds nation, its people, Xi says. 22nd February 2018, *The China Daily*. http://www.chinadaily.com.cn/a/201802/22/WS5a8dfb08a3106e7dcc13d42a.html [Accessed 04/04/2018].

Andreas, J. (2009) *Rise of the red engineers: The Cultural Revolution and the origins of China's new class*. Stanford: Stanford University Press.

Barbalet, J. (2016) Chinese individualization, revisited. *Journal of Sociology,* 52 (1): 9–23.

Beck, U. (1992) *Risk society: Towards a new modernity*. London: Sage.

Beck, U. and Beck-Gernsheim, E. (2002) *Individualization: Institutionalized individualization and its social and political consequences*. London: Sage.

Chou, R. J.-A. (2011) Filial piety by contract? The emergence, implementation, and implications of the 'Family Support Agreement' in China. *The Gerontologist,* 51 (1): 3–16.

Davin, D. (1999) *Internal Migration in Contemporary China*. Cambridge: Polity Press.

Davis, D. and Friedman, S. (2014) *Wives, husbands and lovers: Marriage and sexuality in Hong Kong, Taiwan and Urban China*. Stanford: Stanford University Press.

Davis-Friedman, D. (1991) *Long lives: Chinese elderly and the communist revolution*. Stanford: Stanford University Press.

Feldshuh, H. (2017) Gender, media, and myth-making: Constructing China's leftover women. *Asian Journal of Communication,* 28 (1): 38–54.

Fong, V.L. (2004) *Only hope: Coming of age under China's one-child policy*. Stanford: Stanford University Press.

Friedman, S. (2005) The intimacy of state power: Marriage, liberation, and socialist subjects in southeastern China. *American Ethnologist* 32 (2): 312–327.

Gaetano, A. (2014) Leftover women: Postponing marriage and renegotiating womanhood in urban China. *Journal of Research in Gender Studies,* 4 (2): 124–149.

Giddens, A. (1991) *Modernity and self-identity: Self and society in the late modern age*. Cambridge: Polity Press.

Gillies, V. (2003) Family and intimate relationships: A review of the sociological research. *Families & Social Capital ESRC Research Group Working Paper No. 2*. South Bank University. http://www.lsbu.ac.uk/research/research-interests/sites/families-social-capital-research-group/working-papers-lectures. [Accessed 04/04/2018].

Glosser, S. (2003) *Chinese visions of family and state, 1915–1953*. Berkeley: University of California Press.

Goldstein, J. (2006) Introduction. In: Yue Dong, M. and Goldstein, J. (eds.) *Everyday Modernity in China*. Seattle: University of Washington Press: 3–21.

Greenhalgh, S. and Winckler, E. (2005) *Governing China's population: From Leninist to neoliberal biopolitics*. Stanford: Stanford University Press.

Heilmann, S. and Melton, O. (2013) The reinvention of development planning in China, 1993–2012. *Modern China*, 39 (6): 580–628.

Hong Fincher, L. (2014) *Leftover women*. London: Zed Books.

Honig, E. and Hershatter, G. (1988) *Personal voices: Chinese women in the 1980s*. Stanford: Stanford University Press.

Hwang, G. (2011) *New welfare states in East Asia: Global challenges and restructuring*. Cheltenham: Edward Elgar Publishing.

Illouz, E. (2007) *Cold intimacies: The making of emotional capitalism*. Cambridge: Polity Press.

Illouz, E. (2012) *Why love hurts: A sociological explanation*. Polity Press, Cambridge

Jamieson, L. (1999) Intimacy transformed? A critical look at the 'pure relationship.' *Sociology*, 33 (3): 477–494.

Jankowiak, W. and Li, X. (2017) Emergent conjugal love, mutual affection and female marital power. In: Santos, G. and Harrell, S. (eds.). *Transforming Patriarchy: Chinese families in the twenty-first century*. Seattle: University of Washington Press: 146–162.

Ji, Y. (2015) Between tradition and modernity: 'leftover' women in Shanghai. *Journal of Marriage and Family*, 77(October): 1057–1073.

Johnson, K.A. (2016) *China's hidden children: Abandonment, adoption and the human costs of the one-child policy*. Chicago: Chicago University Press.

Klesse, C. (2014) Book review: Why love hurts by Illouz. *The Sociological Review*, 62 (1): 224–226.

Kuan, T. (2015) *Love's uncertainty: The politics and ethics of child rearing in contemporary China*. California: University of California Press.

Lahad, K. (2017) *A table for one: A critical reading of singlehood, gender and time*. Manchester: University of Manchester Press.

Luo, W. and Sun, Z. (2014) Are you the one? China's TV dating shows and the *shengnü*'s predicament. *Feminist Media Studies*, 15 (2): 239–256.

Marres, N. (2017) *Digital Sociology*. Cambridge: Polity Press.

Meng, B. (2011) From steamed bun to grass mud horse: *E gao* as alternative political discourse on the Chinese internet. *Global Media and Communication* 7 (1): 33–51.

Qi, W., Dongchao, M. and Sørensen, B. Æ. (eds.) (2016) *Revisiting gender inequality: Perspectives from the People's Republic of China.* Basingstoke: Palgrave Macmillan.

Recuber, T. (2017) Digital Discourse Analysis: Finding meaning in small online space. In: Daniels, J., Gregory, K. and McMillan Cottom, T. (eds). *Digital Sociologies.* Cambridge: Polity Press: 47–60.

To, S. (2015a) *China's leftover women: Late marriage among professional women and its consequences.* London: Routledge.

To, S. (2015b) 'My mother wants me to *jiaru-haomen* (Marry into a rich and powerful family)!': Exploring pathways to 'altruistic individualism' in Chinese professional women's filial strategies of marital choice. *Sage Open* Jan-Feb: 1–11.

Wilkinson, E. (2012) The romantic imaginary: Compulsory coupledom and single existence. In: Hines, S. and Cooper, Y. (eds.) *Sexualities: Past reflections and future directions.* London: Palgrave: 130–145.

Williamson, J.B., Fang, L. and Calvo, E. (2017) Rural pension reform in China: A critical analysis. *Journal of Aging Studies*, 41: 67–74.

Wei, L. and Zhen, S. (2014) Are you the one? China's TV dating shows and the *shengnü*'s predicament. *Feminist Media Studies*, 15 (2): 1–18.

Xie, K. (2018) Premarital abortion – What is the harm: The responsibilisation of women's pregnancy among China's 'privileged' daughters. *Journal of the British Association for Chinese Studies* 8 (1): 1–31.

Yan, Y. (2003) *Private life under socialism: Love, intimacy and family change in a Chinese village, 1949–1999.* Stanford: Stanford University Press.

Yan, Y. (2008) Introduction: Understanding the rise of the individual in China. *European Journal of East Asian Studies*, 7 (1): 1–9.

Yan, Y. (2010) The Chinese path to individualization. *British Journal of Sociology,* 61 (3): 203–229.

Yan, Y. (2016) Intergenerational intimacy descending familism in rural North China. *American Anthropologist* 118 (2): 244–257.

Young, J. (2013) *China's hukou system: Markets, migrants and institutional change.* Cambridge: Polity Press.

Zhang, J. and Sun, P. (2014) When are you going to get married? Parental matchmaking and middle-class women in contemporary Urban China. In: Davis, D. and Friedman, S. (eds.) *Wives, husbands and lovers: Marriage and sexuality in Hong Kong, Taiwan, and Urban China.* Stanford: Stanford University Press: 118–144.

Zhao, J. (2015) China and the Uneasy Case for Universal Human Rights. *Human Rights Quarterly*, 37 (1): 29–52.

Zheng, J. (2019) Doing gender in commodification of courtship and dating: Understanding Women's experiences of attending commercialized match-making activities in China. *Frontiers: A Journal of Women Studies*, 40 (1):176–199.

9

Chasing Happiness: The Role of Marriage in the Aspiration of Success Among China's Middle-Class Women

Kailing Xie

Introduction

Chinese society over the last four decades has gone through profound social and economic changes initiated by the party-state's major policy shifts, such as dismantling the socialist planned economy to develop a market economy overseen by the state, as well as implementing the controversial One Child Policy. The process of marketisation led by the party-state has generated an average of 10 per cent GDP growth per year since the early 1990s, which has profoundly transformed the very social fabric within which individuals conduct their lives. In particular, some scholars (Halskov Hansen and Svarverud 2010; Yan 2009, 2010; Moore 2005) have contended that there is a growing individualisation across all sections of Chinese society, from the changing perceptions of the individual to rising expectations for individual freedom, choice and individuality.

K. Xie (✉)
University of Warwick, Coventry, UK
e-mail: Kailing.Xie@warwick.ac.uk

© The Author(s) 2020
J. Carter, L. Arocha (eds.), *Romantic Relationships in a Time of 'Cold Intimacies'*,
Palgrave Macmillan Studies in Family and Intimate Life,
https://doi.org/10.1007/978-3-030-29256-0_9

It is against this backdrop that a unique generation of urban women born as the only child in their family have grown up, living in the 'third world' but enjoying the first-world consumption standard bred by their family expectation to succeed (Croll 2006; Fong 2004). By the time the One Child Policy was replaced by the Two Child Policy in 2016, the first only-child generation born in the 1980s had reached the age of marriage, pregnancy and establishing a career. Based on data collected from a study investigating the gendered lives of China's privileged daughters—well-educated, urbanite women working in white-collar professions born in the 1980s' one-child generation—this chapter looks into the marriage aspirations of urban university-educated women. As part of China's rising middle class (Hird 2008; Liu 2008), I analyse their romantic choice in light of an ideal spouse for marriage to uncover their understandings of love and pathways to obtain it. By sketching out the structural constraints remaining in place, I examine the conditions within which romantic choices are made by drawing some comparison with Illouz's (2012) analysis of Western society to shed light on why women make certain choices to find love and why love hurts for these women in contemporary Chinese society. This chapter presents empirical evidence to uncover the complex meanings of romantic love and gender inequalities in China, which makes marriage based on romantic love a struggle for women's pursuit of happiness.

Methods

Adopting a feminist approach, this research uses qualitative in-depth interviews to make the individual's case visible and make the rich description of women's own experiences and interpretations possible (Rubin and Rubin 2012). Snowball sampling methods through existing social networks were used, which has proven effective in China's relation-based society (Liu 2007). In total, I carried out interviews with 31 women and 11 men in 2015, who self-identified as heterosexual. All of my participants were university educated and were in full-time employment in various white-collar professions, such as schoolteachers, bank managers, government employees and office staff in private firms. At the time of interview, they were between 25 and 35 years old, and were at various life stages, including those who were single, in a relationship, married without children, married with children, two pregnant mothers and one divorced mother. All names mentioned here are pseudonyms picked by participants themselves. Apart from those who are marked as male, the rest are female.

The Necessity of Love Marriage of Free Choice

Compared to the 'embryonic state' of Western romantic love in 1920s' China (Pan 2015), when the relationship was neither free nor equal, today's younger generation seems to have fully taken the concept of romantic love on board (Farrer 2014; Zhang and Sun 2014). One iconic marker of increased individual choice since the economic reform is the emergence of the so-called sexual revolution, where Pan (1994) observed some well-educated women started to take romantic love as their major sexual purpose. Zhang (2011) contends that China's sexual revolution has gone through three stages: the re-emergence of romantic love in the 1980s after the Cultural Revolution, the awakening of female desires in the 1990s and the new millennium's pleasure-centred sexual practices to enhance individual happiness. Sexual intimacy is increasingly realised outside of wedlock, through one-night stands and cohabitation, as well as non-heterosexual relationships. Romantic love, containing both sex and intensive emotions, is hot in the air, especially among the young, which resembles what Illouz (2012) described as the sexualisation of romantic choices in modern society.

However, romantic love as a one-off fling is not the most desirable object to be obtained according to my female participants. Instead, it is the relationships that could lead to the happily-ever-after which carry the most powerful allure, since these promise to preserve romantic excitement into a stable future. Meanwhile, distinct from previous generations, young couples are increasingly becoming emotionally expressive (Evans 2010). Zheng's (2017) examination of young Chinese women's mate selection also shows that the desire for affection is a central concern, in contrast to the traditional meaning of marriage as the means to survival and merely about providing mundane daily support (Pan 1994). Research on Chinese youth finds that 'true love' is understood as both emotionally expressing one's passionate feelings and a long-term commitment through marriage (Jankowiak and Moore 2012; Farrer 2014). My participants reaffirm such belief in 'true love', which holds a stable happily married family as the most socially desirable life trajectory for themselves, despite the fact that many struggle to fulfil it.

One of the factors that contributed to love's transformation in postmodern individualised society diagnosed by Illouz (2012) is the normative deregulation in the mode of evaluation of prospective partners. When family is no longer in charge of matchmaking for marriage, the individuals gain far more freedom to make their own romantic choices. This individualisation of the criteria of choice of a mate does occur in the Chinese context as well. China's ruling party, the Chinese Communist Party (CCP), since its coming to power in 1949, has issued marriage law that guarantees individuals' right to freely choose their own marriage partner as opposed to allowing parents to matchmake for their children, as in the country's feudal past (Evans 1997). This has significantly reduced parental power over their children, as the party gradually replaced parental authority in individuals' lives, especially under socialism (Parish and Whyte 1978). Since romantic love made its comeback in the 1980s, love marriage of free choice has become a cultural ideal among urban Chinese citizens (Zhang and Sun 2014). Being able to select one's own partner becomes an important marker of being a modern, autonomous self.

During my interviews, participants commonly used language that reflected the importance of the emotional and psychological compatibility, as well as sexual attraction when describing their ideal marriage partner: 'In terms of our thinking and life pursuit, we can generate sparkles and reach consensus with each other, an EQ and IQ match' (Stella); 'We're willing to support each other to chase our dreams, which are not in conflict with each other' (Lixiong, male). Though often described in subtle manners, a potential partner's 'sexiness' that can stir up 'intensive feelings' that would make one 'fall' in love (Maris) is frequently referred to as an important criteria. Similarly, Chain states: '[P]ersonality match is essential, as well as bodily match [laughed]'.

The language used above shows a clear tendency among my participants to apply more subjective criteria to selecting a compatible mate. In this regard, one could argue that the conception of love has been transformed to some extent, which resembles what Illouz (2012: 41) described as 'the sexualisation and psychologization of romantic choices'. What makes the Chinese case different from its postmodern individualised Western counterparts is the co-existence of the traditional moral framework built within family structures and upheld by the state, which functions as a powerful institution to regulate individuals' romantic choice to conform to one standard in the marriage market. In addition, the ongoing class transformation requires individuals' constant self-monitoring to avoid downward social mobility. As a result, individuals' romantic choice, instead of being completely individualised, needs to fit into a world of publicly shared values with others, in order to complete validation of one's self-worth in Chinese society.

The Pressure to Commit

Enshrined by the 1950 Marriage Law, since the beginning of CCP's rule as the central pillar of its explicit goal of gender equality, the universality of heterosexual monogamous marriage has not been a choice for private enjoyment but an obligation to serve the interests of society as a whole (Evans 1997, 2002; McMillan 2006). From giving explicit advice to young people about marriage and love in the 1950s, to giving nearly no advice on such topics during the Cultural Revolution (1966–1976), the state's intention has aimed to ensure that the youth have the correct sexual morality and attitude that fits into its political priority of the time. Dramatic social and economic changes have not shaken the foundation of heterosexual marriage as a governing institution in China. Heterosexual family has consistently been viewed as 'the cell of the society' (Sigley 2001). Its role as the most reliable welfare provider for individuals has only been strengthened since the state's dismantling of the socialist welfare regime under market reform (Qi 2016).

What shifted since the reform is the discourse around marriage and family. The state with its controlled media joined with market forces to rebrand a particular type of family: a happy complete heterosexual family (美满家庭, *mei man jia ting*), as a desirable object for the masses to pursue. Nowadays, the state encourages married couples to master sexual knowledge for sexual satisfaction, since it is considered beneficial for promoting modernisation and social stability by avoiding family breakdown (Wong 2016). Meanwhile, family is promoted to embody certain 'traditional values' substantiated by the Confucian discourse, such as filial piety and harmony, elevated as a moral exemplar for responsible citizenship (Zhuang 2012). These values are also enforced by Chinese law, which states that it is adult children's duty to provide care for their parents (Qi 2015). Family carries social responsibilities not only to care for its rapidly ageing population, but also to mitigate public risks posed by low birth rate with a severely imbalanced sex ratio (Wang 2010; Bell 2010). Moreover, it also becomes a site for consumption and displaying personal success acknowledged by wider society. Consequently, a sexually content, economically productive and socially reproductive heterosexual family is promoted as the modern ideal by the Party-state.

Tying individuals' future welfare to one's offspring encourages people to have children. Importantly, marriage remains the only 'right' place for childrearing and single motherhood is frowned upon and practically difficult (Xie 2018). At the same time, reproduction is naturalised for Chinese women as 'a psychological instinct' (McMillan 2006: 69). Widespread eugenic discourses exacerbate pressures women feel to comply with the reproductive norm (Xie 2019). Voluntary childlessness within marriage is often interpreted as a mistake for the woman: 'She will surely regret it when she gets older' (Lulu). Therefore, marriage becomes an ever-increasing necessity, if childbirth is anticipated. Not to mention the importance of carrying on patriarchal lineage exacerbated by the Only Child policy, where parents of both boys and girls are eager to participate in their only child's marriage and reproductive decisions (Xie 2019). Understandably, some anxious Chinese parents have taken to public parks to matchmake their children (Zarafonetis 2017).

The state-engineered public desire to marry also relies on placing women at the centre of its disciplinary control. Since a Chinese woman's self has historically been shaped by her relational positioning to others, within a hierarchical order formed under a long Confucian patriarchal and patrilineal family tradition, the party-state has long assumed Chinese women's dual roles as worker and mother in its policymaking to build a strong nation (Evans 1997). Hong-Fincher (2014, 2018) argues that the state deliberately pressures well-educated middle-class women to marry and give birth in order to procreate a strong stable high-quality nation with the lowest public cost, as reflected in the stigmatisation of single women as 'leftover' in the state media (see Lamont, this volume, Chap. 8). Unsurprisingly, young women's individual freedom is under constant renegotiation with traditional ideologies.

China's newly found individualism from the very moment of its birth is under the powerful grip of the state, which has been actively trying to curtail certain individual desires unleashed by the market and bring it back under its control through various propagandas and policies. For instance, individualism is frequently condemned as 'Western' and collective language charged with national pride, such as 'rejuvenation of Chinese nation' and 'promoting traditional Chinese values', are deployed to discipline Chinese society (Cao and Huang 2018; Zhao 2005; Ong 1997). 'Socialism with Chinese characteristics', the official name the Chinese state use to describe its state-led marketisation, is an attempt to establish greater state control over freewheeling capitalism to build a strong Chinese state. Steele and Lynch (2013) point out that there has existed an intrinsic ideological tension between individualistic pursuit for personal benefits underpinning capitalism and the socialist promotion of the good of the collective over the individual. The intimacy of state power is premised on forging individuals as certain gendered subjects fitting into its designed modern nation (Friedman 2005). Unlike the highly individualised forms of late-modern selfhood posited by theorists of late modernity such as Giddens (1991) and Beck and Beck-Gernsheim (2001), without a long history of individualism, Chinese women's individualistic dreams of autonomy 'often co-exist with more traditional projects' (Jackson 2011: 23). The tension created by contradicting ideologies is acutely reflected among sufferings experienced by middle-class women's romantic pursuit for marital bliss.

The rampant rise of consumerism in Chinese society has sold the public the idea that the capacity to consummate romance through marriage constitutes a woman's self-worth in the market economy (Wen 2013). As

Tong notes: '[N]o matter how successful you are in your career, without a loving husband and children, people would always think you somehow failed as a woman'. In a society that is going through rapid transformations on many fronts, Chinese women's desire for social recognition as a uniquely valued person compels them to find love before it is 'too late', which exacerbates the marriage pressure they experience. Such pressure is widely expressed among my participants. With the state's continued reliance on family to realise its political agenda, individuals' desire to find commitment in marriage is created by both the external social structure illustrated above and the prevalence of romantic ideology sold by a capitalist market. It is the condition of the marriage market, within which these women are striving to succeed, we shall now turn to, in order to understand their romantic sufferings in the Chinese context.

Performing in the Markets

According to Illouz, the forming of the marriage market means that in a postmodern individualised society,

> the process of choosing a mate becomes defined by the dynamic of taste: that is, it becomes the result of the compatibility of two highly differentiated individuals, each looking for specific attributes in a free and unconstrained way. (2012: 52)

Individuals are placed to face overt competition with others like in a market, where different attributes of a person could be traded. In principle, it would mean everyone's choices are expanded both horizontally and vertically since there exists no formalised mechanism that restricts one's choice within certain social classes and groups.

As much as the individual attributes increasingly appear as significant in my participants description of an ideal partner as discussed above, what equally matters in their narratives is the importance of matching social ranking (门当户对, *men dang hu dui*), which could literally be translated as matching doors and windows. It indicates that a partner's 'objective standing', including education, family background, occupation and financial status, still matter, if not even more so in a society where volatile class reformations are still ongoing under marketisation and people are fearful of downward social mobility (Zurndorfer 2016). Women interviewed deployed their cultural capital, such as education (degree level, intellectual capability and smartness), morality (values and beliefs) and taste (common interests) as markers to describe the type of men they would feel comfortable falling in love with. Chain's answer sums up my participants' views of a good match:

> [M]atching doors and windows makes them compatible...I think a similar background means that their education, family and tastes match, which gives a greater chance of matching or similar values and lifestyle. But without mutual affection there is no way people can live together in the long term.

Such accounts reveal that class-coded identity markers are deployed to select a good match through the language of compatibility. This indicates the formal mechanism of selecting one's mate according to their social ranking is not entirely dissolved but is becoming internalised by the individual and justified differently. Matching one's social ranking, for my participants, is often articulated as being for the sake of compatibility, which is to ensure the lasting of romantic love in marriage.

Compatibility for these women does not only mean unique individualised personal attributes as Illouz (2012) observed in the West, but is also used to emphasise the importance of class-coded value-match, whereby an emotional bond can be formed and maintained. It shows that individuals' romantic choices are also bound by their class position, which makes their pool of choice less vertically open than Illouz (2012) has argued. Similarly, Johnson and Lawler's (2005) examination of romantic relationships in contemporary Britain also demonstrates that relationships can become the very site in which class is 'done'. Illouz (2012) acknowledges that material consideration has always been present in mate selection in both the past and present in the West. What makes the Chinese case different from Illouz's observation in the West is that despite a growing emphasis on the unique attributes of the person, Chinese parents' involvement in their children's marriage illustrates clearly how formal mechanisms of mate selection remain relevant. Romantic choice, therefore, is not completely individualised.

Yan (2013) argues that there are some signs of the return of parental power in important domains of Chinese young people's lives in recent years, including marriage and divorce, as the current generation of young Chinese is observed to rely more on their parents for support and protection. Similarly, my participants all point out the importance of gaining parental consent for their marriage decision, and meeting each other's parents as a significant marker of a serious relationship. When it comes to 'seal the final deal' before the wedding, parents on both sides often play an important role including negotiating the size of the dowry, paying for the wedding banquet and so on. It is also expected that the parents of the groom will provide the first marital home for the couple. Moreover, the importance of being filial to both sets of parents is commonly articulated by participants as an essential moral criterion for a qualified partner, which is in line with values promoted by the state. Hence, parental involvement makes the Chinese formal mechanism of mate selection more explicitly visible.

Therefore, love in China has neither completely left the hands of parents, nor is it detached from a publicly shared moral framework; it has added criteria to fulfil on top of individualised attributes. It requires the alignment of the hearts of those involved as well as other practicalities sanctioned by a publicly shared framework. Indeed, for lovers, there exists a complicated romantic habitus described by Illouz (2012) that operates at once economically and emotionally, rational and irrational, which creates internal tension when one has to choose between a 'socially appropriate' and a 'sexy' person. Individuals in China, however, face higher degrees of tension from conflicting demands that might arise from both outside and inside one self. Moreover, the country's remaining patriarchal tradition with an emphasis on moralisation of female sexuality places middle-class women in a particularly awkward position in the marriage market, creating suffering that is specific to their gendered position.

Choice of Romance

Scholars contend that consumer culture has greatly accelerated the sexualisation of the human body, first women, later men in modern society (Illouz 2012; Essig 2019). 'Sexiness', according to Illouz (2012), has become an autonomous and decisive criterion in the selection of a mate in the West. Beauty and a type of femininity that emphasise sexuality are intimately associated with the image of romance. I have noted a similar trend in China, which to some extent has presented opportunities for new social groups, such as the young and beautiful, and the poor and beautiful as identified by Illouz (2012) to enter the marriage market and compete with groups with more established class privileges. However, the rising importance of sexuality as a mate-selecting criterion also co-exists with the revival of a patriarchal gender order in China, where women are expected to 'marry up', trading their sexuality for upward social mobility. This is not necessarily good news for the middle-class women I interviewed.

Due to their relatively privileged position on the social ladder, middle-class women face significantly fewer choices than their male counterparts in China. The concept of Chinese women 'marrying up' does not only apply to her social ranking, but also can refer to various aspects of her in relation to the man, such as age, income, education level or even height, which should render men to be superior in the relationship. Moreover, it is a consensus among my participants that the desirability of a woman is tied to her youth, whereas men's seniority in age adds merit to his attractiveness. It means that not only the privileged social status restricts middle-class women's choices, but time is not on her side.

Despite the noted growing pressure on urban Chinese young men to acquire sufficient economic and cultural capital as a precondition to acquire a socially appreciated marriage (Kam 2015), my male participants explicitly and implicitly expressed a preference for women who do not step outside the normative gender order. Adong (male): She must have high emotional intelligence, be independent but not too much... otherwise what's the point of our marriage, right?'. Similarly, David states: 'I don't feel that girls have to be independent. I feel that if a girl becomes too independent, she won't need a man! There might be a lack of trust'. For these men, a woman's independence could directly threaten his sense of self-worth and manliness. Such an attitude could also explain why high-achieving women's marriage dilemmas and stigmatisation is not news in China, even when the gender ratio indicates a significant male surplus (Hong-Fincher 2014). To (2013) argues that the persistence of the Chinese patriarchal structure is the leading cause of such phenomena.

In addition, state policies have long reflected a naturalised and hierarchical view of gender relations, where woman's obligation within monogamy is to serve her husband's interests and needs (Evans 1997). A popular denunciation of Maoist feminism since the reform era that is believed to have 'emasculated men, masculinized women, and mistakenly equates the genders' (Rofel 2007: 117) has given rise to the post-Mao recovery of 'real men' and 'real women'. Both the state and market forces have co-shaped the normative gender order based on the unchallenged discourse of sex difference and widespread commercialisation of the female body, within which a man's role as the main provider for the family has become re-established (Zuo and Bian 2001). The reconfiguration of femininity around these familial norms, although varied in its forms, requires women to embrace domestic roles as wives and mothers as core features (Evans 2010; Liu 2014).

Being aware of their male peers' attitudes, women consciously perform their femininity as the 'weaker/softer' sex conforming to the normative gender order to secure her 'Mr Right'. *Sajiao* (撒娇, play the woman), often involves behaving in a pettishly charming manner by using a child-like tone and voice, and is one of the popular strategies used by women I interviewed. It allows Chinese women to display their feminine charm and elicit help by taking a lower position to avoid conflicts and persuade others in an unthreatening way (Yueh 2013). As Java recommends: 'I think girls must know how to sajiao in front of men. Because when she sajiao, the man has to concede. Such women are the most formidable'. Moreover, consciously attending to men's emotional needs and protecting their egos is also widely reflected upon by women interviewed including Chain: 'I think it's ingrained in us Chinese women to depend on men. We're ingrained to protect their ego… it is a crucial part of Chinese gender etiquette'. When women do date men who are slightly younger than themselves, like Lisi, attempts are made to deliberately give him opportunities to display his manliness: 'Now when we go out, I will let him take care of me. I feel it's more normal…but sometimes he still complains that I do not rely on him enough'. Regardless of its effectiveness, these strategies require heightened emotional labour from women to be self-aware of their gendered positions and perform accordingly.

With the long-term stability of marriage in mind, it is not surprising that many of my female participants would 'choose' to conform to the normative gender hierarchy, particularly when it relates to the core feature of contemporary hegemonic masculinity: financial supremacy. My female participants widely believed that it is better to avoid potential troubles by marrying a 'stronger' partner who earned more than them. Zhangsan explains:

> Realistically, it's still better if a man earns more than his wife…in China, I feel that even the woman doesn't mind. In the long term, a man would feel sensitive about having a stronger wife. Then problems will arise…one side would lose the psychological balance. The girl might appear bossy as time goes by, so…it's not good for anybody.

Similarly, Stella says it is her 'personal preference' for 'strong and capable men', because:

> I don't think a man would choose me if I earned more than him. Because that would make me look down upon him, and gradually hurt his self-esteem, unless he's not a normal man. If a woman earns more than him, it would certainly put him under lots of pressure. If he's not capable enough to surpass her, he will be annoyed or even become angry. Bad things might happen. [Laugh]

Stella has a well-paid teaching job at a famous school and owns her own flat. Technically, she does not need a man to provide for her, as she is self-sufficient. Her 'personal preference' for a stronger male partner reflects 'how gender ideals are constructed in relation to hierarchical differentiation of persons, thus serving as means of both social control and distinction' (Liu 2017: 2). To focus solely on individual choices and preferences is to overlook the effects of the social surroundings where these choices and preferences are shaped. Johnson and Lawler (2005: 13) argue that 'social space impinges upon, organises, and to some degree dictates, how and whom we love'. Following this, I further argue that the existing gender script within these classed social spaces is not only central to shaping our sympathies and antipathies, affections and aversions, tastes and distastes, but also guides us to choose a compatible partner with whom our ideal of happiness can be fulfilled within the conventional gender framework. In the case of middle-class Chinese women, the normative gender script not only greatly restricts their chances of success in the existing marriage market but also normalises its oppressive nature.

Chain in the past has accepted men who earn less than her. Since 'if a woman earns more, people might think 'she is a bit xiong' (凶, evil, capable, fierce) like nü qiang ren (女强人, female strong man). But nobody would criticise you if you earned less. If a man earns less, people will gossip about it and he would lose face'. Here, it becomes clear that the social penalties of 'losing face' on both sides brought about by transgressing gender norms effectively regulate individual choices and preferences. In another words, social validation gained outside the couple relationship also constitutes an important part of one's self-worth in Chinese society, which differs from the hyper-individualised self Illouz (2012) observed in the postmodern West. It further encourages individuals to conform instead of challenge the norm.

Even nowadays, when Chinese women do perform well at work, they are often stigmatised as nü qiang ren (female strong man), as shown in my data and elsewhere. For instance, Osburg's (2013) research on Chengdu businessmen uncovers men's disdain for women entrepreneurs as they considered these 'nü qiang ren' to be lacking feminine charms and virtues. It is no wonder that the women I interviewed often distanced themselves from being seen as 'nü qiang ren': 'I never wanted to be one' said Joyce, 'if you are a woman but as strong as men, you become an alien, a third gender, subject to social alienation'. Consequently, middle-class women tended to downplay their professional achievements and performed their gender accordingly, or in many cases chose work that suited men's gendered expectation of a female partner in order to gain advantage in the marriage market. This is particularly salient when marriage is presented as essential and urgent for women.

Choice of Work

Although women's high career achievement is not welcomed in the marriage market, it is also widely acknowledged that it is important for women to have paid work outside the home. Contrary to my participants' avoidance of 'female strong man', the 'white-collar beauty' hailed by the Chinese media has become a popular feminine ideal of the middle classes, wherein a woman's professional identity does not pose an overt threat to male dominance in Chinese society. Instead, it embodies desirable attributes such as modernity and female sexuality at the same time. Such femininity contains 'sexiness' at an appropriate dose, which allows respectability to be maintained within China's class and gender structure, just as Adong (male) previously commented: 'be independent but not too much'.

Therefore, women's employment is commonly perceived as an important element to enhance 'marital harmony'. Practically, differing from the male elite, the mostly middle-class men these women marry cannot afford a stay-at-home wife, which makes a dual-income a necessity to maintain the family's standard of living in China's materialistic culture (Croll 2006). Importantly, a woman's paid employment is believed to make her become a more interesting partner, and therefore enhance 'marital harmony'. Women commonly worried that 'without a public role in the society to keep up knowledge exchange' they will 'lag behind' and 'disconnect' with their husbands 'if only he is progressing' (Gingko). Men's responses confirm this 'I don't expect her to achieve a lot, it's good even if it's just to kill time. I think it can enhance marital harmony' (Chouchou, male). 'Spending a long time at home will certainly affect the relationship. I think women should have their own dreams and enact their dreams. Only focusing on housework for too long would be boring and damage our relationship' (Lixiong, male). It might be true that her employment adds merit to her attractiveness as a partner but such concern also restricts her choice of career.

Liu's study (2017a) on white-collar women in Chinese organisations shows that women's sexual reputations are heavily moralised and are tied closely to their social status, which constrains their agency. Good wifely candidates should be 'morally upright': 'She should have a decent stable job, like civil servant or teacher' (Zen, male). The stigmatisation of women working in sales highlights the boundaries of moralised female sexuality, as Roger explains:

Women in sales have a reputation as 'pretty sluts'. Because they need to be able to entertain their clients with sexualised jokes at the dinner table, allowing their sexual advances, even sleeping with them. It's the hidden rules. I've heard too many stories!

In contemporary Chinese society, one's 'sexiness' is counted as important within individual's mate selection criteria. Nevertheless, for a middle-class woman, her moralised sexuality as an important identity marker also prevents her from freely entering professions that are most profitable; the sexualised business culture centres on male desires (Palmer 2015) and the demarcation of her acceptable sexuality/'sexiness' often connotes sexual exclusivity to one man at a time. On the other hand, there is much higher tolerance from Chinese wives towards their husbands' engaging in sexualised entertainment with their bosses for their career advancement (Uretsky 2016). The existing sexual double standard: moralised female sexuality vs. loose male sexual conduct, means that in the Chinese job market, women are not only sexualised but also marginalised due to their sexuality. For middle-class women, who want to forge ahead in their careers, they run the risk of jeopardising their position in the marriage market. Meanwhile, these women also face competition from other younger and 'sexier' women from poorer backgrounds who are more willing to trade their sexuality for upward social mobility. In this sense, the Chinese marriage market differs from Illouz's analysis of the West, where the formal restrictive mechanisms such as class and sexual morality have largely been dismantled (although see McQueen and Osborn, Chap. 5, in this volume for an alternative take on this). In Chinese society, middle-class women's romantic choice reflects a much deeper asymmetry of opportunity-distribution that privileges men over women.

Choice of Self-Realisation

Illouz (2012) argues that the cultural ideal of self-realisation demands one always keep their options open, in order to switch to a 'better' choice at any given time in the future. It entails a fundamentally unstable monitoring of the self, in which to develop and to grow implies that tomorrow's self must be different from today's. It also fundamentally posits the self as a perpetually moving target, as something in need of discovery and accomplishment. This sense of self-realisation is widely observed among the women I interviewed, who endeavoured to become the 'white-collar beauty' on the job market and find love in the marriage market through continuous self-improvement. Both work and romantic love were crucial components for them to complete their modern sense of self. Even after they 'find love' and get married, to realise one's self means to keep validating one's self-worth through engaging with the job market; as Tj said: 'Apart from providing an income, I also hope to grow together with my child by keeping in touch with society, keep discovering the potential in me and realise my value. Work is essential in this process'. This shows that the rhetoric of growth and self-development has been deeply instilled into the psyches of my research cohort. Unlike nineteenth-century Western Europe, noted in Illouz's book (2012), where one's class position is fixed and given, China's ongoing class transformation requires individuals to constantly acquire and perform various class symbols to validate their social worth. Since the 'happy and complete family' was erected by the party-state as the most socially desirable middle-class symbol, which rests upon 'economic security and cultural superiority' (Miao 2017), maintaining class status has become particularly challenging for the women I interviewed. To validate their middle-class identity, they were often torn between performance demands from both the marriage and job market, where they are also discriminated against. Even for those women who manage to follow the conventional life path of marriage and having children before the socially expected deadline, juggling work and family duties often leaves them in a constant battle within themselves and with their partner (Xie 2019). However, the state-sanctioned desire to realise oneself through embodying the most socially welcomed middle-class family ideal drives these women to persevere.

In addition, in a society where job security in precarious (Howard and Howard 1995) and divorce rates are on the rise (CGTN 2019), keeping one's options open for self-realisation also means that marriage and work serve as backup for each other. For women, since security provided through marriage is no longer guaranteed, jobs become even more necessary. One recent TV hit 'The First Half of My Life' (我的前半生, *wo de qian ban sheng*) vividly depicts the reality that Chinese women face. It tells the story of a once pampered full-time housewife abandoned by her husband for his colleague, and her struggle to re-establish herself as a desirable, independent 'beauty at work'. This drama shows the need for urban professional women to juggle between family and work and to strike the right balance in order to keep their desirability in both markets. The popularity of this show reflects the deep relevance of the issue. Just like Muyu puts it: 'I think a woman without her own career but just family, is …not very secure [laugh]'. Java, a married woman whose husband is more financially established than her, also says: 'I think women should be financially independent, I don't want to rely on my husband too much'. Increasingly, women's employment becomes a form of realising her market value, but also a backup plan for potential relationship breakdown.

Mass media in our contemporary consumer culture has sold us the ideal of romantic love, which contains both intensive feelings and a happily-ever-after. It has significantly raised our expectations of modern marriage, but ironically has undermined its stability at the same time. For some, it has become part of the self-realisation project, certainly for those I interviewed. Simultaneously, the same desire of self-realisation through finding romantic love prevents some from making choices. Illouz (2012) points out that romantic love is the site of a paradoxical process, desiring both freedom and commitment. Exercising freedom of choice means the possibility of abandoning or being abandoned, which creates suffering for lovers. She also contends that promise-making in modern society has become a burden on the self. Promises, in the romantic context, are oppressive because they require the permanent exercise of choice that leads to an absence of choice for one's future self. Meanwhile, the increased freedom to choose one's lover according to individual personal preferences in modern societies presupposes a large number of possible partners for both men and women to choose from, which makes it particularly difficult to project one's self along a continuous line linking the present to the future. Since the very ideal of self-realisation disrupts and opposes the idea of the self and of the will as something constant and fixed, to self-realise means not committing to any fixed identity and especially not committing to a single project of the self. Therefore, self-realisation affects the very capacity and desire to choose, which creates what Illouz (2012: 108) calls 'commitment phobia', as 'freedom becomes aporetic'. For my participants who are compelled to make such choices within a limited timeframe in line with various societal expectations, it generates even more hesitation to avoid making the 'wrong choice'.

Despite the intensive time pressure for women to marry, most of them refuse to surrender to this pressure without finding their 'Mr. Right'. Precisely because they believe that they should 'be responsible for their own future happiness' (Maris). Although longing for commitment in marriage, they become extra cautious in the choosing process in fear of making the 'wrong choice'. This often leads them choose to wait for their 'true love for life', while continuously improving themselves through developing new hobbies or cultivating class-coded tastes. The problem is, within China's gender and age hierarchy, women's sexual attractiveness decreases as they age and their continuous self-betterment often presents an even smaller pool of male partners to match with as time goes by. Consequently, their faith in romantic love could have them waiting in vain. In contrast, middle-class men's determination to improve themselves enables them to further increase their romantic choices, as they become more 'mature and cultured', according to social perception. Men might also hesitate to make their marriage commitment, waiting for a better choice to emerge in the future, but their gender privilege could make their waiting more affordable and worthwhile. As a result, despite Chinese men and women both facing external pressure to commit themselves in marriage, the consequences of 'commitment phobia' are gendered (as Illouz also notes).

Facing the abundance of opportunities presented in modern society, men and women both enjoy far greater freedom to choose their romantic partners. However, the open-endedness of one's sense of possibilities and the rising importance of 'sexiness' in mate selection have dramatically shaped both the environment and process within which men and women make their choices. Using Illouz's (2012) terms, the ecology and architecture of sexual choice have been transformed in modernity. Such transformation affects the balance between the two genders to generate a certain degree of emotional inequality between men and women as suggested by Illouz (2012). She believes that the different strategies men and women deploy to gain status in modern societies mean that men are more able to be emotionally detached in sex than women, which gives them greater capacity to exert choice and to constrain the choice of the other. This, to some extent, creates more romantic suffering for women than men.

Less convinced by her judgement of gendered strategies, I am more certain that the pre-existing gendered social structure constrains and compels individuals to make certain choices and believe in their owner-ship of these choices, which intensifies Chinese women's romantic suffer-ings. Parents' supervision in children's big life decisions, including marriage, reflects the formal mechanism that continues to regulate indi-viduals' romantic desire and choice within accepted social and gendered norms. The long-standing sexual double standard embedded within China's patriarchal tradition gives middle-class men far more privilege to wait and choose a desirable partner than their female counterparts. The sexual exclusivity required by monogamous marriage in China often means women are morally judged more severely when they are sexually engaged with multiple partners, even after divorce (Xie 2018). Far from entering the marriage market on a somewhat equal footing with men in a hyper-individualised society as Illouz (2012) describes, middle-class women's suffering for contemporary romance is underpinned by the long existing gender inequality shaped by China's social economical arrange-ment, which exacerbates the pains they experience in finding 'true love'. The classed expectation on women to embody the image of the 'white-collar beauty' further complicates their search for love, which reflects the unique struggle to realise one's gendered and classed subjectivity in China's modernity.

Conclusion

Located in a rather privileged position on the Chinese social ladder, most of my participants display a strong belief in continuous self-betterment to achieve their values through embodying the happy and complete fam-ily ideal upheld by the party-state. Romantic sentiment around 'true love' is utilised to entice individual desires to marry and raise children within the conventional family framework. One interesting observation made by Beck and Beck-Gernsheim (2001: 151) is that the ongoing process of individualisation in the contemporary world often leads to 'a life of one's own through conformity', where individuals are compelled through various modern social institutions including education and the labour market to be proactive and responsible for one's own failure or success. It creates what Bauman (2001: 32) described as 'compulsive and obligatory self-determination'. This is particularly true among my participants, as they were all eager to continuously obtain and maintain their middle-class privileges through both marriage and job markets by making the 'right choice'. This type of autonomous free choosing self is a central feature of contemporary governmentality in China, since the autonomous individual's desire for success is channelled to choose certain compliant gendered behaviours.

Applying the analytical tools offered by Illouz (2012) to examine individuals' romantic choices and how they make these choices while facing love's transformation in modernity, I attempt to uncover the unique constraints women face in finding love and marital happiness in the Chinese context. Though love marriage is equally desired as a middle-class symbol for both men and women, professional women face particular challenges to fulfil this ideal, which affects their sense of self-worth and experience of romantic sufferings. Through analysing the ecology and architecture of their romantic choices, it reveals that the external social mechanism of mate selection represented by parents' involvement in their children's marriage decision co-exists with the patriarchal sexual double standard against the backdrop of sexual abundance. All of these present a disadvantage to these women in the marriage market. They do not only have a smaller pool of men to choose from as women are supposed to 'marry up', but they also face more intense time pressure to commit due to the reproductive norm. Moreover, the sexual double standard restricts middle-class women from freely utilising their sexuality to gain advantage in both markets, which deprives them of certain opportunities offered by modernity.

Simultaneously, the wide purchase of romantic love among these women and their belief in self-realisation mean that they are less likely to settle for less, and adopt the strategy of self-improvement while waiting for their 'Mr Right'. Ironically, the longer they hold on to this romantic vision of love, the more likely they are to be pushed out, as younger 'sexier' women enter the marriage market. This strategy could also push them up higher on the social ladder, which further reduces the pool of available choices they have to find a romantic match in China, creating still more anguish. These women's struggles to reconcile the multiple and often oppositional ideologies arising from the intermingling of tradition and modernity on their journey to marital happiness reveal the deeply rooted patriarchal structure underpinning gender inequalities in China's great social transformation. Attempting to hold conflicting desires and different motivations together in a heightened time span to chase happiness, even if it is possible, how can women not experience pain?

References

Bauman, Z. (2001) *The individualized society*. Cambridge: Polity Press.

Beck, U. and Beck-Gernsheim, E. (2001) *Individualization: Institutionalized individualism and its social and political consequences*. London: Sage.

Bell, D.A. (2010) Reconciling socialism and Confucianism? Reviving tradition in China. *Dissent*, 57 (1): 91–99.

Cao, K. and Huang, C. (2018) People's Daily Internet Commentary: Leading the great rejuvenation of China-Opinions. *Renmin Wang*. [Online]. Available at: http://opinion.people.com.cn/n1/2018/0226/c1003-29833533.html [Accessed 25 November 2018].

CGTN (2019) Marriage in China: High divorce rate affecting China's economy. *CGTN*. [Online]. Available at: https://news.cgtn.com/news/7845544e3349 4464776c6d636a4e6e62684a4856/index.html [Accessed 25 May 2019].

Croll, E. (2006) *China's New Consumers: Social Development and Domestic Demand*. London: Routledge.

Essig, L. (2019) *Love, Inc.: Dating Apps, the Big White Wedding, and Chasing the Happily Neverafter*. Oakland: University of California Press.

Evans, H. (1997) *Women and sexuality in china: Dominant discourses of female sexuality and gender since 1949*. Cambridge: Policy Press.

Evans, H. (2002) Past, perfect or imperfect: changing images of the ideal wife. In: Brownell, S. L. and Wasserstrom, J. (eds). *Chinese Femininities, Chinese Masculinities*. Berkeley: University of California Press: 355–360.

Evans, H. (2010) The Gender of Communication: Changing Expectations of Mothers and Daughters in Urban China. In Evans, H. and Strauss, J. C. (eds.) *Gender in Flux: Agency and Its Limits in Contemporary China: The China Quarterly Special Issues New Series*. Cambridge: Cambridge University Press.

Farrer, J. (2014) Love, sex, and commitment: delinking premarital intimacy from marriage in urban China. In: Davis, D. S. and Friedman, S. L. (eds). *Wives, husbands, and lovers: marriage and sexuality in Hong Kong, Taiwan, and Urban China*. Stanford, California: Stanford University Press: 62–96.

Fong, V. L. (2004) *Only Hope: Coming of Age Under China's One-child Policy*. Stanford, California: Stanford University Press.

Friedman, S. L. (2005) The intimacy of state power: marriage, liberation, and socialist subjects in south eastern China. *American Ethnologist*, 32 (2): 312–327.

Giddens, A. (1991) *Modernity and self-identity: Self and society in the late modern age*. Stanford: Stanford University Press.

Halskov Hansen, M. and Svarverud, R. (2010) *iChina: The Rise of the Individual in Modern Chinese Society*. NIAS Press. [Online]. Available at: http://urn. kb.se/resolve?urn=urn:nbn:se:norden:org:diva-4090 [Accessed 25 November 2018].

Hird, D. (2008) *White-Collar Men and Masculinity in Contemporary Urban China*. PhD dissertation, Department of Politics and International Relations: University of Westminster.

Hong-Fincher, L. (2014) *Leftover women: The resurgence of gender inequality in China*. London: Zed Books Ltd.

Hong-Fincher, L. (2018) *Betraying big brother: The feminist awakening in China*. New York: Verso Books.

Howard, P. and Howard, R. (1995) The campaign to eliminate job security in China. *Journal of Contemporary Asia*, 25 (3): 338–355.

Illouz, E. (2012) *Why love hurts: A sociological explanation*. Cambridge: Polity Press.

Jackson, S. (2011) Materialist feminism, the self and global late modernity: Some consequences for intimacy and sexuality. In: *Sexuality, gender and power: Intersectional and transnational perspectives*. London: Routledge: 15–29.

Jankowiak, W. and Moore, R. (2012) China's emergent youth: Gender, work, dating, and life orientation. In: Hewlett, B. L. (ed) *Adolescent identity: Evolutionary, cultural and developmental perspectives*. New York: Routledge.

Johnson, P. and Lawler, S. (2005) Coming home to love and class. *Sociological Research Online*, 10 (3): 1–13.

Kam, L. (2015) The demand for a 'normal life': Marriage and its discontents in contemporary China. In: McLelland, M. and Mackie, V. (eds). *Routledge handbook of sexuality studies in East Asia*. Abingdon: Routledge: 77–86.

Liu, F. (2008) Constructing the autonomous middle-class self in today's China: The case of young-adult only-children university students. *Journal of Youth Studies*, 11 (2): 193–212.

Liu, F. (2014) From degendering to (re)gendering the self: Chinese youth negotiating modern womanhood. *Gender and Education*, 26 (1): 18–34.

Liu, F. (2017) Chinese young men's construction of exemplary masculinity: the hegemony of chenggong. *Men and Masculinities*, 22(2): 294–316.

Liu, J. (2007) *Gender and work in urban China: Women workers of the unlucky generation*. London: Routledge.

Liu, J. (2017a) *Gender, sexuality and power in Chinese companies: Beauties at work*. London: Palgrave Macmillan.

McMillan, J. (2006) *Sex, science and morality in China*. London: Routledge, Taylor & Francis.

Miao, Y. (2017) Middle class identity in China: Subjectivity and stratification. *Asian Studies Review*, 41 (4): 629–646.

Moore, R. L. (2005) Generation Ku: Individualism and China's Millennial Youth. *Ethnology*, 44 (4): 357–376.

Ong, A. (1997) 'A momentary glow of fraternity': Narratives of Chinese nationalism and capitalism. *Identities*, 3 (3): 331–366.

Osburg, J. (2013) *Anxious wealth: money and morality among China's new rich*. Stanford: Stanford University Press.

Palmer, J. (2015) 'Brotherhood: Chinese yinchou, sex transaction and hidden rules of doing business'. *New York Times*. [Online]. Available at: https://cn.nytstyle.com/culture/20150708/tc08brocode/ [Accessed 6 March 2018].

Pan, L. (2015) *When True Love Came to China*. Hong Kong: Hong Kong University Press.

Pan, S. (1994) A Sex Revolution in Current China, *Journal of Psychology & Human Sexuality* 6 (2): 1–14.

Parish W. L. and Whyte M. K. (1978) *Village and family in contemporary China*. New York: The University of Chicago Press.

Qi, X. (2015) Filial obligation in contemporary China: Evolution of the culture-system. *Journal for the Theory of Social Behaviour*, 45 (1): 141–161.

Qi, X. (2016) Family bond and family obligation: continuity and transformation. *Journal of Sociology*, 52 (1): 39–52.

Rofel, L. (2007) *Desiring china: Experiments in neoliberalism, sexuality, and public culture*. Durham and London: Duke University Press.

Rubin, H. J. and Rubin, I. S. (2012) *Qualitative interviewing: the art of hearing data*. London: Sage.

Sigley, G. (2001) Keep it in the family: Government, marriage, and sex in contemporary China. In: Jolly, M. and Ram, K. (eds). *Borders of being: Citizenship, fertility, and sexuality in Asia and the Pacific*. Ann Arbor: University of Michigan Press: 118–153.

Steele, L. G. and Lynch, S. M. (2013) The Pursuit of Happiness in China: Individualism, Collectivism, and Subjective Well-Being during China's Economic and Social Transformation. *Social indicators research*, 114 (2).

To, S. (2013) Understanding sheng nu 'leftover women': the phenomenon of late marriage among Chinese professional women. *Symbolic Interaction*, 36 (1): 1–20.

Uretsky, E. (2016) *Occupational hazards: Sex, business and HIV in post-Mao China*. Stanford, California: Stanford University Press.

Wang, F. (2010) China's Population Destiny: The Looming Crisis. *Brookings*. [Online]. Available at: https://www.brookings.edu/articles/chinas-population-destiny-the-looming-crisis/ [Accessed 2 February 2018].

Wen, H. (2013) *Buying beauty: Cosmetic surgery in China*. Hong Kong: Hong Kong University Press.

Wong, D. (2016) Sexology and the making of sexual subjects in contemporary China. *Journal of Sociology* 52 (1): 68–82.

Xie, K. (2018) Premarital Abortion – What is the Harm? The Responsibilisation of Women's Pregnancy Among China's 'Privileged' Daughters. *Journal of the British Association for Chinese Studies*, 8 (1): 1–31.

Xie, K. (2019) The Naturalisation of Motherhood Within Marriage and Its Implications for Chinese Academic Women. *Journal of the British Association for Chinese Studies*, 9 (1): 59–84.

Yan, Y. (2009) *The Individualization of Chinese Society*. Oxford: Berg Publishers.

Yan, Y. (2010) The Chinese path to individualization. *The British Journal of Sociology*, 61 (3): 489–512.

Yan, Y. (2013) Parent-driven divorce and individualisation among urban Chinese youth. *International Social Science Journal*, 64(213–214): 317–330.

Yueh, H.-I. S. (2013) Body performance in gendered language deconstructing the mandarin term sajiao in the cultural context of Taiwan. *Journal of Theories and Research in Education*, 8 (1): 159–182.

Zarafonetis, N. (2017) *Gendered change and continuity in china: Sex, sexuality and intimate relationships in the reform period*. London: Routledge.

Zhang, E. (2011) China's sexual revolution, in Kleinman, A. et al., (eds) *Deep China: The moral life of the person*. Berkeley, Los Angeles, and London: University of California Press: 91–126.

Zhang, J. and Sun, P. (2014) 'When are you going to get married?' parental matchmaking in middle-class women in contemporary urban China. In: Davis, D. S. and Friedman, S. L. (eds). *Wives, husbands, and lovers: marriage and sexuality in Hong Kong, Taiwan, and Urban China*. Stanford, California: Stanford University Press: 118–143.

Zhao, S. (2005) China's pragmatic nationalism: Is it manageable? *The Washington Quarterly*, 29 (1): 131–144.

Zheng, J. (2017) Mate Selection and Gender Reflexivity. *Asian Women*, 33 (1): 49–71.

Zhuang, P. (2012) *New standards on filial piety cause unhappiness*. *South China Morning Post*. [Online]. Available at: http://www.scmp.com/news/china/article/1018761/new-standards-filial-piety-cause-unhappiness [Accessed 8 March 2018].

Zuo J. and Bian Y. (2001) Gendered resources, division of housework, and perceived fairness – a case in urban China. *Journal of Marriage and Family* 63(4): 1122–1133.

Zurndorfer, H. (2016) Men, women, money, and morality: The development of China's sexual economy. *Feminist Economics*, 22 (2): 1–23.

10

'I Entered This Life Because My Husband Left Me, I Have to Be Careful Now': A Study of Domesticity, Intimacy and Belonging in the Lives of Women in Sex Work in a Red-Light Area in Eastern India

Mirna Guha

Introduction

Literature on sex work in India has primarily concerned itself with examining modes of entry into the trade (forced versus voluntary) and on forms of organisation of sex work (traditional, i.e. family or community-based, or commercially organised). Within this, the scholarship has tended to focus on experiences of coercion viz. trafficking into sex work, and on labour relations including financial arrangements within sex work versus other forms of work in the informal labour market, as well as on sex workers' physical, psychological and sexual health concerns, and their

M. Guha (✉)
Anglia Ruskin University, Cambridge, UK
e-mail: mirna.guha@anglia.ac.uk

© The Author(s) 2020
J. Carter, L. Arocha (eds.), *Romantic Relationships in a Time of 'Cold Intimacies'*,
Palgrave Macmillan Studies in Family and Intimate Life,
https://doi.org/10.1007/978-3-030-29256-0_10

experiences of stigma. While there is a growing body of literature on the involvement of trans-individuals and men within sex work in India, the focus is overwhelmingly on women from marginalised socio-economic backgrounds.

Literature on women's engagement with traditional forms of sex work in India has explored the role of familial and community-based relationships in women's engagement with sex work. However, there is a dearth of similar literature on social relations within commercially organised sex work, particularly in the region of Eastern India; an exception is Kotiswaran's (2008) work on how labour relations are organised in *Sonagachi*, which is one of Asia's largest red-light areas. While a body of research on intimate relationships within the lives of women in sex work exists, this tends to explore violence within such relationships to draw linkages with vulnerability to HIV/AIDS and other health risks.

Drawing on Kabeer's (1994) social relations framework, my PhD research on the lives of women formerly and actively in sex work, undertaken between 2013 and 2017, explored and highlighted the centrality of social relations within the lives of women formerly and actively engaged in commercially organised sex work in Eastern India. Focusing on peri-urban and rural women from West Bengal, the research found that entries into, experiences within, exit from and re-entry into sex work were shaped by experiences of 'everyday' violence within social relations and women's social positionalities within them—these relations included those with members of their natal and (ex) marital households (outside red-light areas), rural and peri-urban communities of origin, the sex-work labour market and the state.

Experiences of violence within sex work, therefore, were not exceptional but lay on a spectrum of 'everyday violence' within social relations. These experiences took on specific manifestations within sex work but existed beyond these sites as well. This often led to re-entries into sex work due to the persistence of experiences of violence in household and community-based relations after women had left sex work (Guha 2018a).

Violence and Intimacy in the Lives of Women in Sex Work in Eastern India: Concepts, Context and Methodology

In this chapter, I discuss a particular aspect of my doctoral research. Specifically, I look at how full-time residential female sex workers living and working in brothel households in the red-light area of *Kalighat*, in South Kolkata, form everyday relations of intimacy and belonging within their lives. For this analysis, I draw on Illouz's (2007) conceptualisation of 'emotional capitalism' to illustrate how the sex-work marketplace becomes a site for the overlap of economic, social and emotional aspirations and concerns in the everyday lives of women who live and work there. I will also refer to Illouz's (2012) *Why Love Hurts* to discuss how these women construct and perceive their choices regarding work, love, intimacy and safety.

As part of my research,[1] I spent two months in Kalighat conducting participant observations of everyday life in the red-light area. Additionally, I collected life-history interviews with six full-time, two part-time and three retired sex workers. These interviews took place over several days and were 2–3 hours long each time. They were conducted during early and late afternoons, in indoor and outdoor spaces—within one-roomed brothel households and on streets and pavements. In this article, I refer to the life-histories and experiences of four full-time and residential sex workers—Chumki, Jasmine, Sabina and Rima.[2] I describe each respondent's profile when I present their narratives later in the chapter.

Although my doctoral research concerned itself with experiences and negotiations with everyday violence, it should not come as a surprise that these experiences were often situated within existing and potential relationships of intimacy and care. In a patriarchal context, familial control and regulation of women's autonomy, mobility, 'honour' and sexuality are often framed in the language of care and protection. This is especially pertinent for women who come from socio-economically marginalised backgrounds, who have low levels of literacy and low technical skills and are often dependent upon patriarchal heads of their households for social and economic security.

As I have discussed in Guha (2018a), peri-urban and rural women's entries into sex work in Eastern India were influenced by the breakdown of social relationships with their families and communities, which included experiences of violence. The breakdown left the women's positions within household relations precarious—they were viewed as *bhaar*, that is, as social, economic and emotional burdens on their households. Women sought *kono kaaj* or 'any work' for social and economic security, which often entailed them leaving their communities, and looking for work in the informal labour market. Low technical skills and minimal literacy led to reliance on others to help them look for work. This reliance was often exploited, and led to coercive entries into sex work, while others voluntarily entered sex work. Those who experienced violence stemming from coercive entries into sex work from madams, pimps and brothel owners escaped, but often re-entered sex work due to various reasons. These included experiences of violence in other forms of work in the informal labour market juxtaposed with demanding manual labour and low incomes compared to sex work. However, women also re-entered sex work because it allowed them to 'start over'—that is, form new social relationships within their lives which offered friendship, comfort, solace, as well as the potential for domesticity and matrimony. Despite stigma associated with sex work, within the red-light area, women were able to live non-normatively, within households comprising unmarried partners (often long-term customers) as well as children from previous relationships that had ended or were on pause due to entries into sex work.

In this chapter, I explore this further: how the 'marketplace', that is, the red-light area, where sex workers live and work, becomes the epicentre of social and emotional relationships for women in sex work. I am interested in exploring how financial arrangements and aspirations overlap with social ones, (re)producing the sex work labour market as a system of emotional and social arrangements, alongside economic ones.

The Red-Light Area as a Site for 'Emotional Capitalism'

Illouz (2007) defines 'emotional capitalism' as a

> culture in which emotional and economic discourses and practices mutually shape each other, thus producing...a broad, sweeping movement in which affect is made an essential aspect of economic behaviour and within which emotional life – especially of the middle classes – follows the logic of economic relations and exchange. (2007: 5)

Within emotional capitalism, then,

> market-based cultural repertoires shape and inform interpersonal and emotional relationships, while interpersonal relationships are at the epicenter (sic) of economic relationships. (2007: 5)

Drawing on this, this chapter explores the various ways in which economic and interpersonal relationships intertwine in the lives of full-time brothel-based residential female sex workers in Kalighat. It examines how through these overlaps and interlinkages, the sex-work marketplace becomes a space which offers women in sex work opportunities to build 'fictive kin' relations, modelled on kin relations while providing the social and material structures to support and sustain existing consanguineal bonds.

I examine two specific relations of intimacy and belonging: (i) romantic relationships with long-term customers, and (ii) motherhood. I explore how economic, social and emotional concerns overlap within these relationships, and how these overlaps affect decisions about the future of the co-existence of fictive kin relations with consanguineal ones in the red-light area. Additionally, as Illouz (2007) has argued, 'social arrangements are also emotional arrangements', which is particularly true for socio-economically marginalised women within gender-unequal contexts: social security and emotional security go together. These affect economic decisions that sex workers make—in terms of not only relationships but their sexual labour too—whom to 'sell' sex to versus form relations of sexual intimacy with. The co-existence of the social, sexual and domestic within brothel households has been highlighted by Kotiswaran (2008: 586) who argues that

> [The] structural and cultural aspects of brothel-based sex work are fundamentally shaped by the spatial concentration of brothels in a red-light area. Unlike institutions such as the school, family, church, military, or prison that can be characterised as public or private, **the brothel operates at the crossroads of the market and the family,**[3] harbo[u]ring both sex workers and brothel keepers as well as their families. This permeates every aspect of institutional life in the brothel. For example, brothel rents reflect commercial levels, but the living conditions of the property do not approximate standards of commercial property since the brothel is the living space of its sex workers and brothel keepers, who are its labo[u]ring and entrepreneurial classes, respectively. Similarly, unlike the family where the wife socially reproduces her husband, in a brothel the sexual labo[u]r of several women, managed by the entrepreneurial labo[u]r of a brothel keeper (often a woman herself), socially reproduces a collectivity of male customers. At the same time, the brothel's economy, like that of the family, includes the labo[u]r invested by the brothel keeper in reproducing the sex workers as laborers as well as the reproductive labo[u]r that both sex workers and brothel keepers invest in their families who reside with them in the brothel.

Over this chapter, I look at how the Kalighat red-light area, located in the southern part of the Eastern Indian city of Kolkata, lies at the 'crossroads of market and the family'. But first I highlight how unlike other red-light area, the influence of the middle-class is literally and symbolically omnipresent in the everyday lives, labour and social relations of the women who live and work there.

Middle-Class 'Respectability' in the Kalighat Red-Light Area: Influence on Space and Sartorial Choices

Spatial Characteristics

The middle-class influence in the lives of women in sex work in Kalighat manifests in the form of norms on respectability and female propriety which emanate from the red-light area's particular location within a bustling middle-class neighbourhood—with residences, schools, an institution of higher education and an underground metro station located within it. Kalighat is also home to a renowned temple for the Hindu goddess *Kali*, which is a national and local pilgrimage spot for Hindu devotees.

During the day, the neighbourhood is abuzz with activity—worshippers to the temple intermingle with throng of daily commuters going about their everyday lives. Like other red-light areas in South Asia, the Kalighat red-light area is not a gated community but there are unspoken rules about soliciting zones for female sex workers. During the day, full and part-time sex workers[4] primarily solicit on Kalighat road and the adjoining alleyways which are dotted with brothel households. However, during the evenings they leave the confines of the area and solicit on the main streets as well as on the Kalighat bridge. Young women who live in the red-light area aged between 18 and 25 years often 'fly' or travel to other spaces in the city to solicit for customers during the night.

The prominence of the neighbourhood increased in 2009 after the All India Trinamool Congress's (a political party) ascension to power in West Bengal; the Chief Minister, Ms. Mamata Banerjee's residence is located in Kalighat, in close proximity to Kalighat Road. After the party's victory in the Municipal Corporation elections, which cemented its political control of the city, Ms. Banerjee declared her wish to install a 'grand gate' measuring 40 ft × 60 ft at the entrance of Kalighat Road as a commemorative entry point for devotees visiting the temple. The location, however, was critiqued by the opposition; its proximity to the Chief Minister's residence was indicated to criticise the decision as a sign of political opportunism for which public finances (to the tune of 60 lakhs/£65,000 to a crore/over £100,000) would be utilised. The criticism also referred to the choice of Kalighat Road over S.P. Mukherjee road, a parallel street which is used more commonly by pedestrians and has an absence of female sex workers occupying public space. Nevertheless, the gate was installed in its pre-determined destination and stands as an unwittingly iconic and ornate entrance to one of the prominent streets of the red-light area. This has also meant a near-constant presence of police officers in jeeps stationed under the gate, to provide security to the Chief Minister's residence across the street.

The increased significance of this neighbourhood and the constant police presence have increased the spatial restrictions for the women who live and work in the red-light area. This often leads to tussles between younger female sex workers and the police when the women defy unofficial soliciting-prohibitions near the Chief Minister's residence; the women are often arrested and need to be bailed out by a 'sex workers' organisation' that employs peer workers from the sex-work community, runs a health clinic and implements health-centred interventions in the red-light area. My field guide and part-time sex worker, Bandana, who works as a peer outreach worker for the NGO in Kalighat and as a sex worker in Sonagachi, explained:

> These policemen [...] they don't like putting our girls in jail. They say, 'We know. The women here are doing this out of desperation. To fill their stomachs. That's why we tell these young girls to respect [these rules and] their clients. But who listens? They constantly get into trouble, soliciting in front of the Chief Minister's house, doing *chinn-tai* [pickpocketing]; sometimes they sell drugs to customers too. All this is unnecessary. They get arrested, and we must go get them out, every time. [Bandana, September 2018]

Bandana's comments reveal how middle-class influences produce ideas of 'respectable' sex work, which entails abiding by rules about no-go zones in and around the 'bhodro' (respectable,[5] particularly of a middle-class nature) areas surrounding the red-light area. The middle-class influence permeates right into the red-light area, too, and affects the lives of women who live and work there. In Guha (2018b), I discuss how middle-class norms on respectable female behaviour shape sartorial norms for women in sex work: unlike other red-light areas, where women would often wear shorts, dresses and skirts—considered 'revealing' and 'titillating'—in Kalighat, female sex workers are expected to wear sarees. When quizzed on this, Jasmine, a 27-year-old full-time residential female sex worker explained, 'this is a *bhodroloker para* (middle-class and 'respectable' neighbourhood). Kali Ma's temple is also nearby. Here, we have to dress respectably. We cannot wear skimpy clothes'.

When I asked Jasmine what would happen if female sex workers violated this unspoken rule, she said, shrugging and half-jokingly: '*Para-r chele-ra mere felbe* [the neighbourhood boys will kill us]'. Donner (2008: 9) argues that '[f]or Calcuttans, *paras* [neighbourhoods] are very significant spaces in the lives of women'. '[C]onversations about a specific para and its role in women's lives [...] are often related to behavioural codes and ideas about femininity and proper conduct' (Donner 2008: 9). The middle-class norms that shape the Kalighat *para* and the middle-class households also govern the lives of women who engage in an otherwise socially subversive act, that is, selling sex. However, the women took advantage of this by manipulating the norms to their own social and economic advantage. In particular, symbols of matrimony, that is, the *sindoor* (vermillion worn by married women in the partings of their hair) and the *shankha-pola* (white and red bangles worn as symbols of fertility), were repeatedly adopted by unmarried female sex workers both as a 'marketing tool' and to keep themselves safe. Chumki, a 23-year-old full-time sex worker, who had entered sex work after leaving her violent and alcoholic husband and was not keen to initiate romantic relationships with customers explained:

It's saaj (dressing up). A woman looks beautiful with *sindoor* and *shankha-pola*. This helps me attract customers and keeps me safe, too. An unmarried (looking) young woman is an easy target in this world.

Middle-class norms in the red-light area shaped the 'sexual field', which Illouz (2012: 54) describes as the

social [arena] in which sexual desire is autonomized, sexual competition is generalized, sexual appeal is made into an autonomous criterion for selection of a mate and sexual attractiveness is made into an independent criterion by which to classify and hierarchize people.

Chumki's deployment of bridal beauty markers to increase her sexual appeal and attractiveness in a site where sexual relations lie outside of conventional domesticity highlight the persistence of these norms even within the sex work market. However, in their deployment, Chumki was also able to navigate the adverse effects of the sexualisation of women, which render them vulnerable to violence and harm. These norms also affected the 'architecture of choice' (Illouz 2012: 20) available to these women. I discuss this in the next section.

'Sex Work' and *shongshaar* (Family) in a Red-Light Area

As mentioned earlier, many women I met who lived and worked in the Kalighat red-light area came from natal and marital households where they had experienced violence and power inequalities. Despite, and probably because of it, many were keen to build new romantic relations which would eventually lead to domesticity and marriage—which, in keeping with middle-class norms, were perceived as desirable for women. However, the hardships encountered by the women which were of financial, social and economic nature led them to adopt certain strategies to ensure that domesticity still enabled the women to hold considerable 'bargaining power' within intra-household relations (Agarwal 1997). This implied that emotional decisions about establishing 'relatedness' (Carsten 2000) in the red-light area were laced with social and economic concerns. Carsten (2000: 1) argues that studies on the 'cultures of relatedness' do not take the 'content of kinship for granted [but rather] build from first principles a picture of the implications and lived experience of relatedness in local contexts'. This involves accepting and acknowledging the 'truism that people are always conscious of their connections to other people…and that some of these connections carry particular weight – socially, materially, affectively [which] can be described in genealogical words but they can also be described in other ways' (ibid). In this chapter, this refers to the ways in which women in sex work established domesticity and built families in the red-light area through fictive kin and consanguineal bonds. I discuss this below.

Women living and working in the red-light area often formed long-term intimate relations with customers—these were initiated by the men, who would express romantic feelings for the women, promise marriage and offer avenues for them to leave the red-light area. The relationships would start once the women stopped 'selling sex' to the men and the sexual interactions would become encoded in an agreement and language of intimacy. However, the men were expected to provide social security, take on 'masculine jobs', for example, fixing things around the household and running errands, and eventually fulfil the promise of marriage and domesticity, which would in most cases, enable the women to exit sex work. The women who were in these relationships referred to their partners as *bor*, the Bengali word for 'husband' irrespective of their marital status. They referred to their brothel households as *shongshaar*, which refers to familial and domestic dwelling in terms of the social relations but also the materiality of the settings: one which is supposed to provide social, economic and emotional security and is a microcosm of the world.

Illouz (2012: 20) defines the 'architecture of choice' as 'mechanisms that are integral to the subject and shaped by culture: they concern both the criteria with which one evaluates an object...and the modes of self-consultation, the ways in which a person consults his or her emotions, knowledge and formal reasoning to reach a decision'. The author identifies six components: (i) influence of remote consequences on one's decisions, (ii) the nature of the process of consultation used to decide, (iii) modes of self-consultation used to make a decision, (iv) cultural norms and techniques to hold one's desires and wants in suspicion, (v) accepted grounds for make a decision and finally, (vi) the value of choice for its own sake. (ibid). This is a useful framework to understand how women living in the red-light area constructed and formulated their choices regarding intimacy.

For women living in the red-light area, the influence of 'remote consequences' of their choices regarding intimacy and belonging were omnipresent in their minds. These included a fear of abandonment by their partners leading to social and economic precarity which most had experienced, and which had led them into sex work. Therefore, despite drawing heavily from ideas about normative and idealised (by middle-class standards) intimate relationships, the women took decisions regarding intimate relations in ways that were meant to avoid 'past mistakes' if such relationships ended. This also led to a complete avoidance of romantic relationships, as explained by Chumki: 'Why would I want to end up in the same place that led me here? I am here to make money, not fall in love'.

The dichotomy of aspirations of domesticity as a way out of sex work and a simultaneous fear of abandonment framed the choices the women made about intimacy in their lives. This is exemplified in the domestic arrangement of Sabina, a 25-year old[6] from Bangladesh, who lived next door to her sister Jasmine, who was 27. I discuss this next, embedding it within a discussion of her life-history.

Born and raised in a Muslim household in rural Bangladesh, Jasmine and Sabina's father remarried when they were around the ages of 7 and 5, and this pushed their mother into the informal labour market across the border in India (Guha 2018a). As a family the three of them lived and worked in a brick kiln in North Bangladesh, where Sabina met and eventually married a fellow Bangladeshi living with his family in the same brick kiln and hailing from the same village as her. She returned to the village to live with her husband and her in-laws, and became pregnant with their first child. However, she discovered that her husband was having multiple affairs with other women in the village.

> He was often away, for many days at a time – he said it was work, but we heard that he was with other women. My in-laws blamed me for his behaviour, said I couldn't keep him at home. I was quite pregnant, and it was a difficult time, so I couldn't keep track of where he went. (Sabina, September 2014)

Jasmine had also returned to her village as part of Sabina's bridal party—she decided to stay on in her natal household, while their mother returned to the brick kiln. She was aware of her sister's growing unhappiness but hoped her brother-in-law would change his ways. At one point, her brother-in-law returned to the village after a couple of weeks away and visited Jasmine. He told her he'd seen her mother and that she was unwell and had asked for Jasmine to visit. Worried, Jasmine left with her brother-in-law, after sharing the concerning news with Sabina. Unfortunately, her brother-in-law took her to Kolkata and sold her to a brothel in Park Street, a nightlife hub of the city. Jasmine was able to eventually escape and re-entered sex work in Kalighat, where she could live and work independently, without being under the control of a madam or pimp (Guha 2018a). When she returned to her village and reunited with a beleaguered Sabina who had been fully abandoned by her husband and had no idea about her sister's whereabouts, Jasmine found her living a hand-to-mouth existence. Sabina's in-laws, angered at losing their son, treated her like a burden and deprived her of household resources, including access to food. Saddened at her sister's state, Jasmine shared with Sabina her engagement with sex work and asked her to join the trade for social and economic independence and security. Sabina was hesitant at first but eventually decided to join Jasmine keeping her son's needs in mind:

> If it was just about me, I might have tried some other work first, like domestic work. But I have my son, whom my useless husband had also abandoned. I needed to do something where we could live together, and I could make enough money for his future. This kind of work [sex work] made sense. (Sabina, September 2014)

Sabina's rationale for entering sex work resonated with other women I met in the Kalighat red-light area. As single mothers from broken marriages, the women favoured a form of work which would enable them to keep their children close, while being able to earn more than what domestic work and other forms of manual work would render possible. Sex work also afforded possibilities to meet men in a way that didn't attract constant attention within the communities in which they lived—wider social stigma meant that they barely left the red-light areas and the sex-work marketplace also became the setting for their domestic and intimate lives.

Sabina's past and her memories of hardship caused by her husband's abandonment also affected her 'modes of self-consultation' (Illouz 2012: 21) when it came to making decisions about future relationships. The self-consultation process also included an understanding of the cultural norms that shape vulnerabilities experienced by single, unmarried (or those who have separated from their partners) women in a patriarchal society—this includes sexual vulnerability. Sex work afforded an opportunity to be embedded in a community of other single women, and to draw from each other's experiences. This affected the 'process of consultation' (ibid: 21) through which women made their decisions about intimacy and belonging. While Sabina's own experiences affected her decision-making process, Jasmine's failed attempts at long-term intimacy played a role, too. The two sisters lived next door to each—sharing walls to their one-roomed households, and their lives and experiences within the red-light areas.

In her first two-and-a-half years of working in Kalighat, Jasmine fell in love with a customer. His mother was a retired sex worker living in the area, and she approved of her son's decision to marry Jasmine and set up a household outside the red-light area. However, the approval was conditional—she wanted Jasmine to help her son to establish himself financially. This sparked the eventual end of the relationship:

> She came and asked me to help my future husband economically – to give him money so he could buy a second-hand taxi. I was happy that she was willing to let her son marry me and I wanted to help. I went to the NGO bank[7] and withdrew all my savings. *Didi* [older sister, referring to a peer worker] warned me against it. She said 'You are harming yourself'. But I was madly in love, didn't want to listen. I gave him the money, but in another two months both mother and son wanted more. Meanwhile, no talk of marriage or leaving the *lain-bari (red-light area)* was mentioned. I began to realise that this mother-son duo was trying to ruin me. Take all my money and leave me penniless. I didn't want to let that happen, so I ended it. (Jasmine, 2014)

In the formulation of her initial choice to support her partner, Jasmine reveals how she had prioritised her own emotions and instinct over advice from social workers. However, after terminating the relationship, she decided to prioritise motherhood instead, focusing on her twin children born during her time as a sex worker. Jasmine's decision to prioritise motherhood over relations of intimacy affected Sabina's decisions in this matter, too.

While Illouz's (2012) 'architecture of choice' offers conceptual possibilities for an analysis of the decision-making processes for women in sex work regarding matters of intimacy, its limitations need to be explored. At the centre of her conceptual framework Illouz (2012) imagines a heterosexual female subject; the author acknowledges this. However, this is also unarguably a privileged Western heterosexual subject whose choices in matters of intimacy are mostly individualised. Her 'architecture of choice' therefore, unlike those in the lives of my research respondents, does not operate in a context where the control of female sexuality is 'at the core of both patriarchal and caste relations' (Abraham 2001: 135). It might be tempting to think that in India this only holds true for women from disadvantaged social and economic backgrounds. However, based on fieldwork with middle-class families in Kolkata, Donner (2016: 1147) argues that

> [despite what the] ostensibly overwhelming transformations that individualism, discourses on coupledom and the public display of affection among the young may suggest, the new ways of being intimate, of choosing a spouse and of conducting conjugal relations among middle-class urbanites have to be interpreted in relation to less conspicuous discourses, which are equally powerful and significant, in particular the resilient ideology and practical implications of the joint family.

These families and communities function as sites of everyday violence and power inequalities in the lives of women who are socially and economically dependent on them. Although Illouz's (2012) *Why Love Hurts* strives to place a discussion of 'romantic pain' within a sociological perspective, Illouz's work does not discuss 'pain' from violence inflicted within relations of intimacy, marriage and domesticity. As I have discussed earlier in the chapter, in the lives of women from sex work, violence within social relations with members of their households, communities, market and the state not only affect women's engagement with sex work, but also shape their choices regarding intimacy. Gendered violence as a feature of modern forms of intimacy (and conflicts and power differentials within) need to be acknowledged as a cause for the physical and psychological *koshto* or pain inflicted in women's lives, which determine future trajectories of intimacy.

With the rise of the Hindu right-wing in India, 'love' is now deeply politicised and lies at the crossroads of relations between majoritarian and minority religions in India. This is evident in the escalating hysteria around 'love *jihad*', which are claims of forcible conversions of Hindu women to Islam in the name of 'love', carried out by Muslim men (Gupta

2009; Rao 2011). These larger forces which control intimacy in women's lives, and the role of the state within this, which empowers 'social institutions such as the "community" or "family" as spaces where intimacies are legitimized, valorized or criminalized' (Datta 2016: 175, drawing on Jeejeebhoy 1998; Das (1995) and Mody (2008)) are overlooked in Illouz's (2012) model. But these factors lie at the very heart of choices and decisions regarding intimacy and domesticity within the lives of women in sex work.

These choices also operate in a context where the sexualities and livelihoods of the women in question are considered economically and culturally illicit. In India, the shaping of sex work as socially and legally subversive (in the way it is understood now) traces its historical legacy to the British empire. In its bid to protect its soldiers from venereal diseases, the colonial 'social reform' project removed existing social, political, cultural power from sex workers and zoned them into restricted sites ('red-light areas') which still evoke ideas of 'disease' and decay (Shah 2014) among the populace. This was carried out in collusion with the nineteenth-century middle-class nationalist movement which was both responding to the colonial project of social reform (Chatterjee 1989) and middle-class anxieties about the crumbling institution of the Bengali joint family due to migration, urbanisation and changing conjugal patterns (Sen 1999: 179). In postcolonial India, this legacy continues to hold forth in the lived experiences of women in sex work and persists within their intimate lives which have direct and indirect consequences on their perceived social 'deviance'. I will explore more of this in the next section where I look at how women in sex work balance motherhood with intimacy.

Balancing Romantic Relationships and Motherhood: When the Emotional, Social and Economic Collide

During Sabina's life-history interviews, she showed me pictures of her son and of a man she was in a long-term relationship with. As the interviews progressed over the period of several days, Sabina confided that she was married but didn't share that with everyone. While it was common for the women I met to be in long-term relationships with ex-customers, it was unusual for them to marry the men but continue to stay on in the red-light area. However, for Sabina 'motherhood' was an important aspect in her decision regarding his romantic life. This wasn't particular to her as over the course of my ethnographic fieldwork in Kalighat, 'motherhood' emerged as a strong source of belonging in the lives of full-time female sex workers. Women would often cite their children as reasons for the entry into sex work while expressing concern that their children might stigmatise them in the future for their engagement with sex work. Sabina worried about that too:

I know his friends in the school tell him 'your mother is this, your mother is that'. I only hope this does not go into his head, and that he doesn't end up hating me for this decision and the life I chose – I did it for both of us. I hope he understands that. (Sabina, September 2018)

The importance that motherhood played in the lives of these women as sources of comfort and belonging was emphasised constantly across interviews and conversations with women I met in the red-light area. This was particularly illustrated by Rima's case, a 22-year-old full-time residential female sex work. Born into a village in the South 24 Parganas district of West Bengal, Rima was abandoned by her husband and chose to enter sex work with her parents' knowledge. She left her one-year-old daughter from her marriage with her parents, who agreed to raise the child and became emotionally attached to her. Despite the support with childcare that Rima received from her parents, Rima found herself missing her daughter:

When my husband abandoned me, I decided to come to Kolkata to look for work. I was worried about my daughter, but my parents decided to formally adopt her. It would make it easier for her to have a father figure in the house to grow up around. I was relieved then, but it's been two years here and this life gets lonely. Customers come and go, and sometimes I just wish I had a child to raise here. My parents love my daughter, they don't want to give her to me, for her to live here. But I too want a child. There's no meaning to this life if there isn't a child to feed, to raise, to dream for. (Rima, September 2014)

During the interview Rima asked me repeatedly if I could help her to adopt a child. Rima's yearning for a child 'to feed, to raise, to dream for' underlines how motherhood in the lives of women in sex work is perceived to impart purpose or meaning to a life lived in subversion and framed by social marginalisation. Rao (2018: 2) highlights the 'centrality of reproduction to women's identities' in her work with Dalit women in rural Tamil Nadu in southern India. As Rima's narrative highlights, 'motherhood' is not only a source of belonging within the lives of female sex workers, but also a form of social respectability in an otherwise stigmatised way of life.

In this light, motherhood becomes a key criterion within decisions about romance and intimacy within relationships with men encountered through sex work. This was exemplified in Sabina's hesitation about entering into a long-term monogamous relationship with a customer because she did not want it to cause friction in her relationship with her son. This resonated with what other women in the red-light area expressed too—prioritising their children's welfare over their own romantic needs. When I asked her what swayed her decision, which included accepting her marriage proposal, she cited his acceptance and love for her son as the decisive factor:

> I told him at the start, like I did to other men who said they loved me, that my son is very important to me. He has no father, so I am his everything. If they love and marry me, they also need to love my son and accept him. I cannot abandon him for 'love'. I entered this life because my husband left me, I have to be careful now because now my son is older, and he will feel the hurt too. I want to protect him from that. The other customers, when they heard this, they would change their minds. But this man was different – he seemed to understand right away. I've seen how he (her partner) is with my son. He treats him like he is of the same blood – my son idolises him and is very attached to him. When my husband asked me to marry him, I was unsure. I didn't want to get into a second marriage – but my son coaxed me into it. I know my son needs a father, and I decided to go ahead with it. (Sabina, September, 2014)

Sabina's decision to marry her partner hinged strongly on his acceptability of her son, highlighting how decisions about intimacy and domesticity within the lives of women living in a red-light area depend on the co-existence of consanguineal and fictive kin relationships. However, despite her marriage, Sabina continued to live on in the red-light area. This was unusual, as marriage was usually seen as a way for women to exit the red-light area. When I asked Sabina, what led her to stay on, she underlined her fear of economic and social precarity due to her past experiences:

My previous husband abandoned me, for no fault of my own. I was help-less, relying on the generosity of my in-laws to give me food and shelter. They were angry with me, they considered me a burden and taunted me for not being able to hold on to my husband. I remember those desperate times like they were yesterday. I came into this life to stand on my own two feet – this life, it has many lows, but it does give me economic and social security. I can work, live on my own and with my son, I have friends who look out for me, and I am making good money for son and my future. Yes, I married my partner because he is a good man. But he is not economically strong enough to provide for us as a family, yet. His family – they know me, they love me. Sometimes his mother will send food for me, and I will cook something and send it to them too. His parents want me to move in with then, be a proper wife and daughter-in-law. But I have to think about myself, and my son. I cannot give all of this up before my husband is finan-cially able to provide for us, including my son. And yes, he has accepted my son – but who knows if his mother will? Once I move into their household, I give up my independence and ability to control things. If he leaves me, I am alone and helpless again. I don't want that for myself, and my son. So, I will continue to work and be independent for now, or maybe for as long as I can. (Sabina, September 2014)

Sabina's decision to continue sex work despite her marriage unsettles Illouz's (2012) argument regarding the dynamics of women's (sexually) exclusivist strategies. Illouz (2012: 74) argues 'that heterosexual women who follow an exclusivist sexual strategy are…motivated…by a reproduc-tive orientation'. This differs from Susan Brownmiller (1976)| and Alice Rossi's (1976) arguments that that women are exclusivist to obtain male protection for rape and due to possession of an innate orientation towards men (and towards their young) respectively—which Illouz (2012: 75) draws on to build a counter argument. The author argues that 'biological time now plays a significant role in shaping women's cultural *perceptions* of their bodies and their pairing strategies…[and] in that process, the ecology and architecture of choice within which they operate have changed considerably'. This dominates their decision and strategy to be sexually exclusivist.

However, Illouz (2012) seems to draw on conventional norms of family and kinship. The argument, therefore, does not address what happens when, for example, women with children (from a previous relationship) choose a partner—how do women's strategies of sexual exclusivity (or lack thereof) play out in a scenario where motherhood is not directly connected to the partner under consideration? Or more, simply how do single mothers with limited access to social and financial capital make decisions about future partners? (see also Morris, this volume, for a further discussion of this question).

For Sabina, experiences of gender and power inequalities in her previous marriage and across her life affected the dynamics of her sexual exclusivist (or lack, thereof) strategy. In this context, sexual exclusivity to a future partner threatened her ability to prioritise her relationship with her son from a previous marriage—the former, therefore, depended on the partner's acceptability of her son. Even when this is verbally expressed, the culturally influenced mutual exclusivity of the two, that is, being subsumed into her new partner's family and being economically dependent on him (because of sexual exclusivity through marriage) and caring for her son, compels her to continue to remain in sex work. In this cultural context, sexual exclusivity implies economic dependency—which threatens Sabina's ability to provide for her son.

The overlap of sexual (and romantic) and economic concerns for Sabina also calls into question Illouz's (2012) suggestion of no direct continuity between social spheres. Instead, through Sabina's experiences, it is evident how the collision of the economic, social, sexual and romantic uniquely shaped her strategies and decisions about her intimate life. However, this should not become an argument for exceptionalising the lives and sex workers' experiences. Drawing on Zelizer (2005), Sanders (2008: 411) argues that 'emotional and bodily intimacy can be achieved through commerce and that there is not a necessary corrupting factor when the two spheres merge'. That experiences and relationships formed prior to entering sex work continue to affect decisions regarding intimacy within sex work highlight how different spheres not only collide but do so across space and time in the lives of women affected by life-cycles of power inequalities and violence.

Analysis and Concluding Thoughts

Sabina's decision to stay on in sex work and live apart from her husband and in-laws illuminated how the emotional, social and economic collide in the lives of women in a red-light area. These overlapping concerns become inextricable in their relations of intimacy and belonging in the red-light area which affords them multiple possibilities to 'start over' socially and emotionally. The sex-work marketplace enables the co-existence of what may seem like contradictory relations, for example, labour relations in sex work and relations of conjugality. Crucially, it also allows for possibilities of motherhood and conjugality in the lives of women in sex work even when these do not follow conventional kinship trajectories.

Overall, the red-light area provides a liminal space for the women to live out their liminal identities: engaging with work and a way of life that is perceived as socially subversive but desiring and aspiring towards 'normalcy' in the form of domesticity and marriage and a conventional household. These norms of 'ideal' relationships draw strongly from upper-caste and middle-class valorisations of motherhood and marriage and influence the way of life in the Kalighat red-light area. However, as Sabina's example highlights, the red-light area makes it materially possible for the women to adapt and adjust conventional middle-class norms regarding domesticity and marriage to work to their own social and economic advantage.

This provides expressions of agency in an otherwise constrained context, and highlights how social, economic and emotional concerns overlap to construct unique subjectivities of female sex workers in the Kalighat red-light area. This echoes Butler's (1997) argument that despite an external imposition of power, it is never static. Instead power is engaged with on a subjective level enabling for unique forms of resistance and expressions of agency alongside experiences of victimhood. The ways in which women like Sabina are able to draw on their past experiences to negotiate the terms of their present relations to offset dangers of social and economic precarity, can be read as their attempts to appropriate 'middle-class femininity', which can become 'in itself a kind of symbolic capital that women, especially from the working classes, seek to embody' (Rao 2018: 5, drawing on Skeggs 1997), to suit their own lives. In many ways, the contradictions of selling sex while attempting to build normative domestic arrangements are similar to the paradox of middle-class femininities in India where work and employment are central to the middle-class woman's persona, but their 'everyday practices are contradictory, combining trying work regimes with efforts to reproduce family norms and values, seen as contributing to a 'respectable femininity'' (Rao 2018 drawing on Radhakrishnan 2009; Thapan 2009). As Rao (2018) argues, drawing on Heyer (2014) instead of reading these domestic and family-making attempts as an additional form of subordination, 'it could reflect creative navigations and renegotiations of both conjugal and wider social relations of caste and class' (2014: 5; see also Xie, this volume).

The co-existence of choice and constraint also highlight how female sex workers express 'patiency' (Reader 2007) which are responses to dependency, capability and necessity within their lives. In the conceptualisation of 'patiency', Reader (2007: 593) argues for a broader understanding of personhood which incorporates 'patiental features', where a 'patient' is a being that is acted upon, and is different from an object: 'When I am a patient, I am not thereby an object, but remain as much of a subject, a human person, as I am when I act'. In acting to form relations of intimacy in a life marred by violence and power inequalities in household relations, and in acting to appropriate middle-class institutions of marriage and motherhood to suit their own aspirations for social and economic stability, women in sex work like Sabina exercise patiency and resilience that deserve to not be overlooked, or dismissed as victimhood, alone.

These negotiations can also be read as the making of 'emotional capitalism' within the lives of women in sex work—where emotional decisions about intimacy and belonging become invested with matters of financial importance, and where social and emotional arrangements are also economic arrangements. While these can be sources of violence and exploitation, in Jasmine's case for example, they can also be a source of comfort and belonging. These hint at the complexity and dynamism in the lives of women in sex work where agency exists alongside victimhood, commerce alongside emotion, and sexual labour alongside domesticity and intimacy.

Notes

1. The research received ethical approval from the International Development Ethics Committee, School of International Development, University of East Anglia.
2. All names have been changed to protect confidentiality.
3. Emphasis added.
4. Women who live outside the red-light area, for example, in towns or villages close to the city of Kolkata. They travel to the red-light area and rent spaces for the day, and return to their residences in the evenings.
5. I am aware of the problematic connotations of the term in its usage.
6. All ages are self-reported.
7. A 'sex workers' NGO in the red-light area runs a financial cooperative bank.

References

Abraham, L. (2001) Redrawing the Lakshman Rekha: Gender Differences and Cultural Constructions in Youth Sexuality in Urban India. *South Asia: Journal of South Asian Studies,* 24 (s1): 133–156.

Agarwal, B. (1997) 'Bargaining' and Gender Relations: Within and Beyond the Household. *Feminist Economics,* 3 (1): 1–51.

Brownmiller, S. (1976) *Against our will: Men, women, and rape.* New York: Bantam Books.

Butler, J. (1997) *The Psychic Life of Power: Theories in Subjection.* Stanford: Stanford University Press.

Carsten, J. (2000) *Cultures of relatedness: New approaches to the study of kinship.* Cambridge: Cambridge University Press.

Chatterjee, P. (1989) Colonialism, nationalism, and colonialized women: The contest in India. *American Ethnologist* 16 (4): 622–633.

Das, V. (1995) *Critical Events: An Anthropological Perspective on Contemporary India*. Delhi: Oxford University Press.

Datta, A. (2016) Another Rape? The Persistence of Public/Private Divides in Sexual Violence Debates in India. *Dialogues in Human Geography* 6 (2): 173–177.

Donner, H. (2008) *Domestic Goddesses: Maternity, Globalization and Middle-Class Identity in Contemporary India*. Hampshire: Ashgate.

Donner, H. (2016) Doing it our Way: Love and marriage in Kolkata middle-class families. *Modern Asian Studies* 50 (4): 1147–1189.

Guha, M. (2018a) Disrupting the 'life-cycle' of violence in social relations: Recommendations for anti-trafficking interventions from an analysis of pathways out of sex work for women in Eastern India. *Gender & Development*, 26 (1): 53–69.

Guha, M. (2018b) Sartorially weaving their way through *bhodrota* (respectability): Georgette sarees, bangles and selling sex in a Kolkata neighbourhood. *International Journal of Fashion Studies*, 5 (2): 399–405.

Gupta, C. (2009) Hindu Women, Muslim Men: Love Jihad and Conversions. *Economic and Political Weekly* 44 (51): 13–15.

Heyer, J. (2014) Dalit Women Becoming 'Housewives': Lessons from the Thiruppur Region, 1981/2 to 2008/9. In C. Still (ed.) *Dalits in Neoliberal India: Mobility or Marginalisation?* New Delhi: Routledge: 208–35.

Illouz, E. (2007) *Cold intimacies: The making of emotional capitalism*. Cambridge: Polity.

Illouz, E. (2012) *Why love hurts: A sociological explanation*. Cambridge: Polity.

Jeejeebhoy, S. J. (1998) Adolescent Sexual and Reproductive Behaviour. *Soc Sci Med* 46 (10): 1275–1290.

Kabeer, N. (1994) *Reversed Realities: Gender Hierarchies in Development Thought*. London: Verso.

Kotiswaran, P. (2008) Born unto Brothels – Toward a Legal Ethnography of Sex Work in an Indian Red-Light Area. *Law & Social Inquiry*, 33 (3): 579–629.

Mody, P. (2008) *The Intimate State: Love-Marriage and the Law in India*. Delhi: Routledge.

Radhakrishnan, S. (2009) Professional Women, Good Families: Respectable Femininity and the Cultural Politics of a 'New' India. *Qualitative Sociology* 32: 195–212.

Rao, M. (2011) Love Jihad and Demographic Fears. *Indian Journal of Gender Studies* 18 (3): 425–430.

Rao, N. (2018) Fertility, Reproduction and Conjugal Loyalty: Renegotiating Gender Relations amongst Dalits in Rural Tamil Nadu. *South Asia Multidisciplinary Academic Journal* https://doi.org/10.4000/samaj.4575

Reader, S. (2007) The other side of agency. *Philosophy*, 82(4): 579–604.

Rossi, A. (1976) Children and Work in the Lives of Women (Paper delivered at the University of Arizona, Tucson, February) cited in Rich. A (1980) Compulsory Heterosexuality and Lesbian Existence. *Signs: Journal of women in culture and society*, 5 (4): 631.

Sanders, T. (2008) Male sexual scripts: Intimacy, sexuality and pleasure in the purchase of commercial sex. *Sociology*, 42 (3): 400–417.

Sen, S. (1999) *Women and labour in late colonial India: The Bengal jute industry.* Cambridge: Cambridge University Press.

Shah, S. P. (2014) *Street corner secrets: Sex, Work, and Migration in the city of Mumbai.* London: Duke University Press.

Skeggs, B. (1997) *Formations of Class and Gender: Becoming Respectable.* London: Sage.

Thapan, M. (2009) *Living the Body: Embodiment, Womanhood and Identity in Contemporary India.* New Delhi: Sage.

Zelizer, V. (2005) *The Purchase of Intimacy.* Princeton, NJ: Princeton University Press.

Section IV

From Romantic Fantasy to Disappointment

11

'Utterly Heart-Breaking and Devastating': Couple Relationships and Intensive Parenting Culture in a Time of 'Cold Intimacies'

Charlotte Faircloth

Introduction

[I]t's seen as a really, really bad thing to have anybody who's dependent on you. So, in relationships, like with [my husband] and with … previous relationships and so on, and all my girlfriends and I would always establish this thing, 'You must never have someone who's dependent on you', that's a sort of the revolting thing to happen and [if it happens] you should get rid of them immediately. And as an extension of that it feels like you're not really allowed to have children either because they're also dependent on you and that's like … not a very nice thing to happen. (Claudia, 32, expecting her first child)

Changes to what has been termed 'Parenting Culture' have now become a well-established field of social science scholarship (Lee et al. 2014; Hays 1996; Hendrick 2016; Nelson 2010). This scholarship,

C. Faircloth (✉)
University College London, London, UK
e-mail: c.faircloth@ucl.ac.uk

© The Author(s) 2020
J. Carter, L. Arocha (eds.), *Romantic Relationships in a Time of 'Cold Intimacies'*,
Palgrave Macmillan Studies in Family and Intimate Life,
https://doi.org/10.1007/978-3-030-29256-0_11

largely based on research in Euro-American settings, has called attention to an 'intensification' of parenting in the last 40 years, suggesting that raising children has become, culturally, a more demanding and complex task. So far, the majority of this work has looked at the effect of these changes on individuals, and particularly on women. Mothers (more than fathers) are recognised as increasingly 'torn' by the competing expectations to parent intensively on the one hand, whilst participating in the labour market on the other (Hays 1996; Miller 2005). More recent work has documented the experiences of men grappling with shifting ideals of a more intensive 'involved' fatherhood (Dermott 2008; Miller 2011; Shirani et al. 2012). No research to date, however, has looked at the impact of these changes on couples.

Focusing for the first time on couple relationships in the context of an intensified parenting culture, this chapter reports on a longitudinal study with first-time heterosexual parents (in London, UK) over a five-year period. The suggestion is that new parents are caught in an uncomfortable confluence between competing discourses of ideal relationships and those of ideal parenting. On the one hand, they are (or should be) committed to egalitarian ideals about their relationships. On the other, they aspire to parent 'intensively', in ways which are markedly more demanding for mothers and which makes paternal involvement more complicated.

As Collins has noted, there is a contradiction at the heart of many contemporary family set-ups: a tension between the aspiration for self-realisation through individualism on the one hand and commitment through coupledom and parenthood on the other (Collins 2003). As this chapters explores, and indicative of what Illouz terms 'cold intimacies' (2007), this tension is as difficult to resolve, if not more difficult for contemporary 'egalitarian' couples, than ever. In an era where choice in partner is (apparently) more free and open, Illouz's work in particular points to the gendered nature of 'romantic suffering' such that women are disadvantaged by being more family oriented (2012). In part then, this chapter provides evidence for Illouz's assertion that 'love hurts' (2012) whilst also addressing the empirical lacunae around parenting in her work. At the same time, it points to the limits of her analytical focus on individual or self-reflexive 'choices', to bring tensions around partnering and parenting to the fore. Drawing largely on the narratives of couples who have faced relationship difficulties, this chapter points to the pressures at play in raising the next generation at material, physiological and cultural levels. These tensions are arguably not due to having more or less 'choice' in marriage or sexual markets, but a product of the difficulty in reconciling tensions between partnering and parenting which are based on investments and commitments *beyond* individual choice.

Couple Relationships and Ideals of Equality

Work by Giddens (1992), Bauman (2003), Beck (1992), Beck and Beck-Gernsheim (1995) and Illouz (2007), amongst others, has explored shifting relationship patterns in the contemporary age. Broadly speaking, this body of work argues that, in an age of 'reflexive modernisation', there has been a shift away from traditional, patriarchal couple relationships, based on an inherent inequality between men and women, towards a more equitable, mutually fulfilling model, accompanied by the rise of a more 'plastic' sexuality in particular (Giddens 1992). Giddens argues that in the late twentieth century, in place of traditional patterns of marriage, for example, individuals have become more aware of the need for a fulfilling relationship, based on 'confluent love'; one that is active and contingent. As part of a wider culture of 'individualisation', independence within relationships is highly valued. The 'pure relationship', which is not bound by traditional notions of duty and obligation, has come to depend, instead, on communication, intimacy and a sense of equality.

In line with this thesis, but taking a more critical stance, Illouz has argued that this 'equality' has been modelled on rational, economic systems of bargaining and exchange, indicative of a 'cold' intimacy and a turn towards an 'emotional capitalism' more widely (Illouz 2007). This leads to what she calls 'romantic suffering', in that wider social structures (including marriage) are in contradiction with the 'quest for love', and that this is internalised—by women in particular—as disappointment and personal failing. The separation of romantic relationships from wider social and moral structures, manifest in increasing freedom in our choice of partner, for example, means that even 'love' itself has become individualised, rationalised, an 'object of endless investigation, self-knowledge and self-scrutiny' (2012: 163) and a lonely site for self-validation.

A discursive shift around ideal relationships has arguably been matched by growing legislation in social life (in the UK) around gender equality, which has been concerned to protect individual rights in matters such as pay, political representation and family life (Browne 2013), as well as a growing commitment to gender equality, especially in so far as childcare responsibilities relate to men and women's career prospects and 'work-life-balance'. Parental leave has been one key area for this drive (Gornick and Meyers 2009), with the idea that extending leave alone to fathers promotes their involvement in childcare and housework (Kotsadam and Finseraas 2011). However, 'Shared Parental Leave' (SPL), the current policy iteration in the UK, has had notoriously low up-take amongst parents (Twamley and Schober 2019), and it remains mothers who take extended periods of time away from work, or move to part-time hours, with only 2–8% of parents taking SPL in 2016 (Her Majesty's Revenue and Customs figures in Twamley and Schober 2019). Baird and O'Brien (2015) argue that this is due to an historical emphasis on men's breadwinning roles and women's caring roles in the UK (see also Lewis 1997).

Thus since the work by Giddens et al. was published, scholars working in the field of personal life have critiqued the model of 'plastic' relationships, arguing for a more nuanced perspective, grounded in the realities of everyday experience, which is often less equitable (and more dependent) than either theory or legislation might suggest (Smart 2007). As Gillies says, for example, concepts of 'individualisation' and 'democratisation' that underpin theories of intimacy are much debated, 'with many disputing the claim that personal relationships have become more contingent, negotiated and self directed' (2003: 2). In short, whilst discourses around ideal relationships may have changed, practices have not kept pace (Jamieson 1998)—precisely the gap this chapter, and indeed this volume, seeks to explore.

With respect to parenthood in particular, Collins (2003) has pointed out that in post-industrialised settings, whilst (some) couples might live relatively equal lives before having children, parenthood accentuates the sexual division of labour and still has the potential to divide egalitarian couples along more traditional lines. Where independence and equality might be hallmarks of ideal contemporary relationships, parenthood, instead, is marked by ideals of obligation and permanence (Beck and Beck-Gernsheim 1995). As Beck and Beck-Gernsheim argue, the understood irreversibility of a kinship tie with a child—and indeed the fact that infants require supervision 24 hours a day—sits uncomfortably with a more 'flexible' approach to relationships. At the same time, in a culture which shuns permanence and commitment for the sake of self-fulfilment, there is something existentially appealing, relaxing, even, about a relationship that is beyond the remit of personal preference, such that the parent-child relationship is one suffused with deep meaning (Beck and Beck-Gernsheim 1995; Ribbens McCarthy and Edwards 2002).

Contemporary Parenting Culture

Across the world, and across history, parenting has always been subject to moralising and guidance (Hardyment 2007; Lee et al. 2014). However, the magnitude of the increase in expectations around raising children, particularly in the US and the UK, and particularly since the mid-1970s—the fact that we even use the term 'parenting' as a verb at all—is striking: parenting classes, parenting manuals, parenting experts and parenting 'interventions' are now so common-place as to be unremarkable (Lee et al. 2014). Rather than being something that is simple, straightforward or common sense, parenting today is routinely presented as a task requiring expert guidance and supervision, fuelling a multi-million pound industry of advice and 'support' (Faircloth 2013; Lee et al. 2014).

Drawing on a developmental, psychological rationale, parenting is understood as the source of, and solution to, a whole range of problems—at both individual and societal levels. The transformative potential of parenting to solve what might better be called structural social problems (such as the 'obesity epidemic'), means parenting has been the subject of much policy intervention in recent years, especially under the auspices of 'early intervention' in deprived communities (Gillies et al. 2017; Macvarish 2016; Lee et al. 2014). What scholars of 'parenting culture' observe is that the task of raising the next generation has become highly fragmented and detailed, with a keen focus on the everyday practices of daily life (such as eating or sleeping). Further, rather than 'socialising' children into a set of shared social values, a more individualised perspective means that the aim is to raise 'successful individuals' who are able to 'be themselves', at the same time as acting as an aspect of adult identity work (Faircloth 2013).

Recognising the gendered dimension to these changes, much work has drawn on the concept of 'intensive mothering' (Hays 1996) in understanding the experiences of contemporary women (Faircloth 2013). Arguing that the mother-child relationship represents a sacred bastion in a society otherwise governed by the pursuit of profit, Hays summarises the characteristics of intensive motherhood, as 'child-centred, expert-guided, emotionally absorbing, labour intensive, and financially expensive' (Hays 1996: 8). The 'intensive' mother is one who is considered responsible for all aspects of her child's development—physical, social, emotional and cognitive—above and beyond anyone else, including the father (Hays 1996: 46). Ideally she demonstrates this commitment through embodied means, such as by birthing 'without intervention' or breastfeeding 'on demand', and no cost, physical or otherwise, is considered too great in her efforts to optimise her child (Wolf 2011). As noted, fathers have not been immune from this trend (Dermott 2008; Collier and Sheldon 2008; Shirani et al. 2012), although most scholars agree that it remains mothers to whom these cultural messages are largely targeted and around women's reproductive choices that the fiercest debates reign.

As a body of work, *Parenting Culture Studies* draws on important traditions within sociology around not only the 'doing' and 'display' of family (Finch 2007) but also individualisation and risk-consciousness (Beck and Beck-Gernsheim 1995, 2002). Certainly, a key assumption of contemporary culture is that children are vulnerable to risk in the early years, and therefore require protection and guidance. In a neo-liberal era, with its emphasis on self-management, 'good' mothers are therefore reflexive, informed consumers, able to 'account' for their parenting strategies (Murphy 2003; Faircloth 2013).

Of course, the perception of what is a 'good parent' is largely culturally, historically and ideologically rooted, and thus in continuous change. A Euro-American cultural script does not affect all individuals in the same way around the world—class, ethnicity and gender all affect its internalisation, and there may be a curious combination of adoption, resistance or adaptation according to specific time and place (Faircloth et al. 2013; Hamilton 2016). What is important, however, is that this ideal script is widely recognised as the 'proper' way of 'doing' parenting, an injunction to which most people must respond (Arendell 2000).

In a similar vein, Jamieson (1998), whilst a critic of Giddens' argument around the emergence of the pure relationship, agrees that disclosing intimacy and equality is an *ideal* within contemporary relationships, through which individuals narrate and idealise in their own aspirations, with 'real love' being particularly important for women in the quest for self-worth (where public forms of fulfilment, such as careers, remain more readily open to men) (Illouz 2012; Twamley 2012). This means, of course that, the transition to motherhood and the return to so-called traditional gendered roles—even if only temporarily—can be felt particularly acutely by contemporary women; a trope common to much current sociological and popular literature (Cusk 2001; Miller 2005).

In sum, there is a contradiction between two ideals at play: couple relationships which value equality, intimacy and independence and parenting relationships (seen as permanent and dependent) which value a highly gendered, ever present and embodied form of motherhood. What implications does this have for the lived experiences of couples themselves?

Methodology

To explore the implications of competing expectations around personal and family life, this study was designed as a longitudinal one, which included repeat in-depth interviews with 30 participants (15 first-time parent, heterosexual and dual-professional couples) over a five-year period (2011–2017). These interviews were part of a wider mixed-methods study into shifts in parenting culture, which also included one-off interviews with a further ten participants (five couples who were lesbian, gay and/or second time parents) and a survey with a sample of 125 parents (distributed via *Qualtrics* to a demographically diverse panel of parents in the UK with children under a year old) although those data are not referred to in this chapter.

Building on previous research (Faircloth 2013), the intention was to find parents who internalised the injunction to 'parent' intensively, and who consciously reflected on and articulated their decisions as an element of their 'identity work'. Furthermore, the aim was to work with couples who were committed to, and might technically be able to afford, an 'equitable' division of parental leave, even if they chose not to. Bringing together these objectives, parents were contacted through a range of antenatal education classes and courses in London—such as the National Childbirth Trust—recognised by a number of scholars (Thomson et al. 2011) as being primarily made up of this higher-educated, dual-professional, middle class and high earning demographic.

Analytically and methodologically a largely narrative approach to research is taken here. Whilst appreciating that narratives are not a straightforward reflection of experience (Craib 2004), many scholars have emphasised the role of language in the constitution of personhood, and have argued 'that human beings actually live out their lives as "narratives", [and] that we make use of the stories of the self that our culture makes available to us to plan out our lives ... to account for events and give them significance, to accord ourselves an identity' (Rose 1999: xviii; Riessman 2008). Looking at how couples 'accounted' for the division of labour within their respective partnerships, and particularly the contradiction between 'equitable' relationships and unequal 'intensive' parenting, was the intention of the study, analysing both anticipation and outcomes before and after children were born.

Couples were interviewed in various areas of London.[1] After meeting one or both of them at an antenatal group or similar, and a discussion with the aid of a study information sheet, they were asked to fill out a brief online survey (designed and administered via *Qualtrics*) to collect demographic data, using sections from the 2011 census as a template (e.g. age/marital status, etc.). These couples were then interviewed, usually in their homes, at times convenient to them. The first interview (both together and separate) was before their child was born, and then jointly when their child was 1–2 months old, at 6 months old, and then finally at 12–13 months old, when we also repeated the individual interviews where possible. Recordings were transcribed and coded thematically as a whole, with the aid of relevant software. However, to avoid fragmentation of the data too far, a 'listening guide' approach was adopted with a sub-sample of the transcripts (see, e.g. Doucet 2006) to try to grasp the 'deep' narratives in the accounts. Couples were contacted again (by email) for follow-up questionnaires when their first children were two-and-a-half and five years old. Eleven of the original 15 couples responded, by which point all of them had had at least one further child, and two of them had two more.

The majority of the couples interviewed were middle class (in that they overwhelmingly had higher educational qualifications and professions), middle aged (between 45 and 29 though typically 34 or 35), white, heterosexual and married (all were living in long-term relationships, though if they were not married 'partner' is used, rather than 'husband' or 'wife'). The average household income for the group ranged between £30,000 (in the case of a couple where the wife was undertaking a PhD) and over £200,000, with the majority between £50,000 and £150,000. All interviews were conducted in English, though some participants were born outside the UK.

A final note on context before moving to the findings, which is important in understanding couples' accounts not only of parental leave but also decisions about work: childcare provision in the UK has been recognised as some of the most expensive in Europe (nearly £10,000/annum for a nursery place, or in the region of £25,000 for a full-time nanny, Family and Childcare Trust (FCT) 2017). Childcare therefore represents a major household outgoing second only to a mortgage for most couples, particularly if they have more than one child. There are no government subsidies to assist with this until children reach the age of three (or two in some means-tested cases), at which point children are entitled to 15 hours of free care a week (which has recently risen to 30 hours for some families, albeit with some concern about the feasibility of such provision, due to the on-costs to providers themselves, FCT 2017).

Findings

Introducing the Couples

Indicative of their age, class and educational capital (not to mention the availability of contraception and abortion), all couples were fully invested in their 'decision' to have children, and none of the pregnancies were unplanned or unwanted (one couple had sought fertility treatment to this end).

Furthermore, parenting was understood as a 'fulfilling' and 'rewarding' activity that both parents were looking forward to, with fathers committed to being as 'involved' in as possible. However, despite a discursive commitment to equality, of the 15 couples none formally planned to split parental leave, and all stuck to the traditional division, with mothers taking longer periods than fathers. In fact, at the time of first interview, only three couples seemed to know about the possibility of splitting leave, but had decided against it as it would be financially too constraining for the family (see discussion below). This is curious not least because these couples are those who are most likely to be literate about their own policy entitlements.

To give an example, this couple, Laura (32, a teacher) and her husband James (a barrister, also 32) have been together since the age of 17 years, are highly committed to ideals of equality and spoke highly of their 'independent' social lives and equally active careers. They had a 'gentleman's agreement' that they would have an 'equitable' division of parental leave, such that Laura would take an extended period away from work after the birth of the their first child, whilst James would do so after the second, because Laura wanted James to 'experience the whole thing' and not set up 'damaging gendered patterns'. As Laura says, '[James] and I have been together for 14 years and we've grown up together, we've done everything together which may or may not be a good thing, but that's been what we've done. We're kind of intellectual equals, we're roughly at the same stages in our career. Then suddenly, kind of almost without us realising, we've made a mutual decision to have a child and now I feel like we're on these different paths, at least I guess until I go back to work'.[2]

There are clearly many ways of understanding equality in couple relationships, especially as they relate to parenting, and not all of them will be a straightforward '50/50' split of each task or activity (e.g. feeding, changing or scheduling activities), but take a more holistic approach to family contributions. However, the findings from across the sample point to a gap between 'ideals' around equality (expressed in current policy discourses and indeed by many couples themselves) and the realities of caring for a small child. Perhaps not surprisingly, for those couples who were most explicitly committed to an 'equitable' division of labour, like Laura and James, navigating this gap was harder than for those who had anticipated a more traditional gendered set up, and it was their accounts that revealed the most tension and that are the focus here.

Whilst the majority of the 11 couples remained together (i.e. those of the original 15 with whom follow-up was possible), two had separated (but one was making attempts to stay together). Whether or not their relationships had suffered, all of the accounts pointed to the extent to which having children had re-entrenched gendered stereotypes around the division of labour, and the unique kind of pressure that had created in the context of an ostensibly 'egalitarian' relationship. This study therefore provides empirical evidence for Collins' (2003) assertion that equal partners can, in spite of their best intentions, become unequal parents. Furthermore, they highlight the danger of focusing too much on suffering as the result of individual 'choice' (Illouz 2012), but show the need for a *relational* perspective on everyday constraints to combining partnering and parenting, which become far more enmeshed at the birth of a child. The findings are presented with a focus on material, physiological and cultural factors in turn.

Material Barriers: Parental Leave and Social Institutions of Care

In only one case was the female partner out-earning their male partner in this sample, and in no instance would it have made financial 'sense' for men to take longer periods of leave than women, particularly because at this point it was rare for the father's employers to offer enhanced SPL packages (meaning they would be only eligible to statutory pay).[3] This reflects a gender pay gap across society as a whole (FCT 2017).

Heather, (29) is a PhD student and freelance teacher and David, (44) a freelance web-developer. They are expecting their first child and talk about how they would have liked to have divided childcare:

I mean our original plan … I seem to remember as saying, 'wouldn't it be good if I worked two days a week and looked after the baby for three and [my husband] did the other way round'. Because I couldn't really imagine not working (Heather, 29, one child)

Unfortunately, this was just not financially feasible, in part because if her husband were to take any leave (which would have to be unpaid due to the restrictions on SPL) she would not earn enough to cover their outgoings (unlike other couples in the sample who may have been able to afford it for a few months at least). Once the child was born, she was therefore looking after it full time indefinitely, with some support from grandparents, something she described as a bit 'demoralising' having just finished her PhD. This couple went on to have two other children within the next three years. Whilst Heather talked about the way in which David 'carries them' financially, he spoke about finding this responsibility a 'strain' and in a 'money-no-object' world, would like to have more time with the children, although felt very grateful to be able to work from home so much.

Many critics point out that despite the ideological emphasis on equal parenting, the financial backing to make that a reality for couples is simply not there, particularly given the restrictions on SPL. Instead, there is a tendency to advocate the importance of what Dermott calls the 'caring about' activities of childcare to men—swimming clubs, reading classes and so on (2008) rather than actually legislating to facilitate the 'caring for' activities (the day-to-day care children require). Whilst *discursively* fathers may be encouraged to be 'involved' in parenting and take more of an equal load of childcare, in reality, it is women who continue to shoulder most of the responsibility for care, something which many men are complicit with, consciously or otherwise (Dermott 2008; Gillies 2009).

At the same time, of course, there were also certainly cases where fathers would say they would *like* to spend more time with their children (e.g. if facilitated by paid parental leave) but when pushed admitted that in fact 'just something like a month might be nice … but I couldn't be a stay-at-home Dad' and that 'my kind of work doesn't really allow [part-time working]' (James, a barrister, husband of Laura who talks of the 'gentleman's agreement' above). What was also noticeable was the way in which many couples justified the mother's decision to work by their ability to pay for childcare with their own salary. This accountability strategy (Faircloth 2013) was noticeable by its absence in men's accounts. This yet again reflects Baird and O'Brien's assertion around the residual stereotypes around men and women's roles in society, such that care-giving and home-making should be a woman's first priority, and if not, her responsibility to 'outsource', rather than a cost for the household (2015).

Practical and Physiological Barriers to Equal Parenting

Explicitly or otherwise, as the literature around intensive motherhood has argued (Hays 1996; Wolf 2011) it is women to whom the majority of messages about 'good parenting' are directed, not least because there is a physiological element to so much of what is considered appropriate care.

As numerous authors have discussed, this gendered, embodied ideal about good parenting is one which stretches from pre-conception well into a child's youth. A conception that is 'prepared for', in the form of the mother focusing on both her physical but also emotional health (Lee et al. 2014), or a pregnancy that is carefully monitored and well regulated (in the form of maternal diet, exercise and wellbeing) might be considered an extension of a more formalised 'parenting culture' which focuses around the avoidance of risks to the child once it is born. Later examples such as play, or indeed sleeping habits, such as co-sleeping, which centre around creating secure attachments and establishing 'optimal neural pathways' were regularly mentioned by my informants, with many mothers attending classes such as 'baby sensory' or 'baby massage' under the same rationale (Macvarish 2016).

Space does not allow here to examine fully the ways in which these discourses around 'optimal' or 'natural' care are highly gendered, or what their implications are (Faircloth 2013), but to give an example, this is the account of Claudia, an academic working at a London University, who is at this point 36. She took six months of maternity leave with her first son and seven with her second. In both cases, her husband, Anthony was made redundant whilst she was on maternity leave (albeit with a generous financial pay-off from his job in the City). Claudia was so strongly committed both to her career and to ideals about equality that like Laura and James, her and Anthony made a 'pact' that the only way they would try for a baby would be with the agreement that it would be equally cared for. (This was one of the couples aware of the possibility of splitting parental leave, although this turned out not to be financially feasible in their case, due to the large discrepancy in their salaries). The plan had been, however, that when Claudia went back to work after maternity leave, they would both work a four-day week, and only pay for three days of childcare. In spite of this, when her husband asked to have compressed hours he was made redundant (for the first time). This couple have separated several times since the birth of their second child, but are taking steps to stay together.

Like many other women in the sample, Claudia felt that the way she fed her children had a lot to do with the division of labour between her and her husband and played a part in their relationship breakdown after her second child was born. In the 'breast is best' culture that has been so widely written about in the UK (Faircloth 2013) many women felt that they were in a bind, in that they were on the one hand encouraged, as per the National Health Service guidance, to 'breastfeed exclusively for six months and for "anything up to two years, or beyond"', whilst at the same time aspiring to an equitable (and intimate) relationship with their partners. For this couple, these two things were difficult to combine, as feeding a baby had knock-on implications for other activities of care, as this mother discovered when she breastfed her second child, having formula fed the first:

> I breastfed Joseph [her second son] and we bottle-fed George. This was often used as a reason for [my husband] not being so involved or bonding with Joseph, and somehow was seen as me blocking him and used as an excuse ... for why he started resenting me ... [but] it didn't actually make sense because yes I would feed him but that doesn't mean I had to be the one rocking him for hours on end to sleep ... [my husband] gave up quite early on trying to get him to take the bottle ... I breastfed Joseph until he was 18 months old and this was blamed by everyone for why he didn't sleep so well (he continued to not sleep well when I stopped, though), and I was told I had 'made my bed' so I deserved to be woken continuously by him

and deserved to have to not only feed him but settle him, which would take 1–3 hours each time, after which he would only sleep for 1–2 hours. It was utterly exhausting and took everything out of me, and yet I was expected to be performing motherly duties to my other child, and on top wifely duties to my husband who complained of the lack of intimacy and I think justified him deciding to switch off entirely from our relationship and fantasise about being out of it and with other people. The whole thing has been utterly heart breaking and devastating (Claudia, 36, two children)

And whilst it was not typical of the majority of the responses, Ellen, 45, mother of two children, and separated from their father speaks about breastfeeding in ways that magnify several of the issues other couples mentioned. Ellen used to work as a digital marketing executive in London, but now lives in Denmark, where the family relocated because her partner (a Danish self-employed fashion designer) had been offered a job there, and the day-care system made their cost of living more reasonable:

Breastfeeding was extremely satisfying, fulfilling and comforting to me. I felt I was doing the best for my babies. It did serve to widen the divide with my partner. He felt I should wean earlier than I wanted to because he was pressuring me to find work and have the baby sleep through the night [Ellen, 45, two children]

There are several interesting points to emerge here. One, an obvious one that breastfeeding (as an embodied form of care) can cause tension in relationships, not least because breastfeeding is so much more than about providing nutrition for a child, but has cascading effects on all sorts of parenting practices, including couple intimacy and individual's sense of personhood (Tomori 2014). Second, the point that because men *cannot* breastfeed there is no option but for the father or partner to do less in terms of direct care for the child, particularly in the early days (although as Claudia says, this sets up patterns well into children's infancies). Many couples acknowledged that mothers were 'better' and 'quicker' at settling children at night, even once they had stopped breastfeeding, and even when both had returned to work. This will clearly sit uneasily with couples committed to '50/50 parenting'.

Cultural Barriers: The Intensive Motherhood and the Mental Load

Clearly, although messages about intensive parenting and optimal child development are ostensibly directed at both mothers and fathers today, it is mothers who internalise this injunction more strongly, and who feel that they have ultimate responsibility for its delivery. To draw on Claudia's account again, there is a sense that by not engaging with children intensively and wholeheartedly that one is jeopardising their development.

> [T]hat's one of my regrets, when [my first son] was small, he could've sat in his bouncy chair and I could've done my hair but I didn't want to split my attention from him because I thought that would damage him for life. So it's just mental and you completely neglect yourself ... [and] then you just judge everybody else because they've managed to put some makeup on! (Claudia, 36, two children)

This 'self neglect' appeared very gendered, leading many women in the sample to talk about how they envied their husbands and their ability to 'shut off' their sense of self from their domestic or childcare obligations, at the same time as being frustrated by it. Indeed, most mothers said that although they were 'lucky' that their partners 'helped out' more than fathers in the past, they were still the ones who were expected to shoulder the burden of managing the household and family, something which they felt was both exhausting and unfair (at the same time, of course, as deriving a culturally sanctioned source of 'identity work'). Whilst they had—in the majority of cases—been managing the bulk of household tasks before the birth of their children too, once children actually arrived, the scale of this task multiplied dramatically.

This was a typical response, again from Laura. At this stage (the five-year follow-up questionnaire) she and James have two children, aged five and a half and two and a half. She works four days a week, and looks after both children one day a week. (As her husband James says, 'I think both of us feel that it's not ideal to have a nanny bringing up [our children] more than is necessary', although he has not changed his hours from full-time since the birth of their first son.) They have a nanny the other days, who does the school-run for the older child as they often both have to leave the house by 7.30/8 am and are not home until at least 6 pm.

Having spoken in earlier interviews about how they had expected to parent equally, when asked *'Do you and your partner parent equally? If so, how? If not, why not?'* Laura replied with the following (referring to a recent comic in the Guardian newspaper about the 'Mental Load' carried by women, which portrays the invisible labour of running a household):

> This basically sums up my life! [James] helps out (and to be fair he does most of the cooking for us, not for the kids) but I am the one keeping the show on the road and keeping a vast amount of plates spinning in terms of schedules and just remembering all the hundreds of things that need to get done every day relating to the kids (clothes, school stuff, health stuff – doctor, dentist, injections etc), the house, the dog, the car, birthday presents, family commitments, social life, holiday planning etc etc. This is of course on top of trying to keep two jobs going ... I also have a nanny and a cleaner so I am not a domestic drudge but they also need managing and there is always extra housework to be done (which I invariably do). I am mostly happy with my life (although I am cutting back on my school teaching hours next academic year as the sheer volume of what I was trying to do became untenable this year) but we are VERY far from having attained gender equality in terms of parenting and domestic life in general in this country (Laura 37, two children, five-and-a-half and two-and-a-half years old)

As numerous scholars have noted (Collier and Sheldon 2008) one of the consequences of a shift towards a model of 'involved' fatherhood is that breadwinning has been (ideologically, at least) downplayed as an important parental contribution. In its place, there is a greater cultural emphasis on the importance of 'being there' for the child.

Certainly an ideological commitment to 'being there' has not been matched by men's actions in terms of longer leaves or more flexible working, and breadwinning clearly remains central to men's identity work (and indeed often crucial to family finances—see James' comment above). In an interview when their first child was a year old, Anthony and Claudia reflect on what 'equality' means in this sense. '[Anthony] was saying 'isn't it really important that I'm bringing money into the house?' and I was like, 'No, that's not what matters to me', says Claudia. Instead, what really seems to matter is an equal division of the 'mental load', as well as splitting the *emotional* labour of parenting with your partner and sharing the 'worrying enough' about a preferred parenting 'path'. So whilst it was not unusual to encounter couples in this sample who had spreadsheets divvying up household tasks (e.g.), Illouz's comments around 'emotional capitalism' are salient here, notably the assertion that techniques of rationalisation and standardisation have entered intimate relationships *psychologically* as well as practically (2012).

Many men were aware of this imbalance, but did not see it as either desirable or feasible to ape their partners' intensive interest in their children. Alex, a father in a couple—both working in the university sector—and at this point (the 2.5-year follow-up interview) expecting their second child, says in response to the question 'Do you and your partner parent equally?' 'Probably not—I imagine it's [my wife] 60% and myself 40% … I am probably more willing to catch up with friends in the evening and at weekends, whereas [my wife] is often interested in spending every possible moment with the kids. I'd also say that [she] is more willing to assert her views and preferences when it comes to the children … whereas I am more agnostic'.

This, of course, was the cause of much argument and tension amongst couples. Michael (currently with one small son, and another on the way, his wife is currently on maternity leave from her job in the city, where he also works) says: 'I feel [she] watches me intent on spotting the smallest error or point of disagreement, when I am taking care of our son … and mainly talks to me to offer criticism. She tells me I am not involved enough as a father, which has some truth to it—though I also feel I don't get enough recognition for the amount of cleaning and cooking I do'.

Discussion: Individuals, Couples and Parenting

As the accounts here point to, the emergence of a more 'intensive' parenting (or, mothering) ideology has negative implications for couples. In the example of Ellen, where she talks about breastfeeding being 'extremely fulfilling', for example, the partner is arguably trying to 'de-intensify' his wife's mothering, in ways that he presumably believes to be beneficial to her, or them as a family (e.g. ceasing breastfeeding to make it easier to go sleep through the night and be able to work). In an intensive mothering culture which puts the child's needs at the centre, however, this can be read as undermining her very identity. A partner who is committed to ideals of 'good parenting' (i.e. breastfeeding) is meant to be 'supportive' of what his partner decides to do, and suggesting otherwise is a threat to her bodily rights and therefore 'pressuring' her. Arguably then, an intensive parenting culture has the potential to displace men and make it harder for them to know how to be 'involved' (and easier for them to 'check out', as in the example of Claudia and Anthony), at the same time as heaping demands on women and leaving them overwhelmed. Ellen writes in a follow-up questionnaire, five years after our initial meeting, for example:

Given this research was originally titled 'Gender, intimacy and equality', how would you say having a baby has changed things between you and your partner, if at all?

It has ended our relationship. Having children made clear to both of us how different we are and how we are complete opposites when it comes to raising children. Before children I had no idea about how I felt about parenting and I'm surprised at the path of parenting I prefer (respectful) ... I do not recognise the man I spent 12 years together in a relationship with. (Ellen, 45, two children)

And Claudia says at the same point:

Yes definitely—intimacy is now a luxury, equality is far more acutely negotiated, and gender has become much more obvious in terms of expectations ... There was a lot of dancing around issues and treading on eggshells with each of these issues you list: gender, intimacy and equality (Claudia, 36, two children)

It is worth re-iterating the point that the couples who are the focus of this paper are not entirely representative of the sample. Many other couples did weather the 'ebb and flow' of day-to-day intimate life without suffering from relationship breakdown and spoke about the maintenance of family life in ways that were more affectionate in their narratives (Twamley 2019). Instead, ironically, it seemed to be those couples (or rather, those women) who were most highly committed to ideals of equality (such as Claudia and Laura) who struggled the most.

In her later work Illouz notes, 'much of the anger or disappointment in marriage has to do with the way in which marriage structures gender relations and mixes institutional and emotional logics: say, a desire for genderless fusion and equality, and the distance that inevitably emanates from the performance of gender roles' (2012: 12). She sees this as linked to our inability to reconcile an abundance of choice in (e.g.) partners, with ideals of romance, not least because these 'choices' are increasingly reversible ones: where once these decisions were influenced by wider, shared moral communities, backed up by external structures, they are more lonely and unstable now than ever. Furthermore, our 'choice' in relationship partner has become an 'interminable process of "validation", part of the "demand for recognition" and "reconfirmation of one's own individuality and value"' (2012: 119), or an 'anchor' in an individualised era.

This is gendered since women are more likely to engage in 'exclusivist' strategies of marriage (2012: 74) such that the pressure for their chosen partner to 'reflect back' their sense of self-worth becomes almost untenable. This leads to what she calls romantic suffering: we are told we are equal, but women are still expected to find solace in a market where men retain more power and control. Relationships are therefore inevitably about transactions (ensuring the 'best deal'), and calculated in 'cool' terms (see also Hochschild 2003). Thus an increasingly economic rationale of bartering and exchange has entered intimate relationships under the auspices of securing 'equality'. To follow this logic, in a contemporary culture of individualism which arguably devalues love and commitment to a partner in place of an orientation towards independence and self-reliance, there is a potential that the foundation for intimate relationships can be threatened—what Illouz might call a threat to the 'emotional glue' of society (2007).

However, whilst this analysis offers much in understanding the case studies of romantic disappointment presented in this chapter, it does not help us understand the way in which parenthood complicates the notion of suffering as product of individual 'choice' alone. The suggestion here is that a more relational perspective is required which foregrounds the fact of infant dependency such that couple relationships are not (only) about individual choice. In her study, *When Couples Become Parents* based on interviews with couples in Canada, Fox observed changes in couples' relationships as they made the transition to parenthood. In nearly half of her sample, relationships deteriorated, and were 'riddled with tension and worn down by the upset and anger of one or both partners' (2009: 252). This was 'fostered by the gender-based divisions organising their daily lives and sometimes enhanced by the insularity of their families ... men's detachment from the care of their babies and the dramatic differences in the men's and women's daily experiences—especially when the women were home full-time—were usually what undermined mutual understanding and often support. When both parties were stressed by the high demands of their daily work, that stress could further erode empathy, negate any hope of mutual gratitude, and produce considerable anger' (2009: 265).

Writing about the emergence of the 'companionate marriage' (as opposed to the more traditional patriarchal one), Collins (2003) notes that the 'keywords of companionship were intimacy and equality. Intimacy was at once achieved and expressed through privacy, closeness, communication, sharing, understanding and friendship' (2003: 24). However, he identifies a problem with this once children come along: parenthood accentuates the sexual division of labour and has the potential to divide companionate couples every bit as profoundly as their patriarchal counterparts. Whereas spouses are able to live 'almost identical lives' before they had children, any resulting intimacy comes under pressure from the inescapable differentiation between the two sexes once there is a child.

Certainly, if maintaining a sense that relationships are fulfilling, equitable and intimate is not one which is helped by an approach to intimate life which is individualist and transactional, it is certainly not made any easier by the arrival of children, who, as Claudia says, require 24/7 attention, turn your time as a couple into 'a zero-sum-game' and become a form of 'competition' for intimacy. The precarity of the relationships highlighted here is not necessarily to do with the idea of finding a better romantic partner then, but rather about not being able to reconcile the tension of balancing ideal partnering with ideal parenting in material (and mental) realities. The suggestion is that the kinds of investments and commitments of parenting, which endure beyond individual self-reflexive choices, create novel kinds of tensions not accounted for in theories of romantic suffering per se. Indeed, what seems to emerge in these accounts is that as much as women want their partners to share in the 'mental load' of parenting—managing the activities of running a household—they also want them to recognise and share in the *anxiety* of parenting itself (Faircloth and Gürtin 2017).

Conclusion

This chapter has argued that there is an uncomfortable contradiction at the heart of many contemporary family set-ups. On the one hand, couple relationships are idealised as 'loose' equitable and intimate. On the other, parenting relationships are idealised as 'permanent', intensive and highly gendered. The tension between these ideals is uncomfortable for many couples, and this chapter has explored how these are played out at material, physiological and cultural levels. These were keenly monitored and sources of considerable strain, resentment and disappointment, particularly in the division of the mental and emotional load of parenting. In extending the work of Illouz to go beyond individual self-reflexive choice to consider the embodied and relational realities of parenthood, we therefore see more clearly the toll of balancing partnering and parenting, particularly on women.

Afterword

I'm a woman who is like a man because I've always looked after myself financially, and I'm independent and I go and do my things and I don't have anyone dependent on me, except now I do, and now I suddenly have to be a woman *and* a man ... I have to be loving and a mothering nurturing person ... and that's a massive conflict in my identity because that's something I've always shunned because I always wanted to be an independent masculine (essentially) woman!

I don't know how that leaves us and that's probably why [my husband] is saying, 'I don't really understand what 50-50 is because you're doing everything and now you want me to do everything that you're doing in the same way you're doing it but you seem to have everything covered'.

But obviously I'm not actually coping. (Claudia, 32, 1 child)

Notes

1. The study was given ethical approval by the University of Kent Ethics Board, in line with BSA guidance.
2. Sadly, in part due to post-natal depression, this 'gentleman's agreement' did not come to fruition, with Laura taking 12 months of leave with their second child, and also the one working part-time; further discussion about this couple is included below.
3. See, however, Twamley on the 'twilight zone' that many similarly earning couples enter when justifying women's extended maternity leaves, where an economic rationale is used to by families to account for women's desire to take longer periods of leave, even in cases where this would not actually result in a reduced household income (forthcoming).

References

Arendell, T. (2000) Conceiving and Investigating Motherhood: The Decade's Scholarship. *Journal of Marriage and the Family* 62: 1192–1207.

Baird, M. and O'Brien M. (2015) Dynamics of parental leave in Anglophone countries: The paradox of state expansion in liberal welfare regimes. *Community Work and Family* 18.

Bauman, Z. (2003) *Liquid Love: On the Frailty of Human Bonds.* Cambridge: Polity Press.

Beck, U. (1992) *Risk Society: Towards a new modernity.* London: Sage.

Beck, U. and Beck-Gernsheim, E. (1995) *The Normal Chaos of Love*. Cambridge: Polity Press.

Beck, U. and Beck-Gernsheim, E. (2002) *Individualization: Institutionalized Individualism and Its Social and Political Consequences*. London: Sage.

Browne, J. (2013) The Default Model: Gender Equality, Fatherhood, and Structural Constraint. *Politics and Gender:* APSA. 9 (02): 152–173.

Collins, M. (2003) *Modern Love: An Intimate History of Men and Women in Twentieth-Century Britain*. London: Atlantic Books.

Collier, R. and Sheldon, S. (2008) *Fragmenting Fatherhood, A Socio-Legal Study.* Oxford: Hart Publishing.

Craib, I. (2004) Narratives as bad faith. In M. Andrews, S.D. Sclater, C. Squire and A. Treacher (eds.) *Uses of Narrative*. New Jersey: Transition.

Cusk, R. (2001) *A Life's Work: On Becoming a Mother*. London: Fourth Estate.

Dermott, E. (2008) *Intimate Fatherhood: A Sociological Analysis*. London: Routledge.

Doucet, A. (2006) *Do Men Mother? Fathering, care and domestic responsibility*. Toronto: University of Toronto Press.

Faircloth, C. (2013) *Militant Lactivism? Attachment Parenting and Intensive Motherhood in the UK and France*. Oxford and New York: Berghahn Books.

Faircloth, C., Hoffman, D.M. and Layne, L.L (eds.) (2013) *Parenting in global perspective: Negotiating ideologies of kinship, self and politics*. London: Routledge.

Faircloth, C. and Gürtin, Z.B. (2017) Fertile connections: Thinking across assisted reproductive technologies and parenting culture studies. *Sociology* 52 (5): 983–1000.

Family and Childcare Trust (FCT) (2017) Childcare Survey 2017. Available here: https://www.familyandchildcaretrust.org/childcare-survey-2017 [Accessed 25 June 2019].

Finch, J. (2007) Displaying families. *Sociology* 41 (1): 165–181.

Fox, B. (2009) *When couples become parents: The creation of gender in the transition to parenthood*. Toronto: University of Toronto Press.

Giddens, A. (1992) *Transformation of Intimacy: Sexuality, love and eroticism in modern societies*. Cambridge: Polity.

Gillies, V. (2003) *Families and Intimate Life: A review of the Sociological Research*. Families and Social Capital Research Group.

Gillies, V. (2009) Understandings and experiences of involved fathering in the United Kingdom: Exploring classed dimensions. *The Annals of the American Academy of Political and Social Science*, 624: 49–60.

Gillies, V., Edwards, R. and Horsley, N. (2017) *Challenging the Politics of Early Intervention: Who's saving children and why?* Bristol: Policy Press.

Gornick, J.C. and Meyers, M. (2009) *Gender Equality: Transforming Family Divisions of Labor.* London: Verso.

Guardian (2017) 'The gender wars of household chores: a feminist comic' Available here: https://www.theguardian.com/world/2017/may/26/gender-wars-household-chores-comic [Accessed 25 June 2019].

Hochschild, A.R. (2003) *The Commercialization of Intimate Life: Notes from Home and Work.* Berkeley and Los Angeles: University of California Press.

Hamilton, P. (2016) The 'Good' Attached Mother: An analysis of postracial thinking in birth and breastfeeding policy in neoliberal Britain'. *Australian Feminist Studies*, 31 (90): 410–447.

Hardyment, C. (2007) *Dream Babies: Childcare Advice from John Locke to Gina Ford.* London: Francis Lincoln.

Hays, S. (1996) *The Cultural Contradictions of Motherhood.* New Haven and London: Yale University Press.

Hendrick, H. (2016) *Narcissistic Parenting in an Insecure World. A history of parenting culture 1920 to present.* Bristol: Policy Press.

Illouz, E. (2007) *Cold Intimacies: The Making of Emotional Capitalism.* Cambridge: Polity Press.

Illouz, E. (2012) *Why Love Hurts: A sociological explanation.* Cambridge: Polity Press.

Jamieson, L. (1998) *Intimacy: Personal relationships in modern societies.* Cambridge: Polity Press.

Kotsadam, A. and Finseraas, H. (2011) The state intervenes in the battle of the sexes: Causal effects of paternity leave. *Social Science Research* 40: 1611–1622.

Lee, E. Bristow, J. Faircloth, C. and Macvarish, J. (2014) *Parenting Culture Studies.* Basingstoke: Palgrave Macmillan.

Lewis, J. (1997) Gender and Welfare Regimes: Further Thoughts. *Social Politics* 4 (2): 160–177.

Macvarish, J. (2016) *Neuroparenting: The expert invasion of family life.* Basingstoke: Palgrave Macmillan.

Miller, T. (2005) *Making Sense of Motherhood: A Narrative Approach.* Cambridge: Cambridge University Press.

Miller, T. (2011) *Making Sense of Fatherhood* Cambridge: Cambridge University Press.

Murphy, E. (2003) Expertise and forms of knowledge in the government of families. *The Sociological Review,* 51 (4): 433–462.

Nelson, M. (2010) *Parenting Out of Control: Anxious parents in uncertain times.* New York and London: New York University Press.

Ribbens McCarthy, J. and Edwards, R. (2002) The individual in public and private: The significance of mothers and children. In A. Carling, S. Duncan and R. Edwards (eds.) *Analysing Families: Morality and Rationality in Policy and Practice.* London: Routledge.

Riessman, C. (2008) *Narrative Methods in the Human Sciences.* New York: Sage.

Rose, N. (1999) [1989] *Governing the Soul: The Shaping of the Private Self.* London: Routledge.

Shirani, F., Henwood, K. and Coltart, C. (2012) Meeting the challenges of intensive parenting culture: gender, risk management and the moral parent. *Sociology,* 46 (1): 25–40.

Smart, C. (2007) *Personal Life: New Directions in Sociological Thinking.* Cambridge: Polity.

Thomson, R., Kehily, M.J., Hadfield, L. and Sharpe, S. (2011) *Making Modern Mothers.* Bristol: Policy Press.

Tomori, C. (2014) *Nighttime Breastfeeding: An American Cultural Dilemma.* Oxford and New York: Berghahn Books.

Twamley, K. (2012) Gender Relations Among Indian Couples in the UK and India: Ideals of Equality and Realities of Inequality. *Sociological Research Online* 17 (4).

Twamley, K. (2019) 'Cold intimacies' in parents' negotiations of work-family practices and parental leave? *The Sociological Review* (Online First) https://doi.org/10.1177/0038026118815427

Twamley, K. and Schober, P. (2019) Shared parental leave: Exploring variations in attitudes, eligibility, knowledge and take-up intentions of expectant mothers in London. *Journal of Social Policy* 48 (2): 387–407.

Wolf, J. (2011) *Is Breast Best? Taking on the breastfeeding experts and the new high stakes of motherhood.* New York: New York University Press.

12

'I Wanted a Happy Ever After Life': Love, Romance and Disappointment in Heterosexual Single Mothers' Intimacy Scripts

Charlotte Morris

Introduction

This chapter probes the theme of 'disappointment', highlighted in the work of Illouz (2007, 2012), and traces the contours of this often over-looked emotion in relation to love and romance. More broadly, as Illouz (2012) argues, this work reflects a need for sociology to attend to suffering and everyday emotions, including disappointment, 'resentment, hurt and humiliation, unreciprocated desire, feelings of anxiety and worthless-ness' (2012: 20). However, what the research focussing on single mothers presented here suggests is the importance of situating such emotions within the realities of everyday material contexts and wider socio-economic structures. Narrative research on which this chapter draws sought to capture experiences and perceptions of intimacy among a generational cohort of UK heterosexual single mothers in relation to broader

C. Morris (✉)
University of Sussex, Brighton, UK
e-mail: C.A.Morris@sussex.ac.uk

© The Author(s) 2020
J. Carter, L. Arocha (eds.), *Romantic Relationships in a Time of 'Cold Intimacies'*,
Palgrave Macmillan Studies in Family and Intimate Life,
https://doi.org/10.1007/978-3-030-29256-0_12

social changes around intimacies, personal biographies and choice (Beck and Beck-Gernsheim 1995; Giddens 1992; Illouz 2012). Participants reflected on experiences, hopes and aspirations for intimacy; in many cases these were in the process of being reworked following relationship breakdowns in a context where they frequently found themselves and their families judged as 'lacking' without a male partner and father figure. This chapter focuses on three key aspects of disappointment, linked to Illouz's (2012) work: First, it identifies ways in which aspirations and fantasies around intimacy did not lead to fruition, exploring expressions of disappointment that idealised 'intimacy scripts' were unrealised. Secondly, it interrogates perceptions of ways in which male partners did not measure up to expectations with regard to 'emotional competency' which Illouz (2007) conveys as carrying increasing value in contemporary capitalist societies, positioned through both psychology and feminism as vital for 'successful' relationships. Thirdly, following from this, it discusses perceptions of a lack of suitable male partners in terms of commitment and responsibility (Illouz 2012), thereby constraining choices. Whilst Illouz's work is useful in strengthening understanding of the processes in which people choose partners, it could be more fully and explicitly situated in relation to social and sexual script theory (Gagnon and Simon 1973) and simultaneously attend more to the material gendered realities of everyday lives and relationships where for many women, including the single-mother participants in my study, priorities are the care, well-being and safety of dependents.

Literature on Love and Intimacy

Individuals are immersed in a post-feminist culture seemingly obsessed by idealistic, normative images of romantic love (Evans 2003), combined with expert guidance and advice on how to conduct relationships (Barker et al. 2018; Illouz 2007, 2012). We do not live out our intimate lives and make choices in a cultural vacuum; rather intimacies are influenced by and mediated through normative ideals, images, expectations, therapeutic interventions and advice (Barker et al. 2018; Illouz 2012). Beck and Beck-Gernsheim (1995) suggest that expectations of love, conceived as a deep, emotional bond, are increasingly high, meaning that relationships are understood as being over as soon as feelings of love are in decline. This may contribute to high levels of relationship breakdown and divorce, alongside continued tensions between men and women as they adjust to new gender roles and attempt to find new ways of conducting relationships in the absence of traditions. Illouz (2012) suggests that this particularly affects women, positioned as responsible for achieving 'successful' relationships in a neoliberal era which stresses individual responsibility alongside the dominance of a therapeutic culture which delineates 'good' relationships. This may be especially acute where women's sense of self-worth is tightly bound up with romantic love in the current milieu (2012: 164).

Conceptualisations of contemporary intimacy are largely underpinned by theories of individualisation, with a contention that intimacy has undergone a radical transformation (Giddens 1992), marked by increased choice, flexibility, experimentation and egalitarianism with broadly positive social effects (Weeks 2007). According to this thesis, people are now free to enter and exit relationships in accordance with the level of personal satisfaction they bring (Giddens 1992). In the light of increased sexual freedom and gender equality, Giddens (1992) argues that a more democratic way of conducting relationships is emerging in the form of the 'pure relationship' based on individuals' reciprocal pleasure. This thesis has been strongly contested in the light of continuing gender inequalities (Jamieson 1998); inter-generational continuities and adaptations of tradition (Duncan 2011; Gross 2005; Plummer 2001); lack of empirical grounding (Jamieson 1998; Gabb 2010; Smart 2007); absence of attention to care and interdependencies (Fineman 2004) and the assumption of white, western, heteronormative and middle-class positionalities (Gillies 2007; Skeggs 2005). However, the notion of individualisation has still provided a touchstone for exploring contemporary intimacies, particularly in terms of experimentation and adaptation (Budgeon 2008; Duncan 2011; Roseneil 2005). While the 'transformation thesis' (Giddens 1992) is a point of reference for Illouz (2012), enabling understandings of ways in which choices around romantic partners have become disembedded from formalised social settings (2012: 42), she argues that it overlooks new forms of gendered inequalities. Specifically she considers ways in which the current 'free market' of sexual encounters has created new forms of emotional domination over women, whereby men may withhold emotional intimacy and commitment. Further, such theories have not fully interrogated ways in which new norms of equality transformed the quality or 'emotional texture' of relationships (Illouz 2007: 30), particularly regarding the negotiation of relationship terms. Crucially, the thesis does not fully take into account complexities around choice-making; for Illouz (2012) there is a need to attend to 'ecologies of choice'—or the social conditions in which romantic choices are made—and 'architectures of choice', the cognitive processes and repertoires through which choices are formed. However, everyday material realities which shape intimate lives still tend to be missing from her analysis which foregrounds more privileged positionalities and experiences.

Romantic love relationships are often regarded as increasingly unstable and vulnerable to volatility and deterioration, reflected in high divorce rates. For Beck and Beck-Gernsheim (1995) individualisation is understood as having contradictory consequences, a heightened need for close relationships reflecting the unreliability of individualised trajectories where we are responsible for carving out personal biographies. While love is seen as increasingly significant, they are concerned with the lack of social support for lasting love relationships and, with complex labour markets leading to fragmented existences and I would argue, in an era of widespread precarities, the effects of this could be taken more fully into account in the field of intimacy (Pugh 2015). Beck and Beck-Gernsheim argue that individuals invest their hope in love as a *central pivot giving meaning to lives*' (Beck and Beck-Gernsheim 1995: 2); this centrality of romantic love is understood as a modern phenomenon in post-industrial societies. It is emphasised that, in an era marked by technological advances and rationalism, love provides a means of transcendence and authenticity, equivalent to religion in secular times. This seems to run counter to Illouz's emphasis on heightened rationalism around intimate choices, to be discussed further (see also Carter and Smith in this volume). However, it is likely that both a desire for authenticity and an attempt to make rational choice come into play when pursuing and managing relationships.

Heteronormative love, romance and commitment can certainly be viewed as some of the most powerful, pervasive images prevalent in consumer society, with advertising, cultural productions and technologies perpetuating cultural ideals of heteronormative monogamous couple-based family living an idealised lifestyle, entailing high levels of consumption. Evans (2003), working within a feminist tradition, critiques continuing ideologies of love and romance, challenging assumptions of the sexualised romantic couple as the ideal basis for family life. Nevertheless, the power of normative expectations, informed by popular discourses of heterosexual romance (Evans 2003; Illouz 2012), should not be underestimated as influencing intimate aspirations. This interlinks with what Berlant (2011) describes are dominant, enduring cultural fantasies of 'the good life', combining idealised intimate lives with material comfort. Jackson (1999) asserts that the continued prevalence of love and romance in our culture are indicative of a continued search for romantic fulfilment and enduring partnerships as opposed to temporary, contingent 'pure relationship' forms (1999: 121). Simultaneously, the fantasy of the romantic couple-based family is often undercut by negative experiences. In their study of heterosexual lives, Hockey, Meah and Robinson (2010) identified frequent expressions of disappointment. There is a discernible distinction between intimacy as imagined and as lived, between intimacy scripts and experiences, creating layers of ambivalence (Budgeon 2008; Illouz 2012).

Illouz (2007, 2012) enables an understanding of ways in which economic and emotional lives—typically presented as separate spheres—interconnect, suggesting that rationalised market-based repertoires inform relationship practices. Her work considers the impact of neoliberal, marketised values and practices on the quality of relationships, alongside the popularisation of psychology and higher expectations of gender equality. Through psychology, the idea of 'healthy relationships' came into being, interacting with the notion of 'equitable exchange' which has brought processes of rationalisation to intimacy. This is set in a context of rapidly expanding emotional literacy, resulting in increased calculation, decontextualisation and objectification of emotions, amounting to an 'intellectualization of intimate bonds' (2007: 37). Illouz's (2007, 2012) insights offer an understanding of broader cultural narratives and productions in shaping intimate selves and lives. We may consider these as forming part of a composite of culturally available 'intimacy scripts' in interplay with a search for romantic love as a panacea for meaning, commitment, care and authenticity (Beck and Beck-Gernsheim 1995).

The concept of social, sexual scripts (Gagnon and Simon 1973) is referred to in the work of Illouz (2012) and has provided a theoretical framework for the research on single mothers presented here: Scripts are seen as continually developing, dynamic cultural blueprints for social, sexual lives. Simon and Gagnon (1999) define scripts as metaphors for understanding the production of social behaviour and repertoires; resources used to construct lives by offering a range of possibilities and selves which people may adhere to, negotiate or remake. This involves reconciling wider, more abstract cultural narratives with individuals' social contexts, interactions and internal (intrapsychic) worlds of desires, fantasies and expectations. While the concept of 'scripts' does not offer wider analyses of structural constraints, which I contend also need to be brought to bear in understanding contemporary intimate lives, it enables understanding of the cultural availability of intimate forms. Scripts are linked to social expectations in terms of the life course; individuals may assume that they will follow conventional paths of falling in love, getting married and starting a family. However, in a time of increasing complexity around family life, relationships and sexuality, this may not necessarily occur in anticipated ways. In 'postparadigmatic societies' (Simon and Gagnon 1999), with fewer shared meanings, greater demands are placed on individual actors to make sense of available possibilities, potentially leading to experiences of personal anxiety (anomie). Where dominant cultural narratives begin to lose coercive power to structure behaviour (such as the married nuclear family as imperative), they may still retain an important point of reference (shaping imaginaries of intimacy). The concept of scripting allows for the interrelation of individuals, their social contexts and the wider cultural milieu, enabling a nuanced approach to understanding intimate lives, recognising social and cultural forces which at least partially shape them. This fits with Illouz's (2012) insight that experiences need to follow cultural patterns in order to be intelligible and indicates the need to take cultural narratives, psychic resources and institutional constraints into account to enable understanding of intimate lives.

Participants in my study held shifting positions in relation to intimacy, gender and family, moving between foregrounding couple-centred nuclear intimacy scripts, egalitarian relationships and romantic fantasies which in the course of their narratives were revisited, critiqued and reworked. I will briefly outline the methodology and then move on to explore the disappointment which frequently arose in response to unsettled intimacy scripts.

Methodology

This chapter draws on a study of heterosexual single mothers' narratives of intimacy undertaken and ethically approved at the University of Sussex (Morris 2014). Drawing on life history methodology (Plummer 2001), 24 narrative interviews provided participants with an opportunity to reflect on experiences of intimacy, to consider their present situation and future possibilities in an unstructured format. This method elicited rich, detailed data, enabling participants to explore personal trajectories in the light of shifting contexts. A short set of semi-structured questions complemented the narrative content, providing a focus on specific aspects of experiences of single motherhood and intimacy.

In terms of the sample, participants were heterosexual single mothers aged between 30 and 55 years in the South-East of England who self-identified as such. All participants had become single mothers through relationship breakdown. An overarching purposive sampling strategy was utilised in seeking to capture a diversity of perspectives, particularly in terms of class. Recruitment took place via a local lone parent network; a locally run course for unemployed lone parents; schools, community and children's centres; professional and social contacts and through deploying the snowballing technique, asking participants to identify further contacts (Bryman 2012). In terms of ethnicity, the sample was mainly white with one mixed-race participant and participants self-identified as either working-class or middle-class with an even balance between these categories. The study specifically set out to explore heterosexual women's experiences to shed light on the dynamics of these relationships, while recognising that heterosexuality is an imperfect category. Following

Riessman (1993), data was transcribed verbatim then analysed at thematic, narrative and discursive levels, attending to broad cross-cutting themes alongside formal features of the narratives and the discursive resources participants drew on in order to make sense of their experiences.

The 'Hollywood Effect': Aspirations of Romantic Intimacy

Illouz (2012) describes a sense of longing linked to romantic fantasy as a key feature of contemporary imaginaries of love. The assertion that 'I wanted a happy ever after life' in my study came from Chloe, a 34 year-old single mother of three young children who had recently moved back to the UK to escape from an abusive relationship (one of eight participants who reported abusive relationships with the fathers of their children). The phrase encapsulates what many participants conveyed; they had not anticipated or desired being single mothers but rather held deep-rooted scripts reflecting normative trajectories, expecting to grow up, fall in love, get married, have children and remain in a lifelong monogamous partnership. The transition to single motherhood therefore brought disappointment, entailing emotional, financial and practical upheavals, frequently accompanied by a sense of shame in now occupying what is perceived to be a stigmatised identity (Morris and Munt 2019).

Jacquie, a professional and mother of one in her early forties, described the loss of a projected intimate trajectory based on the ideals of romantic love which did not come to fruition. Alongside personal and material loss, the fantasy of romance, of 'living happily ever after' was destroyed by lived events. Her narrative began by drawing on a cultural discourse of romance—'I met somebody and fell in love'—setting up the anticipation of following a normative intimacy script of getting married, settling down with the person she loved and having children. This narrative ended abruptly with her partner leaving, underlining the speed at which these events occurred, leaving her in shock. An 'anti-romance' narrative was detectable, subverting the fairytale storybook outcome of 'living happily ever after', rupturing the romantic genre and emphasising disappointment, a painful and abrupt ending to intimate aspirations. Jacquie frequently became emotional during the interview, demonstrating how much these events 14 years earlier still affected her, comprising a painful rupture as she had no control over her circumstances: 'It wasn't like it was this one day and something else another day—there was no discussion around it so it was probably worse' [Pause—becomes upset].

A sense of disappointment that life had fallen short of an anticipated positive trajectory was apparent. For some participants, the loss of intimacy scripts, fantasies and expectations they had grown up with regarding love and family life was experienced as emotionally devastating. Juliet, an unemployed professional with one child in her mid-forties, explained how her life had not turned out the way she imagined—a source of continuing sorrow. Hockey, Meah and Robinson (2010) likewise indicated that the imagined world of idealised heterosexuality is often in conflict with real life experiences. What Juliet thought was the beginning of a long-term partnership and settled family life—following the romantic culmination of being told she was loved—did not transpire as the father decided he was not ready to become a parent or partner. This can be linked to Illouz's (2012) observations of men achieving dominance through emotional withdrawal and refusal to commit (explored further below). For Juliet, this was the beginning of a chain of events which spoiled her life, disrupting her anticipated 'intimacy script' and precipitating what she presented as an unfulfilling lone parent family life, which fell short of the traditional couple-centred scenario she had envisioned.

Participants emphasised sacrifices they had made for partners, for example, moving away from family, friends and jobs. When relationships broke down there was a sense of injustice that the other side of the 'bargain'—a stable father figure and lasting partnership—went unmet, interlinking with notions of emotional exchange (Illouz 2007). Romantic aspirations were frequently bound up with desires for material comfort, especially for those from middle-class backgrounds (Morris and Munt 2019), with fantasies of a 'Prince Charming' and 'nice houses' in idyllic settings in the countryside. This chimes with Illouz's insights (2012) into intertwining emotional and economic domains in shaping romantic aspirations, although western, middle-class privilege inherent in such considerations should be emphasised (Morris and Munt 2019). It further reflects the commercialisation of conventional heteronormative lifestyles and unrealistic ideals resulting in disappointment (Illouz 2007). Such desires are reminiscent of Kaufman's (2008) observations of a recentering of ideals of the couple and family life to provide a sense of security and grounding against a backdrop of heightened existential threat (from nuclear war, terrorism and, we can add, climate change), alongside nostalgia for secure, predictable lives (Berlant 2011) under conditions of economic precarity.

Narratives indicated concerns about the lack of male commitment, a theme which Illouz (2012) takes up, suggesting that men are now less normatively compelled to seek or remain in families comprising monogamous domesticity, reproduction being understood as women's imperative (Illouz 2012: 74). What this research highlights is the devastating consequences of such dynamics in material as well as emotional terms. Karen, a 46 year-old unemployed mother of five, contrasted the life she had before she met the father of her children in a different UK region, where she had enjoyed relative material security and was surrounded by family, friends and a supportive community, to being isolated and homeless as a single mother. As with other participants, the transition to single motherhood was narrated as sudden and shocking, triggered by a partner abruptly changing his mind and resisting the role of father and partner:

> When I look back now I gave up a three bedroom house and my work to come out there to be with him so yeah I gave up security but at the time – well you're not going to know unless you get out there. We survived in the relationship for about 10 months and then he just turned around said, 'I just can't handle the thought of bringing up a child and I don't know if our relationship is going to work'. I was out in the world in the South, I didn't know anybody here, didn't know the place, it was totally alien to me and so … I went straight down to the DHSS with a broken heart and said, 'Right, what do I do now?'

As with other narratives, there is a discernible sub-text where participants portray themselves as victims not just of poor partners but of an uncaring wider society, offering little support for challenging circumstances, further impacting on the quality of lives and contributing to a sense of them being 'spoiled'. Zoe's narrative followed a similar trajectory: An unemployed single mother of 30, with one child, Zoe began her narrative with being 'head over heels in love', referencing the romantic genre. Zoe reflected on what went wrong, describing the mistake of romantically believing her partner had a 'loving soul' who would make a good father—although in reality he had a prison record and was unemployed. In retrospect he was identified as an unsuitable partner, fitting with contemporaneous political and media tropes of the 'feckless father', and reflective of Illouz's (2012) emphasis on the importance of rational evaluation of partner choice, potentially in conflict with romantic ideals. As with other participants, being a lone parent was not part of Zoe's life plan and came as a shock, rupturing an imagined intimacy script based on idealised romance and couple-centred family life.

Similar to Karen, the material realities of single motherhood were as shocking to Zoe as the breakdown of the relationship; her narrative moved from a romantic depiction of being in love to heartbreak and the harsh experience of poor housing and financial deprivation:

I was quite young, quite a young pregnancy I was only 17 and head over heels in love as you are when you're 17 … I was with him until [my child] was 1 – things were a bit strained emotionally because it was a lot of pressure. He was a bit older than me and had a history – he'd just got out of prison when we met – dodgy family –terrible, terrible father material but I thought he had a loving soul so I didn't care! But we split up after a year because the obvious things that were going to happen happened – he didn't want to work, he spent all the money, he wasn't really there enough and so … I thought 'hang on, this isn't really working out' and so I confronted him about it and he left.

When he left, he kind of pretty much went. It didn't really occur to me that I was going to be a lone parent, I probably thought we were just having a big row and he'd come back but he just disappeared and didn't come back for about six months and I was a real emotional wreck and then he came back and said 'I love you' and I said 'I love you too' and we had about a month of wondering if it was going to work and then he was with someone else – I found out he was seeing someone … It all feels really young – looking back over a decade on but then it wasn't, I was a single parent and it was all quite heartbreaking

Participants, in making sense of their experiences, often held conflicting perspectives on love and romance, reflecting cultural contradictions (Illouz 2012). For some, disappointment engendered a questioning
of previously held ideals of romance; Zoe portrayed herself as having
become more politically and self-aware, able to critique her previous
naïve self and the flawed ideology of romance she had subscribed to.
She adopted the role of social commentator in making sense of her
experiences, at times invoking a celebratory sense of intimacy becoming more open, allowing opportunities for sexual self-expression and
diverse intimate forms (Weeks 2007). However, her narrative was
ambivalent (Illouz 2012); contemporary intimate lives are also understood as containing overly high expectations and a tendency to move
on quickly from relationships where these are not met—reminiscent of
the 'pure relationship' (Giddens 1992). Zoe, however, attributed this to
the prevalence of romantic discourse—'the Hollywood effect'—where
people are influenced by romantic images into always seeking something better (echoing Beck and Beck-Gernsheim 1995; Evans 2003;
Illouz 2012; Plummer 1995). This also echoes Illouz's (2007) analysis
of internet dating which highlights consumeristic aspects of choosing
partners. Indeed Sofia, a 39 year-old unemployed mother of two, presented a vision of a world of cold, transactional intimacies based solely
on desires for sex, material goods and financial security when asked
how relationships had changed:

> Number one technology – you can use so many options to make a relation-
> ship, you can be sitting down and still make a relationship, there's so many
> ways of doing that … traditional way is completely different – traditionally
> people don't have that much patience because it's more … Maybe people
> are more confident with themselves … if not happy, if not things going
> well they just finish

> Charlotte: 'And in what ways have relations between men and women
>   changed?'
> Well … nowadays it's mainly sex … I think so, this is the main big change,
>   not much love … emotionally people are much more materialistic in
>   their relationships now.

The majority of participants did hope to settle into fulfilling romantic relationships in the future, retaining their aspirations. Several were in the process of forming new relationships, although their narratives did not constitute idealised romantic 'Hollywood' endings (Plummer 1995), rather they entailed tentative, precarious and complex negotiations with new partners (Morris 2015; Illouz 2007; Ribbens McCarthy et al. 2003). While participants aspired towards re-partnering, their ability to do so was dependent on multiple factors, including economic survival, emotional stability and the age of their children. Yvonne, a 55 year-old full-time employed mother of two, typified the trajectory of moving from the rupture of her initial romantic intimacy script through making the decision to leave an unhappy marriage to basic survival and then eventually, when the circumstances were right (when her children were older), re-exploring intimate possibilities. This is condensed in the following extract which captures the movement from being naïve, innocent and unquestioning about cultural narratives of romance to what she implies is a more mature approach to relationships, based on shared values and enjoyment of life. It demonstrates how participants reflected on and evaluated experiences, distancing themselves from previous identities and reformulating intimacy scripts. Nevertheless, while moving on from what are conveyed as superficial, romantic ideals, there remains a vivid sense of the romantic couple relationship as providing ultimate fulfilment and completion (Beck and Beck-Gernsheim 1995; Illouz 2012):

I made a big, big mistake – I mistook falling in love with actually having an infatuation for this man when I was 24. I'd never really had a serious relationship, I thought this was it. Really made a big mistake – I thought, 'You're married now for better or worse, have to make the best of it' and we had the children so you stay on until … and I thought, 'hang on', I thought, 'I was staying because it was the right thing to do for the children but if they're unhappy because we're together then I have to be brave enough to say I'm going and it can't go on' … I didn't even think of looking for another relationship … I wasn't in the right state of mind to begin thinking about meeting any other men at that time and with the ties of having the children, they were too young to be left on their own and when they got a bit older I realised I've always, always wanted to meet somebody really special who has the same values as I do and who is really passionate about life and me.

'Flights from Commitment'? Gender and Emotional Competencies

Many participants described unfulfilling, at times detrimental, relationships with the fathers of their children; these fell short of expectations they had grown up with in a culture saturated by idealised romance (Evans 2003; Illouz 2012), combined with psychologised ideals of relating and negotiating as equals (Illouz 2007). Underpinning many narratives was an understanding that 'emotion work' (Hochschild 1983) was highly gendered, a 'fair exchange' of emotional labour lacking in their relationships (Illouz 2007).

Susan, a 55 year-old full-time employed mother of one, for example, described a lack of commitment, love and sense of responsibility from her daughter's father which triggered her decision to leave, despite emotional, financial and practical upheavals. She conveyed a sense of disappointment at his failure to 'fight' for the relationship, reflecting Illouz's (2012) insights into men's lack of responsibility and emotional competencies:

> It was a long and difficult process but in the end I decided I had to leave and so I came back to England and truly became solely responsible for her and at the time I had no job to come back to, I had no home, I had two suitcases and three hundred pounds but anything was preferable to staying there by then and I think it upset me that he didn't put up more of a fight, not for me, for her and he said something very odd when I left which was, 'No matter how much I love her, you love her more' which struck me as a very odd thing for a parent to say, as though you can apportion these things out, and I imagine he was upset when she went but he's never made any effort really to maintain what I would call a proper relationship with her.

Idealisations of couple-based family life are undercut by negative experiences although there were exceptions to the predominantly high expectations of participants. For Sam, a 30 year-old, full-time employed mother of one, lasting marriages were not her childhood norm and she saw it as important to leave unhappy relationships. She inferred that her inability to trust was problematic, describing herself as cynical, identified by Illouz (2012) as one potential response to disappointment: 'modern selves are infinitely better equipped to deal with the repeated experiences of abandonment, break-ups or betrayals than ever in the past through detachment, autonomy, hedonism, cynicism, and irony' (2012: 282). Sam advocated that you should get out of a relationship if you are not happy, to some extent reflective of the 'pure relationship' (Giddens 1992) but possibly also awareness of ongoing gender inequalities and the riskiness of relationships. It was unclear whether her assumption that men were unlikely to 'stick around' indicated that she did not expect her relationships to last due to her inability to trust, or that she viewed men generally as untrustworthy. Prevalent throughout these interviews were such perceptions and examples of men rejecting commitment (Ehrenreich 1983; Illouz 2012):

> My background is that a lot of my family are married into the family, they've split up, got together with someone else so, you know, I don't really see marriage as a long term thing or relationships as a long-term thing – I lived with my Nana and Grandad and my Nana was my step-gran. My mum left when I was four so there was my father but he then married again and they buggered off to another country so you know I've never seen relationships as something – when you hear about these couples who've been together for fifty years it's like 'Oh, stupid people!' [laughs] yeah, so coming from that background I think I've never seen relationships – if you're happy with a relationship then fair enough but if you're not happy in it then get out. I've probably always had that attitude which is not good because I've never been one to trust completely that they're going to stick around for a long time, they're going to get bored, they're going to get fed up ... I like to think of myself as a realist – cynical maybe but there you go!

Sam later conveyed being influenced by attitudes of previous generations, including notions that you have to 'stick with it', demonstrating competing intimacy scripts. Sam described being caught between generational positions, describing the conflict of believing, to an extent, in 'old fashioned ideas' about staying in a marriage 'no matter what' but at the same time unable to trust men or the possibility of enduring happiness in a relationship. Ultimately, she resisted the idea of marriage, due to the risk of being trapped in an unhappy relationship. She emphasised how long-term relationships were not considered the norm for her generation, pertinent in relation to the 'transformation of intimacy' thesis (Giddens 1992). However, her version of reality is far from the notion of democratic relationships, suggesting that it is men specifically who reject long-term relationships, in line with notions of men's 'flight from commitment' (Ehrenreich 1983; Illouz 2012).

According to Cristina, a 42-year-old part-time professional mother of one, changes in intimate relationships were highly gendered. Countering assumptions of women's emancipation having been achieved, she disputed that women are now better off as there is still an expectation that they take full responsibility for childcare, echoing other participants (Fineman 2004; Lewis 2001; Morris 2015) and chiming with Illouz's (2012) observation of women's higher investment in family and relationships. Consequently, while some women of this generation grew up expecting to 'have it all' in terms of career and family, in reality many women remain financially and emotionally disadvantaged, whereas men do not necessarily have to take childcare into consideration when making career (and intimacy) choices. As Illouz (2012) observes, this lesser responsibility means it is primarily men who have the freedom to freely choose, experiment and be more fluid in relationships. Cristina saw intimacy as becoming more materialistic, disposable and high-risk and, echoing Illouz (2012), saw this in gendered terms; men being more likely to leave relationships and less likely to value them, apart from a minority of 'thinking men':

> I don't think that men are as serious about families or see their responsibilities … and maybe I'm doing them a disservice – I mean don't get me wrong, I know lots of nice guys … but I think they're kind of a rarity, they're a bit more kind of thinking men

Following unsatisfactory relationships, children tended to be the emotional priority over romantic partnerships (Beck and Beck-Gernsheim 1995); the emotional impact on children was a key consideration when selecting potential partners, placing further constraints around ecologies and architectures of choice (Illouz 2012). While a long-term partner in a father-figure role was portrayed as the ideal, there was recognition that it might be difficult for a partner to fit into established close-knit units.

Furthermore, the responsibility of managing a family alone precluded taking care of someone else. The perception that a male partner might create additional emotional and practical burdens was echoed in several accounts. As Teresa, a 42 year-old part-time employed mother of two elucidated, relationships were considered to be too much to cope with in terms of increased 'emotional labour' (Hochschild 1983) and care of another, alongside the challenges of single parenthood, encapsulated in the statement that, 'They're looking for someone to take care of them and I've already got a child—not another one!'

Some participants encountered negative experiences of boyfriends becoming attached to children with difficult emotional consequences if they were inconsistent, dishonest or through subsequent relationship breakdown. Karen described how such experiences increased protectiveness over her children's wellbeing and created barriers to developing partnerships:

> Alarm bells started ringing in my ears because at first he was all about taking my daughter to Florida for her birthday and everything like that and then one day she turned round and said, 'When are we going to go?' and he totally cut her off saying, 'I'm not going'. She was totally broken-hearted and I thought, 'That's it'– I'm not going to let another guy get that close to me or her again

With children's needs prioritised, participants were often highly discerning about potential partners, even when this limited possibilities. This follows Illouz's (2007, 2012) notions of instrumentality in choosing partners and evaluating traits. However, participants were not necessarily thinking individualistically, rather their ecologies of choice were shaped through taking into account the needs of dependents and maintenance of family units. Some reported deeper levels of emotional relating with female friends and children than with male partners (Morris 2018a). Many described finding it difficult to achieve the emotional as well as sexual fulfilment they sought through heterosexual relationships and there were reworkings of narratives to foreground other relationships including friends (Morris 2018a). Decisions not to enter relationships or to adopt subordinate roles were potentially empowering for

some participants, perceived as a positive break with previous generations where women were seen as more likely to be trapped in abusive
relationships.

Lack of suitable partners was a running theme, channelling perceptions of a male 'flight from commitment' which Ehrenreich (1983)
depicted as embedded in late twentieth-century western culture, locat-
ing it as a reaction against imperatives to provide within normative
nuclear family structures and as influenced by 'playboy' culture. Illouz
(2012) further theorises this phenomenon, suggesting that increasing
numbers of potential sexual partners combined with less social and biological imperative to reproduce than women, has meant men may
ascribe less value to relationships and retain control over their terms.
Women can be positioned in this milieu as dependent, needy and desperate to commit thus threatening men's freedom and autonomy,
resulting in male detachment and manipulation. This closely aligns in
my research to perceptions of risk to single mothers and children from
men, encompassing physical, sexual, financial and emotional threats
which placed limitations on choices around intimacy. Karen felt she
was more vulnerable when at home alone with her children and learned
to negotiate sexual relations to protect herself, for example by not invit-
ing men she dated into her home. She related experiences of having
been 'played' by men on internet sites who gave the impression of wanting a relationship in order to have sex (Morris 2018b). In line with
Illouz (2012), she consequently avoided becoming too emotionally
attached, not wanting to appear vulnerable (see below). The subsequent
quotation from Zoe indicates ambivalence (Illouz 2012) in the tension
between a desire for intimacy and fear surrounding the potential for
relationships to fail:

> I'm a bit more guarded about my emotions … where I may have issues
> with children, with parenting, with upsetting emotional issues, I don't tend
> to share those as much with a man now – partly because they won't under-
> stand because they're not family and also partly because I'll make myself
> vulnerable by getting attached to them so I keep detached I suppose which
> … impacts on how relationships are going to go in any case but it's just part
> of protecting myself. (Karen)

I do crave it, I definitely crave intimacy – right now I would love to be in a loving relationship but if anyone approached me, I'd chase them off with a stick because, you know … what might go wrong, the energy it takes to make it go right … the way I see it the probability is if I meet somebody it will go wrong, it's just such a high risk venture. (Zoe)

Desires for intimacy, closeness and trust were tempered by an awareness of emotional, sexual and physical risks presented by men, exacerbated by concerns about protecting themselves and their children from further emotional pain and upheaval. Responses are indicative of how women may experience what Walklate describes as a *'permanent state of ontological insecurity and precariousness'* (Walklate 2004: 97) engendered through a constant need to negotiate threat. However, there is a danger, as Walklate (2004) specifies, of seeing women solely as victims, thus ignoring ways in which women engage in pleasure seeking and risk-taking behaviour. Single motherhood provided possibilities for experimentation, for taking control over intimate lives, risk-taking and pleasure-seeking conventionally associated with masculinity. Some participants tried internet dating, met a wide variety of men and experimented with relationships (Morris 2018b). Experimentations were narrated as part of processes of self-discovery, echoing insights about the predominance of therapeutic narrative forms (Illouz 2007; Plummer 1995). Nevertheless, new relationships were viewed as containing potential risks, especially in view of previous intimate experiences which led to disappointment and suffering, this perception thereby constraining choices.

Conclusions

This chapter sought to illuminate the theme of 'disappointment' in relation to love and romance with reference to the narratives of single mothers. Illouz (2007, 2012) interrogates this emotion, arguing that a consumeristic framework creates unrealistic ideals of potential partners, resulting in disappointment when reality does not live up to imagined projections. Here, I have considered disappointment more broadly in relation to intimate lives which have failed to live up to scripted expectations. Western culture continues to be infused with narratives of romantic ideals of love, at once presented as an authentic counterpoint to a fast paced, technologised world (Beck and Beck-Gernsheim 1995) and yet paradoxically bound up with highly commercialised, classed constructions of romance and 'the good life' (Berlant 2011; Evans 2003; Illouz 2012), requiring high levels of consumption. Nostalgic notions of love and family in the western context thereby combine desires for intense, enduring love partnerships, couple-based family forms and images of consumeristic comfort—aspirations which, as Berlant (2011) observes, are increasingly unavailable to the majority of people in a precarious neo-liberalised world. Yet, testimony to the power of these cultural narratives is continual longing and searching for romantic fulfilment (Illouz 2012). We might also consider that increasing socio-economic precarity and awareness of potential threats in a context of global insecurity may serve to solidify for some the desire for security in the form of conventional intimacies (Kaufman 2008). As we have seen, these ideals may simply be out of reach and not worth the risk, especially for those from emotionally and economically precarious backgrounds (see also Silva 2013). Despite discourses around increased choice, many participants experienced material and emotional constraints, shaping their ecologies of choice (Illouz 2012), in the context of a highly gendered, unequal cultural milieu. The loss of anticipated intimate lives was experienced as devastating, disappointment and grief adding a further layer of pain amid already fraught, precarious situations.

Expressions of disappointment at the quality or 'emotional texture' (Illouz 2007) of relationships alongside failures to meet expectations of gender equality were in evidence; there were perceptions that men had failed to develop the 'emotional competencies' (Illouz 2007) required for 'successful' relating. It is necessary here to consider the narrative function of disappointment and its complex interplay with other emotions such as shame; single women—particularly mothers—in our culture are frequently shamed for not achieving desired femininity culminating in heteronormative couplehood (Morris and Munt 2019). Narratively conveying disappointment can invoke a sense of having *been failed* (by others or by the condition of modern life) rather than having 'failed'. As Illouz (2012) observes, it is women who are most often attributed responsibility for 'successful relationships'; against neoliberal emphases on self-responsibility, women may experience feelings of 'self-blame' and therefore seek to reapportion this. Disappointment can entail a sense of disenfranchisement, the withdrawal of an entitlement or dream which, given the powerful hold of romance as a cultural narrative, is likely to be pervasive. In the light of 'cold intimacies' (Illouz 2007), disappointment may follow from the failure of a 'fair exchange' with one side of a bargain not being met, perhaps reflecting processes of rationalisation. Less cynically, expressions of disappointment may mask profound feelings of loss of a source of identity, meaning, connection and solidity (indeed optimism) through coupledom amid complex and fragmented social settings. Promises of egalitarian relationships do not always come to fruition in the everyday lived realities of women's lives (Illouz 2012; Morris 2015) and neither do consumeristic images of a 'happy after life' which rather function as a form of cruel optimism (Berlant 2011), alongside the realities of widespread precarities. The prevalence of disappointment throughout these narratives is indicative of its significance as a cultural emotion (Illouz 2012) which here serves to illuminate the gendered workings of intimacy scripts and ongoing primacy of romantic love. In order to more fully comprehend the emotional dimensions of the contemporary western landscape of intimacy (Layne 2015; Morris 2015), there is further work to be done in understanding the manifestations and meanings surrounding disappointment and to contextualise it more fully against the backdrop of an increasingly uncertain world.

References

Barker, M.-J., Gill, R. and Harvey, L. (2018) *Mediated Intimacy: Sex Advice in Media Culture*. Cambridge: Polity Press.

Beck, U. and Beck-Gernsheim, E. (1995) *The Normal Chaos of Love*. Cambridge: Polity Press.

Berlant, L. (2011) *Cruel Optimism*. Durham, NC: Duke University Press.

Bryman, A. (2012) *Social Research Methods*. Oxford: Oxford University Press.

Budgeon, S. (2008) Couple Culture and the Production of Singleness. *Sexualities*, 11: 301–321.

Duncan, S. (2011) Personal Life, Pragmatism and Bricolage. *Sociological Research Online*, 16 (4).

Ehrenreich, B. (1983) *The Hearts of Men: American dreams and the flight from commitment.* London: Pluto.

Evans, M. (2003) *Love: An Unromantic Discussion.* Cambridge: Polity Press.

Fineman, M.A. (2004) *The Autonomy Myth: A Theory of Dependency.* New York: The New Press.

Gabb, J. (2010) *Researching Intimacy in Families.* Basingstoke: Palgrave Macmillan.

Gagnon, J. and Simon, W. (1973) *Sexual Conduct: The Social Sources of Human Sexuality.* London: Hutchinson.

Giddens, A. (1992) *The Transformation of Intimacy.* Cambridge: Polity Press.

Gillies, V. (2007) *Marginalised Mothers: Exploring working-class experiences of parenting.* London: Routledge.

Gross, N. (2005) The Detraditionalization of Intimacy Reconsidered. *Sociological Theory*, 23 (3): 286–311.

Hochschild, A. (1983) *The managed heart: Commercialization of human feeling.* Berkeley: University of California Press.

Hockey, J.L., Meah, A. and Robinson, V. (2010) *Mundane heterosexualities: From theory to practices.* Basingstoke: Palgrave Macmillan.

Illouz, E. (2007) *Cold intimacies: The making of emotional capitalism.* Cambridge: Polity Press.

Illouz, E. (2012) *Why Love Hurts.* Cambridge: Polity Press.

Jackson, S. (1999) *Heterosexuality in Question.* London: Sage.

Jamieson, L. (1998) *Intimacy: Personal Relationships in Modern Societies.* Cambridge: Polity Press.

Kaufman, J. (2008) *The Single Woman and the Fairytale Prince.* Cambridge: Polity Press.

Layne, L. (2015) A Changing Landscape of Intimacy: The Case of a Single Mother by Choice. *Sociological Research Online, Special Issue on Intimacy and Equality,* 20 (4).

Lewis, J. (2001) *The End of Marriage? Individualism and Intimate Relations.* Cheltenham: Edward Elgar.

Morris, C. (2014) *Unsettled scripts: intimacy narratives of heterosexual single mothers.* Doctoral thesis (PhD), University of Sussex. Available at: http://sro.sussex.ac.uk/48918/.

Morris, C. (2015) Considerations of Equality in heterosexual single mothers' intimacy narratives. *Sociological Research Online, Special Issue on Intimacy and Equality*, 20 (4).

Morris, C. (2018a) The significance of friendship in heterosexual single mothers' intimate lives. *Families, Relationships and Society* (Online first) https://doi.org/10.1332/204674318X15262010818254.

Morris, C. (2018b) Mum's the word: Single mothers talking (or not) about sex. In Morris, Boyce, Cornwall, Frith, Harvey and Huang (eds.) (2018) *Researching sex and sexualities*. UK: Zed Publishing.

Morris, C. and Munt, S.R. (2019) Classed formations of shame in white, British single mothers. *Feminism & Psychology, Special Issue on Shame*. 29 (2): 231–249.

Plummer, K. (1995) *Telling sexual stories: Power, change, and social worlds*. New York: Routledge.

Plummer, K. (2001) *Documents of Life: An Invitation to a Critical Humanism*. Sage: London.

Pugh, A. (2015) *The Tumbleweed Society: Working and Caring in an age of insecurity*. Oxford: Oxford University Press.

Ribbens McCarthy, J., Edwards, R. and Gillies, V. (2003) *Making Families: Moral Tales of parenting and step-parenting*. Durham: British Sociological Centre.

Riessman, C.K. (1993) *Narrative Analysis*. Newbury Park: Sage.

Roseneil, S. (2005) Living and Loving beyond the Boundaries of the Heteronorm: Personal relationships in the 21st Century. In Cunningham-Burley, S. and Mckie, L. (eds.) *Families in Society: Boundaries and Relationships*. Bristol: Policy Press.

Simon, W. and Gagnon, J.H. (1999) Sexual Scripts. In Parker, R. and Aggleton, P. (eds.) *Culture, Society and Sexuality: A Reader*. London: University College London Press.

Skeggs, B. (2005) The Making of Class and Gender through Visualizing Moral Subject Formation. *Sociology*, 39 (5): 965–982.

Silva, J. (2013) *Coming up short: Working-class adulthood in an age of uncertainty*. Oxford: Oxford University Press.

Smart, C. (2007) *Personal Life: New Directions in Sociological Thinking*. Cambridge: Polity Press.

Walklate, S. (2004) *Gender, crime and criminal justice*. Cullompton: Willan.

Weeks, J. (2007) *The World we have won: The remaking of intimate and erotic lives*. London: Routledge.

13

The Affective Politics of Progress Narratives: Women Talking About Equality in Heterosexual Relationships

Raisa Jurva

Introduction

The sociology of personal life has proposed that there has been major changes in the ways intimate relationships are organised and lived out in the contemporary global West.[1] The individualisation thesis suggests that human bonds are no longer maintained by tradition or moral codes regarding family life, which would also promote democratisation of the intimate social sphere. The thesis has been debated within different areas of sociology since the 1990s (May and Nordqvist 2019: 7) and claims regarding shifts in romantic relationships have not escaped criticism (Gabb 2008; Holmes 2004; Jamieson 1999; Roseneil 2007) as empirical studies indicate continuities in the organisation of relationships that maintain inequalities. Moreover, while institutions such as marriage might have somewhat lost their power to give meaning to heterosexual

R. Jurva (✉)
Tampere University, Tampere, Finland
e-mail: Raisa.Jurva@uta.fi

J. Carter, L. Arocha (eds.), *Romantic Relationships in a Time of 'Cold Intimacies'*,
Palgrave Macmillan Studies in Family and Intimate Life,
https://doi.org/10.1007/978-3-030-29256-0_13

relationships (Jallinoja 2000), it might still be misleading to downplay their role. Neil Gross (2005: 297) points out that while the regulative traditions of institutionalised heterosexuality, such as marriage, have declined, meaning-constitutive traditions which promote romantic love remain significant in the organisation of intimate relationships. Moreover, the suggested liquidity of romantic relationships also evokes insecurity (Bauman 2003). However, from analyses of people's lived experiences, it appears that insecurity frames some relationships while others are free from it. For example, in the experiences of bisexual women in Finland, heterosexual relationships enjoy strong social support which same-sex relationships lack (Lahti 2015: 436–437). Perhaps the diversification of intimate relationships might best be understood not as a process of individualisation, but as a complexification of how people form, maintain and rely on relationships, as Chris Beasley et al. (2012) suggest.

Continuities seem especially to enter the picture when a gender perspective is taken into account in research. Women continue to struggle between the ideals of gender equality and the lived realities of inequalities in heterosexual relationships, even in countries that foster a rhetoric of equality (Jokinen 2005; Jurva and Lahti forthcoming; Sihto et al. 2018). Illouz (2012: 9) explores intimacy in modernity and argues for two major shifts in heterosexual romantic love in the twentieth century: the economisation of social relationships and the individualisation of lifestyles. In this chapter, I discuss these suggested shifts through 19 mid- to later-life women's narration of their experiences of heterosexual relationships in Finland. In the women's narrations, gendered conventions become politicised in two kinds of progress narratives that portray a development towards more equal relationships. The first progress narrative concerns the sociocultural conditions of heterosexual relationships in Finnish society; the second concerns the interviewees' own senses of living as a man's partner. Both trajectories are depicted as progress towards equality. The Finnish welfare state provides social policies that aim at tackling gendered inequalities in heterosexual relationships, which creates a particular context for economisation and individualisation of lifestyles that Illouz (2012) suggests. Drawing on feminist theory, critical studies of heterosexuality and affect theory, I ask what kind of political potential regarding gender in heterosexual relationships is entailed in the idea of progress.

Politicising Heterosexual Relationships in the Finnish Context

Nordic welfare states are rarely considered to foster male dominance in society; rather, they are seen as woman-friendly (Anttonen 1994: 203). In Finland, women entered the public sphere through participation in paid work and parliamentary politics earlier than in many other countries in Europe, and the male breadwinner model has historically been weak and relatively alien. Moreover, the welfare state ideology in Finland has provided social policies that can potentially tackle some of the inequalities that concern heterosexual couples' reproductive and domestic lives, such as affordable day care for children and the separate taxation of spouses. This way of negotiating issues concerning gender and power on a primarily institutional level has been described as state feminism, and it characterises Finnish society. Gendered conventions seem to pattern public life as well as private. The role that women are assigned in the home also characterises the gendered place assigned to them in parliamentary politics, as the public sphere is defined through motherly attributes for women (Kuusipalo 2011; Pylkkänen 1999). Consequently, women have access to male spheres, but within those spheres, they end up in positions with less power.

Thus, a focus on social policies or women's political participation does not provide a fair representation of gender equality in Finnish society. Even though state feminism has strengthened the conditions for gender equality in Finland, it does not extend to tackling the power dynamics that characterise heterosexuality. Welfare state policies tend to struggle with or even ignore problems that can be situated in the so-called private sphere. It has been argued internationally that heterosexuality has not been the focus of social policies (Carabine 1996), a critique that has been voiced in Finland as well.

Although the two spheres, public and private, are linked together, equality in the public sphere does not directly translate into equality in private and intimate relationships (Halleröd et al. 2007: 151). Moreover, feminist research has pointed out that the division between public and private is itself a way of (re)producing gender and gendered inequalities (Eräsaari et al. 1995: 7). The separation between public and private, which is essential to (neo)liberalism, has been especially problematised in radical feminism (Hekman 2014: 50; Pateman 1989: 118), encapsulated in the slogan 'the personal is political' (Hanisch 1969). While state feminism has provided policies that benefit women, it also enables the avoidance of gender conflict by supporting a conformist strategy for negotiating gendered power dynamics.

One might ask whether the task of seeing the political in the personal is more difficult in Finland than in other Nordic countries. Anu Koivunen (2012) has analysed the reception of Märta Tikkanen's feminist novels during the 1970s. In other Nordic countries, the novel Män kan inte våldtas [Men cannot be raped] (Tikkanen 1975) became a feminist reference point for explorations of power in intimate heterosexual relationships. In Finland, however, the political dimension of the novel went unnoticed in mainstream cultural discussions; instead, critiques portrayed it as the author's unnecessary public dwelling on marital problems that had no resonance beyond her own life. The novel was considered an airing of personal issues, and this was met with hostility by critics (Koivunen 2012). To the extent that feminist ideas were introduced and discussed during the 1960s and 1970s in Finnish women's magazines, they were characterised by a highly businesslike tone, which directed the discussion towards issues in working life and which limited opportunities to problematise and politicise the private (Saarenmaa 2010: 318–320).

Such difficulty in addressing gendered power relations in intimate relationships did not characterise Finnish debate during the 1970s alone. Although feminist groups drew public attention to the highly gendered nature of sexual and domestic violence during the 1970s in Finland, it was not until the 1990s that the gendered nature of the phenomenon was acknowledged more widely. A gender-neutral and individualising research approach to the phenomenon continues to operate alongside more gender-informed approaches, even today (Ronkainen and Näre 2008: 23–25).

It has been suggested that social science fails to provide a suitable vocabulary for understanding social relations within such phenomena (Husso 2003) and also that liberal theories of justice are not productive for the analysis of power dynamics in intimate relationships (Virkki 2004: 90). Consequently, it is hardly surprising that gendered power relations in intimacy remain difficult to grasp in research, politics and everyday life. Moreover, in working life, gender equality is sometimes understood to be best promoted by remaining silent about gender (Ylöstalo 2012: 272).

The history of Finnish women is also saturated with the rhetoric of the 'strong Finnish woman' (Markkola 1997). This rhetoric might be an impediment to understanding the connections between gender and power. Indeed, manifestations of this rhetoric can be seen in the afore-mentioned studies of gendered sexual violence. When the phenomenon finally began to be studied in the 1990s—later than in other Nordic countries—researchers began to collect stories of women's survival, not stories of victims (Koivunen 1998: 24).

Heterosexuality and Female Subjectivity

A sense of dissatisfaction in everyday life that is easy to sense but difficult to pinpoint, let alone change, might be described as a problem with no name, following Betty Friedan (1982). There are, however, culturally available ways of making sense of unsatisfactory situations. When justify-ing gendered conventions in heterosexual relationships, women and men refer to individual character traits, gender stereotypes or claims about practical solutions to the puzzles of everyday life (Magnusson 2005, 2008). Such justifications may enable people to deal with their own situ-ations, but they do not enable them to politicise the dissatisfaction evoked by gendered conventions (Jurva and Lahti forthcoming). Consequently, it has been suggested that it is difficult to take collective action on issues that concern couple relationships (Stocks et al. 2007: 151).

Although difficult to politicise (see Thwaites in this volume), relation-ship problems remain a predominant issue in popular culture and the media. Moreover, services and products offered by therapeutic cultures that target different kinds of problems are widely available for diverse individuals, couples and situations (Illouz 2007). Unfortunately, when these products and services rely on post-feminist perspectives—as they often do—they end up maintaining gendered and sexualised hierarchies (Kolehmainen 2018).

As the gendered conventions that maintain inequalities in heterosexual relationships function habitually (Jokinen 2004) and affectively, the politicisation of such problems has to happen beyond legislation or social policy. In this chapter, I examine the affective politics of progress narratives in order to grasp what kind of political potential such narratives entail in the context of heterosexual relationships, which are saturated with gendered meanings, practices and ideals.

Research Material and Method

My research material consists of 19 interviews with mid- to later-life women (aged 41–68 years) who had experienced relationships with substantially younger men (the average and mean value of the age difference was 14 years). In addition to their age-dissimilar relationships (see also McKenzie in this volume), the women's narrations concerned other relationship experiences throughout their lives. The interviews took place in different locations that provided sufficient privacy, such as my office, meeting rooms in universities or libraries, corner tables in cafes or interviewees' homes. The working class and middle class interviewees lived in different cities and towns in Finland.

The interviews were structured around 12 questions about the women's experiences of heterosexual relationships with younger men and men in general. The questions concerned their relationship with the younger man, such as how they met and the kinds of situation (if any) where the interviewee paid attention to the age difference. Other questions focused on the interviewees' ideas about relationships in general. During the interviews, I posed additional questions connected to the interviewee's responses, in order to hear more detailed narration about their experiences. My role in the interview situation could be described as active interviewing (Holstein and Gubrium 1995), which in my case meant immersing myself in the interviewee's narration and grasping the parts that intuitively attracted me in some way.

In the interviewees' narrations, different temporalities overlapped. Women had experienced relationships and marriages in different decades, from the 1960s to the time of the interviews in the 2010s. Moreover, some of the interviewees had experiences of living in a relationship as a teenager, being a mother of small children, or being divorced.

The interviewees' accounts contained plenty of descriptions of hurtful, unfair and even abusive situations they had faced in heterosexual relationships throughout their lives. After a close reading of the interviews, I identified a narrative structure that organised the women's accounts of gendered power: the structure of progress. In what follows I divide my analysis of this narrative structure into two parts. In the first part, I analyse the progress narratives through which interviewees described a shift in the sociocultural conditions of heterosexual relationships. According to these narrations, the shift has paved the way for more equality in heterosexual relationships as well as for a diversification of relationships, which differs from the shift towards the economisation of social relationships that Illouz (2012) suggests. In the second part of the analysis, I outline a progress narrative that depicts interviewees' strengthening subjectivities through various intimate relationships during their life course. I focus on the affective politics of these progress narratives about heterosexual relationships, approaching affect as 'marking the body's belonging and non-belonging to a world of encounters' (Seigworth and Gregg 2010: 2). I reflect this progress narrative of personal empowerment in relation to Illouz's (2012) argument on individualisation of lifestyles.

The teleological idea of history as progressive development characterises modernism. Feminist critique has pointed out that the idea of inevitable progress hides continuities in gendered power dynamics (Sellberg and Hoogland 2018: xv). Moreover, a common way of making sense of events is to organise them as narratives that depict connectedness and coherence as well as change. Such narrative forms can also be found in research discussions (Gergen and Gergen 1986): one way of describing the previous decades of feminist research draws on the idea of progress (Hemmings 2011). Moreover, the interview technique that I used foregrounded the temporal organisation of events, as I often posed additional questions such as 'has it always been like this for you, or has your understanding of relationships changed throughout your life?'

Sociocultural Progress Towards Diversity and Equality

As the interviewees reflected with hindsight upon their intimate relationships, they depicted how men's control over their female partners' lives had been stronger in previous decades than it was nowadays.

Helena,[2] aged 55, reflects on the control that men can exert over women economically. After describing such situations in her female friends' lives and in her own past, she continues:

> My father was exactly the same. I remember how he always bragged about bringing money into the house while mother was at home. I guess it is a kind of traditional way for men to subjugate the other. Although, nowadays it is not possible to pull that off in the same way, as almost all women work, so one can't, like, disparage the other so grossly.

Leena, 59, recalls that it was taken for granted that changes in her father's workplace would dictate the place of residence for the whole family. Since the family moved often, her mother would give up her own job opportunities. This kind of arrangement, which prioritises the man's paid work and overlooks the wife's labour and earnings, is something that women today would not agree to, Leena maintains.

> Leena: Nowadays, women do not agree to leave their own good jobs. But it was obvious when I was a child that the woman sacrifices her job when the husband gains a better position.
> Raisa: Yes, exactly, yes, and this happens on his terms, kind of…
> Leena: Yes, no matter how nice he would otherwise have been, and the woman did not have to be between a rock and a hard place, but such things were obvious.

Helena's and Leena's descriptions of progress in recent decades depict men's financial domination over women in intimate relationships as a thing of the past. This idea of generational progress towards equality is also projected onto individuals who represent different decades. Leena (59) gives credit to younger men:

Men of my age do not want to be with me [laughing] but young ones can take it, because they think the same way themselves. That a woman does not have to be a slave in the house and that a woman can study, spend her free time as she wishes. My opinion is that younger men are smarter than old men.

In addition to a shift in men's economic domination over women in heterosexual relationships, the interviewees describe a progress towards a greater acceptance of various formations of relationships.

My father's sister was five years older than her spouse, which apparently at that time was quite a difference. [...] But I do remember, actually, how my aunt never let anyone mention the age difference. She even changed her first name, Kyllikki, we were not allowed to ever call her Kyllikki because it sounded like an old woman's name, so she was also Kiti. To make it more youthful. So attitudes have changed. (Tuulikki, 68)

Besides age-dissimilar relationships, Tuulikki points to a shift towards more acceptance of single lifestyles and single motherhood, echoing sociological claims that there has been a historic shift towards greater diversity in the organisation of social and sexual lives (Beck and Beck-Gernsheim 1995, 2002; Giddens 1992) and a decline of normative moral framework (Illouz 2012).

According to the interviewees, in the past, breaking the strict norm of reproduction within marriage could have severe consequences. Marja-Leena, 61, remembers how a close relative of her age, Pirjo, got pregnant at 16. This caused turmoil among their relatives, which Marja-Leena has difficulty understanding even today:

The family made a fuss about it and it became completely [insane]. I think it is a wonderful thing that a child is born but it turned into ... Pirjo's mother, Pirjo is my age, so her mother started to drink and became almost kind of like an alcoholic.

A child born out of wedlock to a teenage girl caused a massive 'fuss' among Marja-Leena's relatives. Moreover, Pirjo's example was used as a warning of the dangers of teenage pregnancy during Marja-Leena's youth.

One of the standard questions that I posed to the interviewees was 'how has your understanding and experience of relationships changed throughout your life, if it has?' The sociocultural changes that the women described overlapped with their own relationship trajectories. In their accounts of their early relationships, getting married was portrayed as a given.

Rauha, 60, reflects upon the function of intimate relationships during the 1970s:

> My very smart sister said that you just transitioned from home to the husband's care, without thinking about anything. It is such a cliché, but that is what you did at that time. It was very common, even.

Rauha's description makes visible how cohabitation with a man was a habitual transition, made 'without thinking about anything'. Moreover, the transition did not move the woman into a life of her own but into 'the husband's care', as Rauha puts it. A transition towards independent adulthood required something else in the interviewees' lives, as I will discuss later.

Even in cases where women's own ideas were not in accordance with the spirit of the times, external pressure towards marriage could be fierce, especially if there were children on the way. Leena, 59, recalls the keen insistence on conformity to marriage in her early adulthood while she was pregnant:

> I remember when I got married, I was married at the time. We were not planning to get married but then I encountered fierce comments like, 'what am I going to say to relatives and what am I going to say to my workmates'.

Leena describes the panic that the prospect of her giving birth to a child out of wedlock caused in her mother in the early 1980s. Even though gender, morality and family life were reinterpreted during the 1960s and 1970s, leading to improvements in the position of divorced mothers and children born outside marriage (Nätkin 2003: 31), in Leena's account, marriage was still the only shield against the condemnation that a departure from reproductive norms would have invoked. Sari, 58, also depicts the combination of marriage and children as self-evident when she recalls her motives for getting married, which she now considers not to have been the right choice. I ask Sari what kinds of motive she is referring to:

> Well, the first marriage happened because I wanted to have children while I was young. And well, at that time you had to get married, you could not even consider ... society was different. So all I was thinking about was to get a good father for children, so that he would be the right type.

In Sari's description of 1970s Finland, reproduction and marriage were inseparable. Anything else was unthinkable, manifested as an empty space in Sari's unfinished sentence: 'you could not even consider'.

Besides avoidance of moral condemnation, the interviewees present motives for getting married that are more practical, reflecting the nature of marriage as a legal contract for financial settlement. Anneli, 62, recalls her situation in the 1970s:

> My partner said that we have to get married now, call the city administrative court to find out if they have slots available for this year. At that time, you would get a tax refund if you were married. It was the last chance, as we got married at the end of December.

The financial benefit of marriage is also present in Sari's description of how she ended up in the second of her three marriages:

> Well, the reason for the second marriage was that we got a mortgage. At that time, it was a better deal; there was no cohabitation in 1997, almost 20 years ago. It was easier with all the practicalities that way. (Sari, 58)

In these progress narratives of sociocultural change in the organisation of intimate relationships, marriage and marriage-like arrangements function to protect women from condemnation in their social circles and as a vehicle to move on in life. Consequently, marriage does not appear as a self-evidently happy object (Ahmed 2010) that would obviously lead to a good life, or even to the promise of one.

According to Neil Gross (2005: 297), regulative traditions of institutionalised heterosexuality, such as marriage, have declined, while meaning-constitutive traditions which promote romantic love remain significant in the organisation of intimate relationships. The progress narrative in the interviewees' accounts depicts a sociocultural shift towards a loosening of marriage's moral grip, resonating with Gross's argument. Furthermore, the interviewees' progress narrative also describes a shift towards more diversity in relationships, and fewer financial or social incentives to get married or live in a relationship. In the women's narrations, the trajectory of this progress narrative wipes out previous obstacles that stood in the way of equality between women and men. This resembles sociological arguments about the connection between women's financial independence and equality in heterosexual relationships (Beck and Beck-Gernsheim 1995; Giddens 1992). In a welfare state context, the economisation of social relationships seems to have loosened, a change different than Illouz (2012) argues.

However, while the sociocultural progress narrative operates on the level of legislation, social policies and social norms, it disregards dynamics within heterosexual relationships that cannot be reduced to (e.g.) legal or financial arrangements. Studies of Finnish heterosexual couples also reveal another kind of change in the handling of inequalities within heterosexual relationships. The equality discourse concerning household chores was widespread in women's narrations in the 1980s, and at that time, women were embarrassed by the unequal sharing of household chores in their heterosexual relationships. Two decades later, instead of being embarrassed, women openly confirm such inequality in their relationships and reflect on how they feel about it (Jokinen 2004: 300).

According to the narrative of sociocultural progress, contemporary conditions should foster the possibility of 'pure relationships' (Giddens 1992), as relationships are no longer constrained by explicit gendered hierarchies or societal pressures. However, the picture becomes more nuanced when we look at progress narratives that depict women's individual evolution from their early relationships to their relationships today. I turn to such narratives in the next section.

Progress from Male Control to Personal Empowerment

Along with the progress narrative of equality and diversity, which depicts a change in the economisation of social relations concerning heterosexual relationships, another kind of progress narrative also emerges in mid- to later-life women's narrations. Even though the interviewees suggest that the Finnish society has undergone changes that delegitimise different forms of male domination in heterosexual relationships, the gendered dynamics of heterosexual relationships linger as an affective residue. The second progress narrative is organised around a trajectory where women reflect retrospectively on their own relationships throughout their lives. This narrative depicts a progression that starts with living according to male partners' interests and desires and ends with women gaining a stronger sense of what they want for themselves. I read this as a progress narrative of personal empowerment.

Even at a time when marriage might already have lost its grip as a regulative tradition that provides vital protection against moral condemnation, marriage and marriage-like arrangements exert another kind of grip on women in this progress narrative of personal empowerment. Sari, 58, describes a phenomenon she has noticed in her relationships:

> I get too much into the other person's life, especially when I was younger, although I am still young [laughs]. I have not held onto my own things but get completely into the other person's sphere of life, in a way that I don't, kind of, have a selfhood at all.

Such feelings of losing oneself have been discussed in terms of asymmetries in heterosexual relationships which emerge as women's needs, wishes and desires are pushed aside while men's get prioritised (Holmberg 1993; Langford 1999). To quote Gunnarsson (2014), women love men as they are. Hence women suppress their own needs in order to prioritise those of their partner, and women's subjectivity gets lost. Although the hope of correcting this by being loved for who one is might involve even tighter attachment to one's partner (Langford 1999), in my study the women described a shift that did not include a different kind of relationship with a man. Rather, my interviewees became whole insofar as they became separate from men.

The grip that attached my interviewees to their partners during early adulthood was tight. Leena, 59, discusses a shift from immersion in her partner towards a more solid subjectivity in her relationships:

> When I was young, I compromised more. As you don't have experience when you're young and perhaps you have lower self-esteem, so I have probably let guys boss me around more. It is only gradually that you start to know your own worth.

In Leena's account, her partners' perspective was prioritised in her early relationships, as she compromised and was susceptible to being bossed around.

According to some interviewees, there might be factors in the life course that make women more prone to lose their selfhood. Susanna, 41, links having small children to dependence on a relationship in her reply to my question about whether her understanding of relationships has changed throughout her life:

> It has probably changed, but I think that it is connected to the general situation of life. When the children were small and we were in the nesting period. When I was, let's say 25 to 35 years of age, perhaps I thought that [pause], well, I wouldn't say that the man was everything but he was much more than at this moment. Later on, my own, independent life entered the picture more strongly. So it has changed quite a bit over the years.

The process of gaining full selfhood resembles the therapeutic narrative that Illouz (2007) connects to feminist narratives of female empowerment. The 'male in the head' (Holland et al. 1998) during the women's early relationships was only gradually overcome during their life course, however.

Helena, 55, recalls her past relationship:

> He [Helena's partner at the time] could not spend a night away from home, he said, and I did not understand that surely I can take myself and my son to the amusement park by car, or take another woman with children with

us so we could go together. Somehow, at that time, I was so stuck and kind of dependent on my partner that I did not realise that I could go on my own.

Helena's account of being stuck in her partner's ways, which limited her time and space for enjoyable activities with her child, highlights her frustration as she recalls the situation. She makes it clear that there were no practical obstacles to her carrying out her own wishes for enjoyable activities with her son, as she could have managed to organise activities by herself or with friends; nevertheless, her partner's refusal to join in guided her actions. The discrepancy becomes clear as she continues, accusing herself harshly of 'being so stupid' and not realising that holiday trips did not have to depend on whether her partner accompanied them. Even though the tendency to prioritise the man's perspective is recognised, it does not free the woman from responsibility in Helena's case. Rather, it demands strong subjectivity (Husso 2003), and it casts the woman as responsible for the situation. Helena further suggests, however, that this might be a phenomenon that characterises young couples in general.

Perhaps young couples or younger ones are always kind of dependent on each other, in a way that it requires the whole family to come along when travelling somewhere. They don't realise that it is possible to travel otherwise as well.

The lifestyle that follows the nuclear family ideal, which organises all the parties' lives as one unit, becomes clear in Helena's account. The reason behind one's loss of willpower is located in youth and the ideal of a tight family unit, but gender is not further considered.

Moreover, the history of male domination is echoed in interactions between spouses. It is possible to exert control over a woman symbolically, even when it is not possible financially. Kirsti, 58, recalls such a scenario in her previous relationship:

If couples have a shared car, it usually is registered to the man. When I needed it, then he would say 'oh, are you going to take my car?' This was always such a crappy, such an economic kind of, like a reminder of what your place is in this house. Even though I used to have a very well-paid job.

Kirsti describes how both she and her spouse contributed to the household, and yet her partner managed to portray his superiority through ownership. The sociocultural changes that the previous progress narrative depicts do not completely eradicate male domination in heterosexual relationships, as liberation from material, financial and social constraints does not guarantee equality in a heterosexual relationship.

The narrative of progress towards female empowerment depicts a shift from being under a man's control towards gaining one's own subjectivity. This is described as nothing less than gaining one's freedom. Sinikka, 56, recalls how her violent ex-husband continued to harass her after they divorced. Despite the dramatic and tragic turn of her ex-husband's later suicide, Sinikka describes her feeling as follows:

> And the thing is that I got this insane feeling of freedom when I got rid of my daughters' father. That is when I felt, for the first time, that I am free and I don't have to consider anyone else than myself and my children.

Insanity, through which Sinikka describes her feelings, connects to cultural understandings of power in heterosexual relationships in other ways as well.

> I have always been kind of a tough guy [laughing], and I have always been able to speak my mind, although I was in such a subordinate position in the countryside, then on the other hand, I have always managed to speak my mind. (Helena, 55)

Helena's pondering points to the special characteristics of power in heterosexual dynamics. She describes taking firm action, for example in her work in the security business, which is a highly male-dominated field with a daily risk of violence. When gendered power dynamics are not grasped beyond clear manifestations of coercion or inequality, such as physical restriction, financial dependence or legal issues, it becomes a conundrum and switches the focus onto the woman's inability to resist.

Women's reflections on their past relationships include descriptions of times when their lives were restricted due to their partners' controlling behaviour. In the interviews, the trajectory of relationship experiences is portrayed as a progress narrative in which women become less dependent on their partners. The main shift in the conditions for living out heterosexual coupledom that the interviewees depict is that the prioritisation of the man's perspective decreases. Even though this trajectory can be considered progress towards female empowerment, it makes that progress by detaching itself from heterosexual dynamics.

The two kinds of progress narrative overlap, as women's experiences of not knowing or having a selfhood are situated in their first marriages or marriage-like arrangements—possibly alongside their responsibility for childcare—which mostly occurred at a time when marriage was considered a self-evident transition in life. Moreover, those experiences are partly situated in times characterised by gendered economisation of heterosexual relationships that would validate such situations. However, the gendered conventions that cast women's needs and desires as secondary continue to organise heterosexual dynamics, despite the sociocultural shift.

Their newly won subjectivity makes it possible for women to keep their distance from their partners and recover their own interests. But as women discuss the inequalities they continue to face in their current relationships, there does not seem to be a narrative that politicises the problem in a feminist way (see Thwaites, this volume). Rather, inequalities in their current relationships evoke non-cathartic emotions (Ngai 2005) such as irritation, a constantly chafing sensation instead of a sharp transformative burst of feeling. Moreover, I have analysed elsewhere how the interviewees' fear of neglect frames their future orientation, as they cannot rely on their younger partners for providing care while being physically or mentally vulnerable (Jurva 2018). The transformative potential of progress operates in hindsight but ends in the present moment.

Conclusion

In this chapter, I have analysed the affective politics of the progress narratives that organise women's narrations of heterosexual relationships. According to my analysis, gender in the context of heterosexuality is politicised through narratives of progress. I have described two kinds of progress narrative that emerge in mid- to later-life women's narrations of heterosexual relationships. The first progress narrative describes legal and economic changes in Finnish society that have weakened women's dependency on their male partners. In contrast to the suggested economisation of social relationships (Illouz 2012), my analysis portrays a development towards a situation where heterosexual relationships are less conditioned by economic benefits or restrictions than before. Furthermore, the problems in their relationship experiences that interviewees depict as explicitly gendered follow the idea that there have been major changes in what is considered possible and desirable in heterosexual relationships. These changes have also enabled a diversification of social bonds. The second progress narrative that I have identified organises women's relationship trajectories as a progression that starts with dependence as a limiting attachment to the male partner and domesticity and ends with solid female subjectivity.

So what is the affective politics of the two progress narratives that I have identified? The first progress narrative, which depicts changes in the ecology and architecture of choice in the context of heterosexual relationships, is affirmative: despite its emotionally charged nature, it provides hope and even proof that profound change is possible in the sociocultural conditions that organise heterosexual relationships. The second progress narrative that I have identified in this chapter, the narrative of progress towards personal empowerment, depicts a trajectory in which women transcend the threat of submersion in domesticity and their partner's life, a threat that risks diminishing women's lives. The final destination in this progress narrative is a selfhood that is somewhat detached from the male partner. According to my research material, this is partly enabled by detaching oneself from domestic and family life, which in the interviewees' narrations entails material as well as ideological constraints that encourage women to lose themselves in their family or partner. The narrative of progress towards empowerment comes close to what Illouz (2007) describes as the self-realisation narrative, whose emergence she locates in the 1960s American context, and whose scope reaches beyond the field of psychology. According to my analysis, the idea of progress towards a more genuine self is also culturally available to make sense of experiences of heterosexual intimacy in contemporary Finland.

My colleague, Annukka Lahti, and I have previously argued that inequalities in intimate (especially heterosexual) relationships are easier to resist and condemn when they are reflected upon on a general level or positioned outside of one's own current situation, for example in other people's relationships or imaginary relationships (Jurva and Lahti forthcoming). Inequalities are made sense of by framing them as tendencies of youth or a stage in the life course, or alternatively as a feature that characterises young couples or families with small children; this might water down the political potential of my interviewees' pointed observations. More importantly, these progress narratives do not enable us to make sense of gender. Rather, the narratives affectively invite us to accept such problems as an inevitable part of a heterosexual life course trajectory, placing no responsibility on men. According to my analysis, a progress narrative about equality in general might not provide relief from male dominance in women's current relationships. Rather, personal progress narratives follow a development-psychological trajectory detached from gendered conventions and power dynamics. Just as the 'personal' problems portrayed in Märta Tikkanen's novels were not received with understanding, so my interviewees remain uncomprehending as they mull over their problems with their former partners (see also Thwaites' discussion on choice and politics, this volume).

Following on from the argument that gender conflict is avoided on an institutional level by resort to the logic of state feminism in Finland, according to my analysis this conflict can also be avoided at an individual level when the overcoming of inequality is made sense of as a story of personal growth that is detached from gendered power in heterosexual relationships.

However, women's reflections of the spirit of the times do not allow them to excuse themselves from responsibility; rather, the demand for strong subjectivity (Husso 2003) remains. The affective politics that progress narratives invite invokes an economy of gratitude (Hochschild and Machung 1990). The notion of progress, however, entails a political potential concerning female ageing. A central feminist question is what happens to womanhood during ageing (Vakimo 2001: 44). The progress narrative of female empowerment enables an affirmative reading of the possibilities that ageing and relationship experiences provide for female subjectivity in heterosexual relationships.

Notes

1. This chapter has been written as part of the research project *Just the Two of Us? Affective inequalities in intimate relationships* (287983), funded by the Academy of Finland.
2. All names are pseudonyms.

References

Ahmed, S. (2010) *The promise of happiness*. Durham, NC: Duke University Press.

Anttonen, A. (1994) Hyvinvointivaltion naisystävälliset kasvot. In A. Anttonen, L. Henriksson and Ritva Nätkin (eds.) *Naisten hyvinvointivaltio*. Tampere: Vastapaino.

Bauman, Z. (2003) *Liquid love: On the frailty of human bonds*. Cambridge: Polity Press.

Beasley, C., Brook, H. and Holmes, M. (2012) *Heterosexuality in theory and practice*. New York: Routledge.

Beck, U. and Beck-Gernsheim, E. (1995) *The normal chaos of love*. Cambridge: Polity Press.

Beck, U. and Beck-Gernsheim, E. (2002) *Individualization: Institutionalized individualism and its social and political consequences*. London: Sage.

Carabine, J. (1996) Heterosexuailty and social policy. In Diane Richardson (ed.) *Theorizing heterosexuality: Telling it straight*. Buckingham: Open University Press: 55–74.

Eräsaari, L., Julkunen, R. and Silius, H. (eds.) (1995) *Naiset yksityisen ja julkisen rajalla*. Tampere: Vastapaino.

Friedan, B. (1982) *The feminine mystique*. Harmondsworth: Penguin.

Gabb, J. (2008) *Researching intimacy in families*. Basingstoke: Palgrave Macmillan.

Gergen, K. J. and Gergen, M. M. (1986) Narrative form and the construction of psychological science. In T. R. Sarbin (ed.) *Narrative psychology: the storied nature of human conduct*. Westport, CT: Praeger/Greenwood: 22–44.

Giddens, A. (1992) *The transformation of intimacy*. Cambridge: Polity Press.

Gross, N. (2005) The detraditionalization of intimacy reconsidered. *Sociological Theory* 23(3): 286–311.

Gunnarsson, L. (2014) *The contradictions of love: Towards a feminist-realist ontology of sociosexuality*. New York: Routledge.

Halleröd, B., Díaz, C. and Stocks, J. (2007) Doing gender while doing couple: concluding remarks. In J. Stocks, C. Díaz and B. Halleröd (eds.) *Modern couples sharing money, sharing life*. Basingstoke: Palgrave Macmillan: 143–155.

Hanisch, C. (1969) *The personal is political*. Available at: http://www.carol-hanisch.org/CHwritings/PIP.html [Accessed 31 July 2018].

Hekman, S. (2014) *The feminine subject*. Cambridge: Polity Press.

Hemmings, C. (2011) *Why stories matter: The political grammar of feminist theory*. Durham, NC and London: Duke University Press.

Hochschild, A. R. and Machung, A. (1990) *The second shift: Working parents and the revolution at home*. London: Piatkus.

Holland, J., Ramazanoglu, C., Sharpe, S. and Thomson, R. (1998) *The male in the head: Young people, heterosexuality and power*. London: Tufnell Press.

Holmberg, C. (1993) *Det kallas kärlek: en socialpsykologisk studie om kvinnors underordning och mäns överordning bland unga jämställda par*. Göteborg: Anamma.

Holmes, M. (2004) An equal distance? Individualisation, gender and intimacy in distance relationships. *The Sociological Review* 52(2): 180–200.

Holstein, J. A. and Gubrium, J. F. (1995) *The active interview*. Thousand Oaks, CA: Sage.

Husso, M. (2003) *Parisuhdeväkivalta: lyötyjen aika ja tila*. Tampere: Vastapaino.

Illouz, E. (2007) *Cold intimacies: The making of emotional capitalism*. Cambridge: Polity Press.

Illouz, E. (2012) *Why love hurts: A sociological explanation*. Cambridge: Polity Press.

Jallinoja, R. (2000) *Perheen aika*. Helsinki: Otava.

Jamieson, L. (1999) Intimacy transformed? A critical look at the 'pure relationship'. *Sociology* 33(3): 477–494.

Jokinen, E. (2004) Kodin työt, tavat, tasa-arvo ja rento refleksiivisyys [Housework, habits, equality and relaxed reflexivity]. In E. Jokinen, M. Kaskisaari and M. Husso (eds.) *Ruumis töihin! Käsite ja käytäntö* [Make that body work! Concept and practice]. Tampere: Vastapaino: 285–304.

Jokinen, E. (2005) *Aikuisten arki* [Everyday life of adults]. Helsinki: Gaudeamus.

Jurva, R. (2018) Independence and vulnerability: Affective orientations in imagining futurities for heterosexual relationships. In T. Juvonen and M. Kolehmainen (eds.) *Affective inequalities in intimate relationships*. London: Routledge: 127–140.

Jurva, R. and Lahti, A. (forthcoming) Challenging unequal gendered conventions in heterosexual relationship contexts through affective dissonance. *NORA – Nordic Journal of Feminist and Gender Research*.

Koivunen, A. (1998) Suomalaisuus ja muita sitoumuksia: kommentteja Tuija Parvikon teeseihin. *Naistutkimus: Kvinnoforskning* 11(3): 23–30.

Koivunen, A. (2012) Kun henkilökohtainen ei ole poliittista. In K. Lempiäinen, T. Leppänen and S. Paasonen (eds.) *Erot ja etiikka feministisessä tutkimuksessa.* Åbo: Utukirjat: 185–209.

Kolehmainen, M. (2018) Mapping affective capacities: gender and sexuality in relationship and sex counselling practices. In T. Juvonen and M. Kolehmainen (eds.) *Affective inequalities in intimate relationships.* London: Routledge: 63–77.

Kuusipalo, J. (2011) *Sukupuolittunut poliittinen edustus Suomessa.* Tampere: Tampere University Press.

Lahti, A. (2015) Similar and equal relationships? Negotiating bisexuality in an enduring relationship. *Feminism and Psychology* 25(4): 431–448.

Langford, W. (1999) *Revolutions of the heart: Gender, power and the delusions of love.* New York: Routledge.

Magnusson, E. (2008) The rhetoric of inequality: Nordic women and men argue against sharing house-work. *NORA: Nordic Journal of Women's Studies* 16(2): 79–95.

Magnusson, E. (2005) Gendering or equality in the lives of Nordic heterosexual couples with children: No well-paved avenues yet. *NORA: Nordic Journal of Women's Studies,* 13(3): 153–163.

Markkola, P. (1997) Constructing and deconstructing the 'strong Finnish woman': Women's history and gender history. *Historiallinen Aikakauskirja* 95(2): 153–160.

May, V. and Nordqvist, P. (2019) Introducing a sociology of personal life. In V. May and P. Nordqvist (eds.) *Sociology of personal life.* London: Red Globe Press: 1–15.

Nätkin, R. (2003) Moninaiset perhemuodot ja lapsen hyvä. In H. Forsberg and R. Nätkin (eds.) *Perhe murroksessa: kriittisen perhetutkimuksen jäljillä.* Helsinki: Gaudeamus: 16–38.

Ngai, S. (2005) *Ugly feelings.* Cambridge, Mass: Harvard University Press.

Pateman, C. (1989) *The disorder of women: Democracy, feminism and political theory.* Cambridge: Polity Press.

Pylkkänen, A. (1999) Suomalainen tasa-arvo: agraarinen perintö ja valtioon kiinnittynyt yksityisyys. In S. Apo (et al.) (eds.) *Suomalainen nainen.* Helsinki: Otava: 24–38.

Ronkainen, S. and Näre, S. (2008) Intiimin haavoittava valta. In S. Näre and S. Ronkainen (eds.) *Paljastettu intiimi: sukupuolistuneen väkivallan dynamiikkaa.* Rovaniemi: Lapin yliopistokustannus: 7–40.

Roseneil, S. (2007) Queer individualization: The transformation of personal life in the early 21st century. *NORA: Nordic Journal of Feminist and Gender Research* 15(2–3): 84–99.

Saarenmaa, L. (2010) *Intiimin äänet: Julkisuuskulttuurin muutos suomalaisissa ajanvietelehdissä 1961–1975.* Tampere: Tampere University Press.

Seigworth, G. J. and Gregg, M. (2010) An inventory of shimmers. In M. Gregg and G. J. Seigworth (eds.) *The affect theory reader.* Durham: Duke University Press: 1–25.

Sellberg, K. and Hoogland, R. C. (2018) Introduction. In K. Sellberg (ed.) *Gender: Time.* New York: Macmillan: xiii–xvii.

Sihto, T., Lahti, A., Elmgren, H. and Jurva, R. (2018) Naisvalitus ja parisuhteen epätasa-arvot. In P. Eerola and H. Pirskanen (eds.) *Perhe ja tunteet.* Helsinki: Gaudeamus: 47–50.

Stocks, J., Díaz, C. and Halleröd, B. (2007) *Modern couples sharing money, sharing life.* Basingstoke: Palgrave Macmillan.

Tikkanen, M. (1975) *Män kan inte våldtas* [Men can't be raped]. Helsinki: Söderström.

Vakimo, S. (2001) *Paljon kokeva, vähän näkyvä: tutkimus vanhaa naista koskevista kulttuurisista käsityksistä ja vanhan naisen elämänkäytännöistä.* Helsinki: Suomalaisen kirjallisuuden seura.

Virkki, T. (2004) *Vihan voima: toimijuus ja muutos vihakertomuksissa.* Jyväskylä: Atena.

Ylöstalo, H. (2012) *Tasa-arvotyön tasa-arvot.* Tampere: Tampere University Press.

Index

© The Author(s) 2020
J. Carter, L. Arocha (eds.), *Romantic Relationships in a Time of 'Cold Intimacies'*,
Palgrave Macmillan Studies in Family and Intimate Life,
https://doi.org/10.1007/978-3-030-29256-0

309